ROBERT BLAKE

Admiral and General at Sea

ROBERT BLAKE

Admiral and General at Sea

BASED ON FAMILY AND STATE PAPERS

BY

HEPWORTH DIXON

With a new introduction by

Barry M. Gough

Regatta Press Limited
Mount Kisco, New York

Regatta Press Limited
Phone: +1-607-277-2211
Fax: +1-607-277-6292
Website: http://www.regattapress.com

First published in Great Britain by Chapman & Hall, 1852

This edition with an introduction by Barry M. Gough
published by *Regatta Press*, 2000

ISBN 0-9674826-1-5

LIBRARY OF CONGRESS CATALOGING-IN-PUBLICATION DATA

Dixon, William Hepworth, 1821-1879.
   Robert Blake : admiral and general at sea : based on family and
state papers / by Hepworth Dixon ; with a new introduction by
Barry M. Gough.
      p. cm.
   Originally published: London : Chapman & Hall, 1852.
   ISBN 0-9674826-1-5 (alk. paper)
   1. Blake, Robert, 1599-1657. 2. Great Britain--History, Naval--
Stuarts, 1603-1714. 3. Great Britain--History--Commonwealth
and Protectorate, 1649-1660. 4. Admirals--Great Britain--
Biography. I. Title.

DA86.1.B6 D6 2000
359'.0092--dc21
[B]
                                                    00-028428

Frontis: copy of original mezzotint engraving and autograph
of Robert Blake. Engraving by R. Young &c. (ca. 1852)

Printed in the United States of America

The paper in this publication meets the minimum requirements of
American National Standard for Information Sciences—
Permanence of Paper for Printed Library Materials,
ANSI Z 39.48-1984

Table of Contents.

PREFACE.

THE story of the renowned Admiral, Robert Blake, and in it
the Naval History of England during one of its most brilliant
periods, has not hitherto been written with either accuracy of
outline or copiousness of detail. Readers of the Commonwealth annals know how prominent is his place in contemporary literature—how many of his letters are preserved in
Thurloe and other collectors—how frequent are the references
to him in the Journals of the House, in broadsides, pamphlets
and the various newspapers. But even these sources of information have almost wholly escaped the attention of such writers
as have formally undertaken his memoirs. The chief authority for such slight notices of Blake as appear in our Encyclo-
pædias and Biographical Dictionaries is an extremely meagre
and incorrect memoir published in a work having the title—
Lives: English and Foreign. 1704. It was on this foundation
that Dr. Johnson based his spirited sketch for the *Gentleman's
Magazine.* After-writers followed his lead; from the author
of the article "Blake" in the *Encyclopædia Britannica*—the
best and most copious of modern accounts—down to Mr. Gor-
ton, who wrote a memoir of twenty-four pages for the Useful
Knowledge Society.

Of these notices it is sufficient to say that, with one or two
exceptions, the writers did not even trouble themselves to consult the Blake Correspondence in Thurloe. Not one of them

appears ever to have seen the two printed documents which
are really valuable originals for the Admiral's life.   These
works are entitled :

1. An Encomiastick or Elegiack Enumeration of the Noble Atchievements and unparallel'd services done at Land and Sea by that Truly
   Honourable General, Robert Blake, Esq., Late one of his Highnesses
   Generals at Sea, who after nine years' Indefatigable Service in that
   high Employment, Exchanged this Earthly Tabernacle for an Eternal
   House not made with Hands, Blessed by dying in the Lord, in
   Plymouth Sound, September the seventh, 1657, aged 59.   London :
   printed by Tho. Roycroft 1658.
2. The History and Life of Robert Blake, Esq., of Bridgewater, General
   and Admiral of the Fleets and Naval Forces of England.   Contain-
   ing a Full Account of his Glorious Atchievements by Sea and Land,
   more especially by Sea; where he obtained surprising Victories over
   the Dutch, French, Spaniards and others, Turks as well as Chris-
   tians.   To which is added a sketch of a comparison between the
   Two Great Actions against the Spaniards at Santa Cruz and Porto
   Bello.   Written by a gentleman who was bred in his Family.   London: printed for J. Millan, opposite the Admiralty Office, near
   Whitehall ; and R. Davis, at the corner of Sackville Street, Piccadilly.
   [without date, but probably written in 1740].

These works are both scarce.   Many of the facts which
they contain are not preserved elsewhere.   They are both
unquestionably genuine.   Yet, so far as I know, they have
never been referred to by writers on Blake or on the Commonwealth history.

The *Elegiack Enumeration* is a rhymed chronicle, of twenty-
eight pages, with little merit as verse, but of importance for
some of its facts and anecdotes, which I have found nowhere
else.   I quote a favourable specimen of the versification from
near the conclusion :

> " If now some British Plutarck, kindly prest
>   With love of vertue sparkling in his breast,

Should in historick style limme out this brave
And English Aristides, and from [the] grave
Redeem his memory,—for his Renown
This one thing more (his worthy Gests to crown)
May added be, the glory of them all ;
That during these long Warres, wherein the fall
Of thousands he beheld, as many rise
To fortunes high (true valour's meed and prize),
Yet he, postponing with heroick zeale
His private interest to the publick weale,
Himself would not advance by these vast spoiles,
Still him attending from those bloudy broiles
(Though millions—siezed by his conduct, so skill'd
In arms and Counsell—the English Coffers fil'd),
Who with his native portion well content,
For his dear countrie's good, was gladly spent."

But a small portion, however, of the existing materials for
a picture of the public and private life of Blake exists in the
printed form. These materials are chiefly to be found in the
voluminous Correspondence of the Navy Commissioners, lately
removed from Deptford to the Tower,—in the Orders and Instructions sent to the Generals and Admirals at sea, preserved
in the Admiralty Office at Whitehall,—in the collection of
Naval Mss. in the State-Paper Office,—in the ancient Rolls de-
posited at Carlton Ride,—in miscellaneous original documents
at the British Museum,—and in Family Papers. The following
list comprises most of the Ms. papers which have been, or are
at present, in my hands, to which I am indebted for valuable
information :

    I. The original Letters written by Blake to the Navy Commissioners
        during the years 1649-1655, in the Deptford Mss.
    II. The originals written by Blake to the officers of the Dockyard
        during the same period, in Deptford Mss.
    III. Copies of Letters written by the Navy Commissioners to Blake,
        in the Admiralty Books at Whitehall.

IV. Various Blake Mss. consisting of Copies of Wills, genealogical notes and other domestic papers, furnished to me by S. W. Blake, Esq., of Venne House, and by William Blake, Esq., of Bishop's Hull, in Somersetshire, the present representatives of the Blake family.

V. The collection of Naval Mss. in the State-Paper Office.

VI. The Parish Registers of Bridgwater from 1563 to 1645.

VII. A list of the mayors of Bridgwater, copied from panels in the Townhall.

VIII. Copies of bequests to the poor of Bridgwater, from panels in St. Mary's Church and in the Workhouse.

IX. The Baker Mss. A collection of inscriptions, drawings and notes on the Blake property in and about Bridgwater, together with extracts from old wills, rent-rolls and title-deeds, placed in my hands by William Baker, Esq., Secretary to the Somersetshire Archæological Society.

X. The Heralds' Visitations of Somerset in 1623, Harl. Mss. 1141.

XI. Michaelis Recorda, 4 Eliz. Rot. 68, Record Office.

XII. Hilarii Recorda, 20 Eliz. Rot. 59, Record Office.

XIII. A Ms. account of the siege of Lyme, belonging to George Roberts, Esq., of that town.

XIV. Various Roberts Mss. including plans, notes, extracts from the contemporary mayor's accounts, and from the Chute House papers, furnished to me by the same gentleman.

XV. Landsdowne Mss., volumes, 733 and 817.

XVI. Burghley Papers (in Lansdowne Coll. 115).

XVII. Ms. Reports of the Judges of the Court of Admiralty, State-Paper Office.

XVIII. Navy Lists in Add. Mss. 17, 503.

XIX. Blake's Letter to Col. Bennett in Add. Mss. 12098.

XX. Copies of Blake Despatches from the Mediterranean, in Add. Mss. 9304.

XXI. Ayscough Mss. 6125.

XXII. An account of Blake's death, from Wood's Mss. in Ashmole Museum, E. 4, No. 8560.

XXIII. Extracts from the Ms. Chronicle of Plymouth.

XXIV. The Order of General Blake's Funeral, in Add. Mss. 12514.

From these copious sources, aided by the results of a careful examination of the squibs, satires and broadsides of that time, I have endeavoured to recover a more distinct image of the Puritan Sea-King—to find, if it were possible, in forgotten nooks and corners the anecdotes and details which were required to complete a character thus far chiefly known by a few heroic outlines. How far the work realises my own idea, or answers the necessity which called it into existence, others must pronounce. But be its faults of execution many or few, it was undertaken with the hope of contributing in its degree to a better appreciation than now obtains of the more moderate men of our revolutionary era—a labour necessary to be undertaken somewhere.

The Portrait affixed to this volume is copied from a mezzotint engraving in the British Museum. There are—or were—four so-called Portraits of Blake. One hangs in the Townhall of Bridgwater, where it has been placed within these dozen years : it is undoubtedly spurious. Another is in Greenwich Hospital; it is a composition by H. P. Briggs, R.A., painted in or about 1828-9 :—yet this fancy sketch has been engraved as a Portrait of Blake ! The third, in the dining-hall of Wadham College, Oxford,—a copy of which is in the possession of William Blake, Esq., of Bishop's Hull,—is probably an original; but its history is not known :—it was engraved fifteen or sixteen years ago by Mr. Charles Knight. The fourth painting was formerly in possession of the antiquary, Joseph Ames, who had it engraved January 24, 1740, by Captain Thomas Preston, and dedicated it "to ye citizens of London." Ames describes the portrait in his " Catalogue of Heads" thus briefly— " Own hair—Laced neckcloth—Buff coat." It is quite possible that the Wadham Portrait and the Ames Portrait may have been painted from the same individual at different ages. They are both fine heads and full of character ; but I consider the latter as of rather better authority—Ames being well acquainted with such matters and almost a contemporary,—and I have consequently chosen it as the illustration for this volume. There are several other pretended heads of Blake on broadsheets and in periodicals; but they are evidently not genuine.

It only remains for me to express the thanks which I owe to so many kind friends for the assistance rendered so readily in my search for the materials here embodied. To T. Duffus Hardy, Esq., Keeper of the Tower Records, I am indebted for many facilities in the inspection and copying of extracts from the Deptford Mss. Hardly less signal are my obligations to William Blake, Esq., of Bishop's Hull, near Taunton; to George Roberts, Esq., of Lyme Regis, author of the *Life of Monmouth;* and to William Baker, Esq., of Bridgwater, for their valued communications, including old deeds, wills, drawings, facsimiles, and local and family traditions, as well as for personal attentions during my visits to the localities connected with Blake's history. Nor must I omit to express my grateful sense of the kindness of Silas Wood Blake, Esq., of Venne House, Wiviliscombe, the present owner of Admiral Blake's property at Knoll and of many other family relics, in furnishing me with various family papers, deeds, wills and genealogies. My sincere thanks are also due to John Barrow, Esq., of the Admiralty, and to W. C. Lemon, Esq., of the State-Paper Office, for aid so readily given me in the inspection of documents at their respective offices. Thomas Ward, Esq., of Overstowey; Henry Bernard, Esq., of Wells; and the Rev. John Poole, of Enmore, have kindly undertaken inquiries or supplied me with local information. The Rev. T. G. James, Vicar of Bridgwater, zealously aided my search among the parish registers; and the Rev. Mr. Jones, Unitarian Minister

of the same town, lent his valuable assistance in the collection
and examination of local traditions and documents. Many
other friends at Bristol, Bridgwater, Taunton, Lyme and Plymouth contributed their time and local knowledge to the completion of my store of biographical materials :—but I will only
further venture to name my obligations to Richard John King,
Esq., of Bigadon, Devonshire, to the Rev. Mr. Warre, and
Messrs. Kinglake and May of Taunton Dean.

W. H. D.

St. John's Wood Terrace,
    Regent's Park.

*** In the extracts made from Blake's Letters in the following work
the spelling has been modernised,—and to prevent any confusion
as to the identity of the ships spoken of, the prefix *St.* (never
used by a Puritan sailor) has been retained in such cases as the
St. George, St. Andrew, &c.

Introduction
to the 2000 Edition

In 1852, at the time of this book's initial publication, the name Hepworth Dixon, more fully William Hepworth Dixon, was well known in both English and American literary circles. Dixon's *Robert Blake, Admiral and General at Sea: Based on Family and State Papers*, published by the prominent London firm Chapman and Hall of 193 Piccadilly, added to his reputation as a writer. The work was soon republished, in 1856, in a cheaper, abbreviated edition, which lacked the footnote references that make the original so valuable. Until now, the work has been unavailable in print, and the original edition is a great prize for persons collecting works in English naval history of the Cromwellian era. For all these reasons, this new imprint is exceedingly welcome.

Hepworth Dixon's life of Blake takes us back to a particularly dynamic and even upsetting era of English history and public affairs. It was a time in which the world seemed upside down. Englishmen fought Englishmen, with the ever powerful Scots a dangerous part of the military equation. The English civil war pitted the forces of Parliament against those of the Crown: it was Roundheads versus Cavaliers, and Congregationalists and Presbyterians against Church of England and, in some cases, Roman Catholics. It was even a social and ideological struggle between existing social orders and those who proclaimed the necessity of eradicating preference and patronage—of levelling the social fabric. The Levellers, so called, never won the day, but it is worth remembering that the English revolution crossed all boundaries of social order and politics. And when the Restoration of the monarchy occurred, as it did in 1660, English life moved beyond its immediate, violent past, and a gradual healing of deep wounds took place. But the legacy of a remarkable division effected in English life would be sizeable.

Then as now England did not stand alone. The English Channel, the Bay of Biscay, and the waters stretching down the coast of France even to the islands off the coasts of Spain and Northwest Africa constituted a seaborne frontier of vital value to the power that could have control of the sea there. In these waters the Dutch ranged almost at will, and they were keenly followed by French and Spanish marine forces. Because nearly all merchant shipping, on which the new and growing wealth of England and Holland depended, had to pass through these narrow seas, they were places of piracy, privateering, ravaging, and cross-ravaging. The naval forces of the English Crown took up station in island haunts such as Jersey, and from them pressed their corsairing work against any and all. Parliament had to check such activities, and it fell to Robert Blake to undertake the work. Blake became master of these narrow seas, and his long and hazardous work against the Royal forces, against the Dutch, and against the Spanish was as adventurous and daring a career at sea as could be imagined.

Blake was the Nelson of his times (though his sea battles were of a different order than those of Nelson). In terms of his primacy in the history of the Royal Navy, Blake stands near the top, out-ranked by Nelson. Drake stands nearby in the triumvirate. Together they represent the great leadership and fighting skill of England's premier admirals of the age of fighting sail. Blake, says Dixon, was the very model of a British sailor, gentle, pious, resolute, and fearless. His supreme military and naval genius placed him in the highest class of great captains.

Dixon was born in Manchester on 30 June 1821 to a well-to-do and old Puritan family. He was privately educated, and, from his teenage years on, he wrote extensively. Dixon wrote variously and prolifically all his life, fulfilling all his aspirations to be a social commentator, travel writer, historian, biographer and playwright. His extensive publication record, which appears in the catalogue of the British Library, lists almost a hundred entries on all manner of matters. As early as 1846, age 24, he was editing a literary magazine in Cheltenham. He went to the Inner Temple in London, apparently taking the requisite number of meals in the course of preparing to take the examination as barrister. He was called to the bar on 1 May 1851 but never practiced. The social conditions of London's poor appalled him, and his writing on the poor and the laboring poor presaged Henry Mayhew's *London Labour and London Poor*, published in 1851. Dixon wrote articles on problems in London prisons, and from these followed his book *John Howard and the Prison World of Europe* (1849). Attracted to the world and influence of the Quakers, he wrote an influential *Life of William Penn* (1851), which brought forth the celebrated Macaulay "charges" against Penn and, in a subsequent edition, Dixon's reply. In 1851, England lived in fear of a French invasion, as it was argued in the press that steam had bridged the channel. Dixon joined that debate too.

In 1852, Dixon's *Robert Blake* appeared, and it had wide-ranging appeal. By this time, Dixon had established a firm place for himself in British letters. The treatment of the subject showed good and thorough research; a grasp of the existing, sparse, literature on the subject; and most felicitous prose. To his credit, Dixon did not exalt the Puritan cause. Charles Kingsley, the novelist, writing in the *Dictionary of National Biography* about his near contemporary said that the book was more successful with the public than it was with serious historians. The same might be said nowadays for a goodly number of popular texts on history written by informed and energetic generalists. That discussion continues in our own times.

Of Dixon's *Blake* there is much more to say presently, but let us not finish our recounting of Dixon's literary output without mentioning that Dixon was as great a traveller as he was a prolific writer. He must have been like postal inspector and novelist Trollope: scribbling all the time during his train journeys. Dixon's love of travel took him to Canada, the United States, Spain, and Turkey, among others and for some destinations a suitable literary deposit occurred: *British Cyprus* (1879) for example. And Dixon continued his pursuit of biography. His work on Francis Bacon, using State Papers to good account, was published in 1861. Its fine reception led to a more elaborate volume on the same subject the next year. But latter years held sad passages for Dixon: personal injury, loss of investments, and the destruction of his house at 6 St. James Terrace, near Regents Park (completely wrecked by a gunpowder explosion in the nearby Regents Canal), all took their toll. He died in bed of apoplectic seizure, and was buried in Highgate Cemetery.

Doubtless Dixon was more lively as a writer than he was advanced as a scholar, but this does not lessen the value of his biography of the great general on land and sea. The sources on which the work is based are clearly indicated in footnotes, and these show a firm grasp of the political and legal documents of the age. In the Preface, at pages xi and xii, he lists the numerous documents as available to him, some residing in offices of government, or libraries and archives, or in private hands. These are, for the modern scholar, a prized roadmap shaping the course for the morrow's research passage. True it is that many more documents are available now than were available to Dixon. Even so, a glance at his sources as given in the Preface and scrupulously cited in the footnotes indicates that his scholarly grasp was in advance of what others gave him credit for at the time. In comparing Dixon to more recent works—the Reverend J.R. Powell's *Robert Blake, General at Sea* (1972) and Michael Baumber's *General-At-Sea: Robert Blake and the Seventeenth-Century Revolution in Naval Warfare* (1989) are the best—it is clear that the general profile as established by Dixon has not changed. Powell provided the first complete *naval* history of the subject and Baumber has done much to enlarge the discussion on tactics, besides telling us much new about Blake at Oxford. However, the general profile of Blake—Dixon's profile—has not substantially changed.

And what does Dixon provide? Above all, he introduces us to a bright, academically competent Oxford student and college fellow who stands slightly outside the power structure of his age, though one who, in his individual strength of character, cannot be denied a place in the pending Revolution. The civil war overtakes Blake, and it provides him with remarkable opportunities—first in land campaigns, of which Taunton's defense is the most noteworthy, and second in the succession of battles against various Royalists and then foreign navies that were to consume the balance of Blake's violent life and eventually end in the great wound that led to his demise before his ship reached England after the celebrated defeat of the Spanish at Santa Cruz. We follow Dixon's story with keen interest. He takes the reader easily from one crisis to the other, and in doing so explains both the Royalist corsairing activity and the Parliamentary necessity of winkling out, so to speak, the opposition's forces from its lairs. We follow Blake through his battles, and we are given ample reasons as to why Parliament, and Cromwell, trusted Blake, though there were differences along the way. Blake's military and naval careers seem to have been one of almost continual success in the fields of battle. He moved with ease from land to an alien sea, and the success of the forces he led induced Parliament to grant him increased administrative obligations, as well as the privilege to write his own instructions as to campaigns against his several enemies.

In short, Dixon's biography of Blake is an excellent introduction to the naval life of England's early genius of tactics and battle capabilities, and it is, besides, a splendid tour through the military and naval aspects of the mid- and late-seventeenth century, when England's forces were first internalized in the civil war and when, in succession, the English navy, the Commonwealth Navy, and, in turn, the Royal Navy came forth as the premier fighting force at sea in Europe. Ahead lay many other wars against Holland, France, and Spain in which England (later Britain) would have to prove itself. But, by the time Blake's lifeless body was brought back home to England, the national momentum that led to world power had been established. In that grand and mighty rise, Blake played a powerful role. We stand in awe that someone could have done so much in so little time—and left such a noteworthy record for History.

Barry M. Gough
January 2000

Barry M. Gough is Professor of History at Wilfrid Laurier University in Waterloo, Ontario, Canada. He is also Editor-in-Chief of *The American Neptune*, as well as author or editor of many books and articles on the subject of maritime history.

ROBERT BLAKE.

CHAPTER I.

1599-1625.

The Scholar.

In the early part of the seventeenth century the counties lying between the South Channel and the river Severn were among the most active, wealthy and cultivated in England. While Liverpool was still a swamp, and Manchester but a straggling hamlet — Leeds a cluster of mud huts, and the romantic valley of the Calder a desolate gorge, the streets of Taunton, Exeter and Dunster resounded with arts and industry; and the merchant-ships of Bridgwater and Bristol were daily going out or coming in from the remotest corners of the earth. The fairest fields, the largest cities, the proudest strongholds lay in this region. The vales of Stroud, Honiton and Evesham still bear away the palm of rural beauty; when the vine was an English plant, it attained its highest perfection on the sunny slopes of Somerset and Devon; and a royal sybarite, whose taste at least has never been impugned, declared that in those days the south-west coast was the only part of England fit for the habitation of a gentleman.

B

The towns were in equal repute with the country. Taunton was famous for its woollens while the Plantagenets were yet on the throne; in later times a band of industrious Flemings, flying from the persecutions of the Duke of Alva, brought their knowledge, enterprise and capital into the town, and under their teaching it soon obtained an equal reputation for serges. Parliament fostered these rising trades, and " Tauntons " were then as well known in the markets of Europe as are now Manchester cottons or Spitalfields silks. While the Yorkshire breeder of sheep was either too indolent or too ignorant to work the wool which grew so plentifully on his native downs into an article of trade, the workmen of the western city obtained by the process wealth, cultivation and political power.[1] Bristol, inferior in population and maritime resources to London alone, had long aspired to the honours of a western metropolis. Its history looked back to the remotest times. Its docks, its streets, its religious edifices, its ancient gates and decaying fortifications, all bore testimony to its long-established grandeur. The city of London barely furnished larger returns to the royal exchequer; commissions, commissioners and pursuivants levied money under many pretexts from its opulent traders, and the armies of Ireland and Scotland were frequently recruited among its hardy and adventurous population. From its excellent situation as a point of departure for the west and south, it gradually obtained a monopoly of Irish commerce; and its vessels visited the harbours of Portugal and Spain, whence they brought

---

[1] Acta Regia, iv. 319; Toulmin's History of Taunton, 368-370.

home the treasures of two worlds in exchange for the
woollen cloths which then constituted our only manu-
facture. As its great houses increased in means, their
enterprises took a bolder range. No longer satisfied to
share their golden harvests with the more fortunate
Iberian, they sought by the path of new discovery to
gain for their own port such advantages as Columbus
had won for the Spaniard and Vasco de Gama for the
Portuguese. Cabot had sailed from their river on his
first adventure, and four of the five small vessels that composed his fleet were supplied by the Severn merchants.
In that and subsequent voyages, undertaken at their
expense, he had added Newfoundland, Nova Scotia, and
North America as far as the inlet of the Chesapeake,
to the known regions of the world,—establishing a connexion with Hispaniola, Porto Rico and the coasts of
Brazil, which was not quite abandoned even after the
government, in virtue of a treaty to that end, gave up
the rights of English discovery in those regions to the
crown of Arragon and Castile. Inspired by these successes in the far west, they fitted out an expedition for
the Arctic Ocean, and sent it forth with orders to search
for a new passage northward to China and Hindustan.
These spirited men pursued their enterprise with admirable zeal, and only failed to rival the fame of more
celebrated discoverers because nature herself had left
nothing for them to find in that direction.[1]

One of the most active of the Severn merchants in
the latter part of the sixteenth century was Humphrey

[1] Hakluyt, iii. 4-700 ; Thurlow, iv. 44 ; Rushworth, ii. 336; Seyers'
History of Bristol, ii. 277-295.

Blake of Plansfield and Bridgwater. This man's father, Robert Blake, a person whose success in life was illustrated by many virtues, had been the first of his family to step out of the narrow circle of a country life and interrupt the old traditions by removing from Tuxwell, the seat of his ancestors for several generations, to Bridgwater, where he hoped to share the harvests then so abundantly reaped in the field of Spanish commerce.[1] The oldest Blake—or Blacke, as the name is sometimes spelt in the Records—whose story is in any way known, is one Humphrey, who lived in the reign of Henry VIII., Mary and Edward VI., and held the estate of Tuxwell, in the parish of Bishop's Lydyard, county of Somerset, in capite, by payment of the fortieth part of a knight's fee.[2] He died towards the close of 1558, and the property then passed to his son John, who immediately conveyed it to one Thomas Blake, probably the deceased Humphrey's brother.[3] This Thomas, who was great-grandfather to the admiral, seems to have been in serious trouble about the middle of Queen Elizabeth's reign, as he at that time made over to his friends and neighbours, James Clark and Mathew Stradling,[4] the titles of his estate; but the occasion for this transfer, whatever it may have been, soon passed away, and the property was re-conveyed to its former owner, from whom it descended in the course of nature to his son

---

[1] Herald's Visitation, 1623, Harl. Mss. 1141.

[2] Michaelis Recorda, 4 Eliz. Rot. 68, Record Office.

[3] Hilarii Recorda, 20 Eliz. Rot. 59, Record Office.

[4] One of the Stradlings married a Blake : Parish Register, April 29, 1582.

Robert.[1] This more active and ambitious personage
married a lady named Margaret Symonds,[2] and settled
in Bridgwater, where he improved his fortune by commercial enterprise, and during a long life retained the
respect and confidence of his fellow-citizens. Three
several times he had the honour to serve as chief magistrate in his adopted town; namely in 1573, 1579 and
in 1587, as appears by the inscriptions still preserved on
panels in the Townhall of Bridgwater. At his death,
which occurred in 1591, he bequeathed 240*l.*, equal to
more than 1000*l.* of our present money, to relieve the
poor and repair the causeways; thus setting an example
of liberality to his townsmen and descendants which
the latter at least piously and honourably followed.[3]
Humphrey, his son, succeeded to the business; but his
temper seems to have been too sanguine and adventurous
for the ordinary action of trade, with its small risks and
quick returns. Although he married a co-heiress, yet
his bold speculations sometimes turned out so ill as to
cause him not only serious losses but even threaten to
involve the family fortunes in ruin. This possible end
of his speculations seemed, however, as yet far off; and in

---

[1] Michaelis Recorda, 4 Eliz. Rot. 68.

[2] Harl. Mss. 1141.

[3] The following is copied from panels in the parish church of Bridgwater:—"Robert Blake of this Town, Gentleman, did give towards pious
uses ye sum of two hundred and forty Pounds, which sum is in ye custody
of ye Common Councell of this Borough, to remain as a stock for ever, y^e
profitt or interest thereof to be yearly distributed at ye discretion of y^e
Maior, Aldermen, and Burgesses for ye time being, towards ye reliefe of
ye poor people of ye said Borough, and reperation of ye Cawsies within
ye said Parish. He died Ano 1592."

the meantime, inheritor of a good estate and a name held in universal respect, he made a considerable figure in the locality, living in one of the best houses in Bridgwater, and twice filling the chair of its chief magistrate.[1]

His marriage with Sara, daughter and co-heiress of Humphrey Williams, made him master of Plansfield— that Plansfield which is described by all previous writers who have treated of Blake's parentage as the original seat of his family. The precise way in which the estate came into his possession is not ascertained; whether it came to him directly in right of his wife, or was purchased with part of her dowry; but it is certain that he was the first member of the Blake family who owned that property, for in the Herald's Visitation of Somerset in 1623, he is styled Humphrey Blake of Plansfield, son of Robert Blake of Bridgwater.[2]

Sara Williams, the admiral's mother, was descended by a collateral line from the knightly owners of Plansfield, an extremely good Somersetshire family. The estate had lapsed to the Crown on the death of Sir Nicholas Williams, in the reign of Queen Elizabeth; but it was restored to his widow Mabel, and probably continued in the family of Williams until carried with the female inheritor to that of the Blakes.[3]

---

[1] Inscription in Townhall.

[2] Harl. Mss. 1141.

[3] What further information has fallen in my way about Plansfield, I throw into a note, for the benefit of any future historian of Somerset.— "4th May, 21 Hen. VII. There is a grant in tail male (hæredibus masculis de corpore legitime procreatis) to Sir John Williams, knight, of the Mannor o' Plainsfield, Wyke, Lenehill, Stogursey, Wortherston, Burnham, Downende, Puriton, Wolavington, Chilton, Edinton, Catcote,

The firstfruits of this marriage, the future admiral and general of England, came into the world about the end of August, 1599, and received the rite of baptism at the parish church of Bridgwater on the 27th of September.[1] He was called Robert in pious remembrance of his grandfather. Many other children followed the first born in rapid succession; in all twelve boys—Hum-

---

Bridgewater, Taunton, Milverton, Durston, Asheholt, Advoc Ecclesiæ de Asholt, Tuxwell, Milverton, Dunster, Netherstowey, Overstowey, Padenoller, in co. Somerset, et Exbridge et Baunton, in co. Devon, or parts of the said lands and mannors.

" It appears by this grant that this mannor was the estate of Thomas Trowe, esq. (held in capite of the Crown), and forfeited by his attainder in Parliament with others, his conferates, for adhering to Piers Warbeck, temp. Hen. VII. Vide Rol. Pal. 19, Hen. VII. n. 21. Vide Inquisition, virtute officii, temp. Hen. VII. n. 224, found upon the attainder of the said Thomas Trowe, that he was seized of the mannor of Plainsfield, with its appurtenances, held in capite (vide Esch. 24 Hen. VII. no. 64). The said Sir John Williams died seized of Plainsfield (Esch. 2 Eliz. pars 2de, no. 67). Reginald Williams died seized of Plainsfield in Sept. (ibid. no. 69). John Williams died seized of Plainsfield in the February following (Esch. 11 Eliz. no. 124). Sir Nicholes Williams died seized of this mannor of Plainsfield and appurtenances without leaving any heir male of his body, whereupon the Crown again seized thereof (Pat. 26 Eliz. p. 16). Queen Eliz. demised the scite of the mannor of Plainsfield for twenty-one years, by lease for twenty-one years (Pat. 33 Eliz. pars nona). Queen Elizabeth granted the mannor of Plainsfield, with all the appurtenances, *in fee*, to Welles and Wytham.

"In the Book of Inrolements (Liver F, fol. 118; Order, 12 Eliz.), there is an entry for assigning dower to Mabell, wife of Rafe Stafford (formerly wife of Nicholes Williams), the mannor of Plainsfield, lands in Tuxwell, Asholt, Mylverton, Durston, Netherstowey, Overstowey, Padnoller, Stogursey, and Wyke, and which Nichs. Williams held in grant from King Henry." There is more information relating to this estate, and also to Tuxwell, in the rent-roll of Lord Egmont, from which these notes are taken. Baker Mss. [1] Register in parish church.

phrey in 1600; William in 1603; George, who died in infancy, in 1604; George, the second of that name, in 1606; Samuel in 1608; Nicholas in 1609; Edward, who died in infancy, in 1611; Benjamin, who died in infancy, in 1612; Edward, the second of that name (he also died in infancy), in 1613; Benjamin, second of the same name, in 1614; John, who died in infancy, in 1617; and Alexander in 1619.[1] The number of girls is not exactly ascertainable in consequence of irregularities in the registers, but the admiral's Will mentions two of his sisters, Bridget, who married a Mr. Bowdich of Chard, and another not referred to by her maiden name. The Herald's Visitation speaks of a Mrs. Burrage as being one of Humphrey Blake's daughters; but this is probably no more than a misspelling of Bowdich.[2] Seven of the sons, Robert, Humphrey, William, George, Samuel, Nicholas and Alexander grew up to manhood. The other sister married Thomas Smythes of Cheapside, a celebrated goldsmith and banker, and went to reside with him in London.[3]

After a lapse of two centuries and a half, it may still be possible to recover an idea, more or less faint, but true in its main features, of the mode in which this interesting family lived down there in the West of England, and of the influences under which the young commander passed the fifteen years of his childhood and early youth.

Bridgwater, on the river Parrett, stands in the centre

---

[1] Registers in parish church under these dates.

[2] Harl. Mss. 1141, folio 107.

[3] Office copy of Blake's will, March 13, 1655, in Blake Mss.

of a rich plain, now covered with orchards and corn-
fields, but in the seventeenth century little better than
a wide morass, bounded on one side by the Quantock
hills, and on the other, at a less distance, by the wooded
slopes of the Poldons. The valley, about three miles
in width, includes several spots famous in English story.
There the victorious armies of the king of Wessex had
been arrested. There our own Alfred had found shelter
from the fury of the Danes. There, in later times,
Monmouth fought and lost the battle of Sedgemoor.
The town was built, as it is now, on both sides of the
river; but at that time the eastern suburb, joined to the
main body of the town by an ancient and solid stone
bridge of three arches, was inhabited almost exclusively
by opulent traders and gentry. High street, leading
through the corn-market—where there was a famous
inn, known to the country gentlemen for miles round
as the *Swan*, and a picturesque old market-cross,—was
filled with fine shops; and the little town had an air
of bustle and business. Lying on the great highway
from Gloucester and Bristol to Taunton, Exeter and
Plymouth, the western traffic of course all passed
through it. Pack-horses, laden with Yorkshire wool,
tinkled their merry bells along its streets and over its old
bridge night and day. Yet even then the town seemed to
have passed its prime. Grass already grew in some of
its outlying streets, and many of its houses wore a fu-
nereal aspect. In former times it had been defended by
a wall and gates; but nearly every vestige of these defences had been swept away. The Castle, once a royal
appanage, held by the Queens of England as a dower,

kept watch and ward over the surrounding country; but though an imposing structure in the feudal era, it too had fallen from its high estate. Some faint rays of light from a distant past lingered about its decaying walls and turrets; in the wars of the Roses it had bravely withstood siege and storm; and in spite of its changed condition it still boasted the proud honours of a virgin fortress.[1]

The first object to catch a stranger's eye as he stands on the iron bridge, which in recent years has replaced the old stone edifice, is a row of young elms on the left bank of the stream; those elm-trees grow in what was formerly Humphrey Blake's garden. On the same bank, a little below the bridge, lie such relics of the old fortress as may still be traced. The house in which the admiral was born, in which he passed his youth, and in which, when at Bridgwater, he lived in the full blaze of his renown, still stands in what was formerly a part of St. Mary's-street; a house two stories high, built of blue lias stone, with walls of immense thickness, heavy stone stairs, oak wainscots and decorated ceilings; altogether a habitation of Tudor origin and of unmistakeable importance in those times. The gardens, bounded by Durleigh brook, the river Parrett and the highway, were about two acres in extent, and seem to have been laid out with simple taste, mingling fruit-trees and flower-beds, scented plants and greenery for the kitchen. Though it stood within a few steps of the church and Corn Hill, the mansion nevertheless enjoyed a complete

---

[1] Collinson's History of Somerset, iii. 75-77 ; Leland's Itinerary, ii. 96; Fairfax Correspondence, iii. 239.

rural seclusion; while the windows looked out over a wide
expanse of valley away to the sunny slopes and summits
of the Quantocks. It was in this secluded garden, by
that old stone bridge, among the ships, native and foreign, lying at anchor in the stream, and under the guns
of that grim fortress, that the ruddy-faced and curly-
haired boy, Robert Blake, played and pondered, as was
his habit, until the age of sixteen. From his father's
garden he could daily see the extraordinary flow of
tide known to seamen as a "bore"—a phenomenon only
met with in the Ganges, the Severn, and one or two
other streams; and the conversation of his father and of
his father's friends would contribute in no slight degree
to fix his young mind on the sea and its affairs.[1]

When it is said that Humphrey Blake was a merchant trading with Spain, it is not to be inferred that
his days were spent in the pacific routine of the desk
and the exchange. The life of a trader was then a life
of peril and adventure. He mostly manned his own
ship and sailed with his argosy. Like later cruisers
among the Pacific islands, his course and his destination
was rarely known before he quitted port. Failing in
one harbour to dispose of his cargo, he spread his canvass
in search of better markets. Experience of strange
lands and stranger people was the daily incident of this
change of place; and he was compelled to hold his own,
not merely against the duties, fines, and exactions of

---

[1] With the aid of William Baker, Esq. secretary of the Somerset
Archæological Society, I have been able, from an inspection and comparison of several old deeds, to confirm the Bridgwater traditions as to the
site of Blake's house.

the more legitimate powers, but against the still more
unscrupulous and formidable corsair.   Piracy was not,
in the sixteenth century, the despicable calling it is now :
in the opinion of that age, a pirate was but a soldier
of fortune on another element.   France, Germany and
Italy were overrun with mercenary heroes, eager to sell
their swords in any cause where good pay and a fair
amount of profligacy were allowed; and hundreds of
distressed English gentlemen, as soon as the civil wars
were over, took to the sea for bread in a similar spirit.
In some parts of Europe entire districts lived on the
plunder of unprotected vessels, long after the close of
these troubles; and many persons still living can re-
member a time when the daring valour of the Greek
and Biscayan freebooters was the theme of winter tales
and popular ballads.   Nor were these unlicensed spoilers
the worst enemies whom the peaceful merchant had to
encounter at sea.   The Moors of Africa had erected
piracy into a national system.   For ages the Salee rover
had been a terror to the south of Europe; and the Tunisian and the Algerine, equal to him in skill, daring, and
fanaticism, had the advantage over him of better ports
and larger privateers.   No coast in Christendom was
free from their incursions; but their favourite stations
were the bays and harbours of Portugal and Spain, as
in these ports they found it easy to attack and capture
stragglers from the fleets of two worlds.   To the ordinary
motives of the pirate, adventure and greed of gold, the
Moor added the fiercer spurs of religious difference and
hereditary hate.   Europeans, it may be justly said, had
forced the Moors into piracy as a measure of defence.

Their expulsion from Granada in the fifteenth century roused the worst passions of their nature ; and that band of armed priests, nestled behind the impregnable ramparts of Malta, and sworn to hold no truce with their race and faith,—a vow which they kept to the last letter, by frequent piratical descents on the coasts of Africa, marking their path along the shore with burning villages, slaughtered peasants and captive women and children, soon to be exposed by these Christian mission- aries in the slave-markets of Venice, Seville and Genoa, —left them no other policy but that of revenge and re- taliation. In their undiscriminating rage, the followers of Mohammed waged war against the commerce of all civilised countries ; when the opportunity offered, they seized both fleets and cargoes; and, like the Knights of Malta, carried off their prisoners for sale to the ba- zaars of Tunis, Tripoli and Algiers.[1]

For protection against these formidable enemies, the merchant had to trust solely to his own bold heart and steady hand. His vessel, however small, carried some means of defence. The crew were well armed. Aids to escape were kept in readiness. From the British Chan- nel to the Straits of Gibraltar the course of the Severn adventurer lay through continual perils. Every rock and inlet along the coast had to be carefully examined for concealed enemies before his little barque could ven- ture on. The adventurer lived on deck, and eat, drank and slept with his mind on the alert and his brain ready

---

[1] Morgan's History of Algiers, c. xviii.; Harl. Misc. viii. 398-402; Warburton's Prince Rupert and the Cavaliers, iii. 308-314 ; John Howard, 329-332, third edition.

for every emergency.   On his return from a successful
voyage, many were the tales of perilous encounters,
chance-escapes and valorous deeds which he had to tell
his friends and children on the dark winter nights:—
and such stories were, no doubt, a part of the food
on which the imagination of young Blake, silent and
thoughtful from his childhood, was fed in the old mansion at Bridgwater.[1]

The rudiments of a more regular education he obtained at the grammar-school, then considered one of
the best foundations of its kind in England.   This
edifice has long disappeared from the streets of Bridgwater; but by a curious coincidence it has been replaced
by another school of similar aims and character, conducted in the very house in which the admiral was born
and in which he lived.   At the grammar-school he made
a decent progress with his Greek and Latin; something
of navigation, ship-building and the routine of sea duties
he probably learned from his father or from his father's
factors and servants.   His own taste, however, his habit
of mind and the bent of his ambition led to the field
of literary endeavour; and, as he was the first of his
race who had shewn any strong vocation to letters and
learning, his father, proud of his talents and his studies,
resolved that he should have every chance of rising to
eminence in his chosen walk that means and education
could confer.   Nor was this early culture thrown away.
At sixteen he was already prepared for the university,
and at his own earnest desire was allowed to proceed to
Oxford, where he matriculated as a member of St. Al-

---

[1] Clarendon, vi. 41; Oxford, 1850.

ban's Hall in Lent Term 1615, in company with Edward Reynolds, afterwards raised to the see of Worcester, and John Earl, subsequently bishop of Salisbury.[1]

But little is known of Blake's college life. It is recorded of him that he rose early, and was extremely assiduous at his books, lectures and devotions; that he took great delight in field-sports, particularly in fishing and shooting. If any credit is to be attributed to an ancient piece of gossip, which, whether false or true, is of respectable age, and is preserved to us by a writer who revered his name and was intimate with several members of the family, — his aquatic sports were sometimes extended to the catching of swans, then as plentiful on the Isis as they still are on the Thames. There is no ground for this report beyond the common scandal of the time, and many writers have rejected it without examination :—but if Shakespere in his youth had a passion for deer, why may not Blake in his youth have had a weakness for cygnets ?[2]

He had not been long at Oxford before his young ambition prompted him to try his strength against Robert Hegge and Robert Newlin in a contest for a scholarship of Christ Church, then vacant; but he soon found that a student without friends or influence had little chance of success in that aristocratic college. The failure of his first effort did not, however, cast him down : —he kept close at his books and looked steadily towards the future. Nevertheless, willing to accept such friendly

---

[1] The History and Life of Robert Blake, Esq. written by a Gentleman bred in his Family, 4; Bliss's Wood's Fasti, ii. 371.

[2] History and Life, 5; Johnson's Works, xii. 42.

support as came in his way unsought, he removed from
St. Alban's Hall, where he had found and felt himself
a stranger, to Wadham College, at the request of his
father's friend, Nicholas Wadham, a Somersetshire man,
who had then recently founded the noble edifice which
bears his name. In this new college Blake remained
several years; there he took the usual honours and completed his education:—and in the great dining-hall of
Wadham, among the effigies of poets, divines and an-
tiquaries, a portrait of the admiral is still shewn with
honest pride as that of its most illustrious scholar.[1]

During the years which he remained at Wadham
College, waiting for an opportunity to establish himself
in some permanent position in the University, the family
prospects were gradually growing darker at Bridgwater.
On the whole, Humphrey Blake had been a decidedly
unprosperous man; many of his most important ventures
in trade had failed to realise a profit; in some his actual
losses had been severe. In these speculations much of
his own and his wife's property was now gone; and in
the decline of life he found himself for the first time in
debt and difficulty.[2] The absence of his former means
chafed his ardent and ambitious mind; the more so as
his misfortunes had fallen on him when the energy and
buoyancy of youth were passed, but not the cares and
responsibilities of early manhood. He had married somewhat late in life; his family had nevertheless increased
steadily and rapidly; and now at fifty-seven or eight he
found himself already an old man with no less than ten

---

[1] History and Life, 5; Johnson's Works, xii. 42.
[2] Harl. Mss. 1141, folio 107.

children, varying in ages from Robert of twenty, down to little Alexander, then in the arms of his nurse.[1] These troubles preyed on his spirits, and with the increasing darkness of his fortunes his health too began to fail.

Robert, in his humble rooms at Wadham College, shared in all the family fears and afflictions. He felt acutely the painful position in which his father stood, embarrassed with debts and surrounded with so many responsibilities; and the feeling gave a new and higher impulse to his desire to obtain a fellowship in one of the colleges. At this very time a vacancy occurred at Merton, and he offered himself as a candidate for the office—not as in the earlier period of his academical career, from a boyish ambition to achieve honours and place, but from an almost sacred wish to be useful to his brothers, and to relieve his father of the modest expense of his maintenance at Oxford. Alexander Fisher, John Earl, Edward Reynolds, his old comrades at St. Alban's Hall, and several other young men of parts and learning were in the lists. Had his efforts been crowned with success, had he gained the fellowship and its humble salary, it is probable that the future life of the renowned admiral would have passed in the seclusion of a college, among the books and studies he already loved so well:— in which case Taunton would in all human probability have remained in royalist hands, the battle of Naseby would not have been fought, Tromp would have remained unconquered, Spain unscathed, Tunis and Santa Cruz

---

[1] Parish register, April 13, 1619.

uncelebrated!   How little did Sir Henry Savile, then
warden of Merton College, dream that in rejecting Blake
from his petty senate, he was turning back on the world
one of those great master-spirits who were soon to over-
turn the government, humiliate his adored sovereign, and
on the ruin of the fallen house elevate England to the
height of human grandeur!   But so it was.   Sir Henry,
a man of sense and acquirements, as witness his fine edition of St. Chrysostom, had an eccentric distaste for men
of low stature, and chose his senators, as the Prussian
king did his grenadiers, by their height.   The young
Somersetshire student, thick-set, fair-complexioned,
and only five feet six, fell below his standard of manly
beauty; and the loss of his election was then and there
commonly attributed to this caprice of the learned warden.   But it is not unfair to suppose that other reasons
may have influenced the adverse decision.   Blake was
already known to profess Puritan sentiments, and with
that fearless frankness which distinguished him through
life, he loudly protested against every attempt of the
court and courtly prelates to impart a papistical character to the rubric of the Church.   Sir Henry Savile, on
the other hand, was a servile supporter of King James's
policy in affairs spiritual.   This difference of principles
would account for the result of the election without the
help of an unworthy and ridiculous caprice.   It must,
however, be stated that no writer of that time makes
any reference to this difference of opinion as a ground
of objection to Blake.[1]

Blake remained five years at Oxford after this inci-

---

[1] Bliss's Wood's Fasti, ii. 371; History and Life, 5.

dent, and in good time took his degree of Master of Arts.[1]
There seems to be no ground for supposing that want
of learning was the bar to his advancement in the University. He had read the best authors in Greek and
Latin, and wrote the latter language at least sufficiently
well for verse or epigram. Even in the busiest days of
his public life, he made it a point of pride not to forget
his classical studies. When out at sea, in chase of the
enemy or fiercely cruising before a foreign station, his
grave humour—and never man had finer sense of sarcasm,
or used that brilliant weapon with greater effect—loved
to find expression for its scorn and merriment in the
satires of Horace and Juvenal; thus in some degree relieving the stern fervour of Puritan piety with the more
easy graces of ancient scholarship. In due course his
brother William joined him at Wadham, where, in
1624, he was already a Bachelor of Arts, and on the
death of the antiquary, Camden, furnished a Latin epi-
graph to the book published by the University :

> Invida quam rapuit vitam parenti,
> Filius en patriæ redidet arte suæ.
> Vixisti nobis satis, ô Camdene, Tibiq.
> Flagitet Annales ni tua vita Tuos.[2]

In the ninth year of his residence at Oxford, and in
the twenty-seventh of his age, Blake was called to his

---

[1] Wood says he only took the degree of B.A.; but Clarendon (vi. 41),
Oldmixon (i. 420), and Bates (Elen. Mot. Part ii. 228), all give him the
higher title.

[2] Camdeni Insignia, Oxon. 1624. Anthony Wood falsely attributes
these lines to Robert Blake; and of course the error has been copied into
all the " notices " of the Admiral.

father's bedside. The old man had grown worse in health, and was probably no longer able to manage his affairs. At last his son abandoned the long-cherished idea of a college life, gave up his rooms at Wadham, and took up his abode in the old house at Bridgwater. In November of the following year, his father died, probably without having made a will, as no reference is made to such a document in the family papers, and as no trace of it exists at Taunton, Wells, or the Prerogative Court in London.[1]

As soon as the funeral rites were all over, Blake surveyed his position. The estate, such as it was, was encumbered with debts. His brothers Humphrey, William and George were of age or near it; Samuel was seventeen, Nicholas sixteen, Benjamin eleven, and Alexander six. Not one of them, with the possible exception of William, was settled in life; and the four youngest had still to be in some measure educated as well as started in the world. There were also the widowed mother and two young girls to support out of the wreck of their former fortunes. The first thing, then, was to ascertain the amount of residue after paying all the debts; and in order to clear off some of these claims, it is probable that Plansfield was at this time sold. When the debts were paid, it would seem that property, exclusive of the house in St. Mary's-street, of about two hundred pounds a year, was all that remained to the family, or rather to himself as the eldest son. The means were slight, the responsibilities heavy; yet he accepted, and in due course achieved the task of rearing, educating and placing the

---

[1] Parish Register, Nov. 19, 1625.

whole of that numerous family in the way of obtaining their own bread. Humphrey lived with him, and followed his fortunes to the last, becoming in due time a commissioner of naval prizes and captain of a ship of war. After the restoration, he was persecuted for nonconformity, and at last quitted this country for Carolina, where some of his descendants still remain. Two of his daughters married in Bridgwater, and there are still Cranes and Normans in that town who claim to be their descendants.[1] William went to London, where he became a learned and successful man; he attracted the notice of scholars, was created a doctor of civil law by the University of Padua, and when he died followed the example of his brother and grandfather in leaving a legacy to the poor of his native town.[2] He also left a number of legacies to his brothers, nephews and nieces.[3] George went to London, and became a goldsmith and banker of Cheapside. In after - life, probably after gaining a competence, he retired to Plymouth, where some of his children remained, but he himself afterwards settled at Minehead, on the Severn. One of his sons, Benjamin, had a taste for letters; and a copy of verses written by him on the death of his uncle, Dr. William

---

[1] Blake Mss.

[2] Ibid. The following appears on a panel in St. Mary's church:— " William Blake, Doctor of ye Civill Law, and Grandchild of the above said Robert Blake, did by his last Will and Testament bequeath unto the Poor of this Towne the sume of one hundred Pounds, which sume is in the custody of ye common Councell of this Borough, and the yearly interest thereof to remain to the poor people of this town for ever." He died 1667.

[3] Blake Mss.

Blake, are still extant.[1] Samuel married early in life, and took to agriculture; as a farm, consisting of a house and about one hundred and fifty acres of land, orchard, garden, meadows and pasturage, at Pawlett, a village about four miles below Bridgwater, on the river Parrett, had been made over to him by his elder brother.[2] When the civil war broke out he joined his brother's company, and was one of the first martyrs of the good cause in the west of England. Nicholas engaged in the Spanish trade like his father and grandfather. He resided chiefly at Dunster and Minehead, successfully cultivated business, and acquired a moderate estate, which his descendants of Venne House still enjoy.[3] Benjamin went to sea, where he so far prospered as to rise ultimately to the rank of captain in the Commonwealth navy. Alexander probably took to farming.

During the nine years spent at Oxford, Blake's character was slowly but soundly developed. When he returned to his native town, and again took up his residence in the family mansion, he was already remarkable for that iron will, that grave demeanour, that free and dauntless spirit for which after-events found employment, but did not create. Simple in his tastes and habits, there was already a dignity and refinement in every line of his noble countenance which bespoke command, and seemed to presage victory. His manners, though somewhat austere in one so young, were relieved by a certain bluntness of address, while his peculiar sense of humour and great vehemence of passion rendered his conversation at once impressive, agreeable, and pictur-

---

[1] Ms. in my own possession.   [2] Blake Mss.   [3] Ibid.

esque. Abuses in Church and State, daily growing more corrupt and incorrigible, afforded an unfailing theme for his satire ; the formal profligacy which reigned at court, the moral laxity and doctrinal intolerance which marked so many religious professors, excited his intense indignation ; and both in public and in private places he never ceased to inveigh against them with bitter sarcasm and solid argument. The weak worldliness of the prelates, the mean subservience of the Church to royal vices and follies, drove young Blake, as they drove thousands of the ardent and uncorrupted, into Puritanism : the despicable pedantry, faithlessness and profligacy of the King, his favourites and his courtiers, insulting from their high station the moral sense of a virtuous, domestic and religious people, made him sigh for the republic of Pericles or of Scipio. The two theories were indeed near allied : the Puritan in religion became by an easy and natural progress a democrat in politics. The head of the State was the admitted head of the Church. The principles of divine right and irresponsibility which ruled in the one ruled also in the other. The King claimed to be the vicegerent of God in affairs spiritual as well as temporal ; and on this point the Church was in complete accord with royalty. After the death of James, his son Charles taught the divine right of kings, Laud contended for the divine right of kings and bishops. Opposition to the ideas which reigned at Lambeth led therefore by a single step to protests against abuses in the secular government. Yet there was scarcely one statesman in that age with sufficient clearness of vision to perceive how nearly the two sets of principles were allied. It was left for time and events to shew that the Puritan, living under the rule of Star-Chambers and Courts of High Commission, became almost as a matter of course an advocate for the Republic. When Blake quitted Oxford in 1624, this startling name had scarcely yet been heard in public; the men who professed a reverence for democratic institutions were few in number and obscure in rank, being for the greater part either poor scholars, fresh from the study of ancient history and poetry, with the glory of that august literature still lingering in their minds, or pious dreamers of an earthly Zion, in which the simple laws and social equality of an early Hebrew tribe should be tried once more amid the complex wants and infinite resources of modern civilisation. But he never made a secret of his opinions.

Long before the throne was considered to be in danger, he was marked by courtiers of sense and observation as a person of avowed republican sentiments. He publicly declared himself of the school of Scipio and Pericles. It was on the model of these ancient heroes that, as a boy dreaming of the classic world, he had endeavoured to form his own character; and in after-life it became his fortune to rival these celebrated men, not alone in their private virtues, but also in the splendour of their public achievements.[1]

---

[1] Clarendon, vi. 41; Laud's Remains (1700), 68.

CHAPTER II.

𝕮𝖍𝖊 𝕽𝖊𝖇𝖔𝖑𝖚𝖙𝖎𝖔𝖓.

For several years after his return from college and final settlement at Bridgwater, Blake's time and talents were chiefly occupied with the care of his aged mother —who outlived her husband thirteen years, seeing her youngest son Alexander arrive at the age of manhood,[1]— and in the education and settlement of his brothers and sisters. But he was a keen observer of public events, a politician by nature and early training; and as the action of the court became suspicious to good Protestants and menacing to the nation's civil liberties, he bent the whole force of his genius to create and organise in his native county a party of resistance to its measures. Nor was this task very difficult. Commercial habits and superior education had already given a strong liberal bias to the men of that district; and the instincts of ancient and unreasoning loyalty which still grew there were rudely disturbed by the King's friends. William Laud, appointed to the see of Bath and Wells shortly after Blake quitted Oxford, in two or three years' administration of that important diocese, contrived by his zeal for high episcopacy and royal right, his personal absence from the see, except when it became necessary to

---

[1] Parish register, Dec. 27, 1638.

appear as a persecutor of conscience, and his fierce denunciation of all classes and degrees of non-conformity, however slight—to rouse a spirit of opposition to the governing powers in Church and State, that increased in violence from year to year, and gradually bore down all counter-influences, until it finally exploded in the civil war. Possessed of the King's ear, Laud felt no scruple in turning the executive arm against his spiritual opponents, and even ventured an attempt to coerce the judges into instruments of his episcopal vengeance. On one occasion, when Lord Chief-Justice Richardson returned to London from the Somerset assizes, where he had heard and disposed of several cases in which the bishop took an interest with a moderation worthy of the bench in its better days, he was attacked with so much fury at the Council-board, that on retiring he remarked to his friends, he had been almost choked with a pair of lawn sleeves. Such a policy, carried out in the immediate vicinity of the town, and finding its victims in men generally respected, gave force and edge to the keen invective of the future admiral; and the still more famous and infamous proceedings of the same prelate, after his translation to Canterbury, in bringing Prynne, Burton, Bastwick, and many other pious and honourable men before the Star-Chamber and Court of High Commission,—the clipping of ears, the branding of temples, the slitting of noses, the burning of tongues, the prisons, pillories, and public scourgings to which he resorted for the maintenance of his Popish dogmas,— continued in the years which followed that event to call forth his most indignant denunciations. Nor was the spur of private resentment long wanting. Bishop Pierce, who after an interval succeeded Laud in the see of Bath and Wells, resolved to put down the famous Lectures with a heavy hand, and suspended Mr. Deverish, the minister of Bridgwater, for preaching as usual a lecture in his own church on market-day, and using a short prayer. But not satisfied with an act of authority which put an end to a system followed by the Church from the days of Elizabeth, Pierce attacked the church-warden, Humphrey Blake, and enjoined him to do penance for the crime of not presenting Deverish for ecclesiastical censure![1] A bold remonstrance against these and similar prostitutions of the power exercised by the courts of conscience was signed by many leading liberals of Somerset, and by Robert Blake one of the first.

The remonstrants prayed the King to put an end to religious persecution, and inveighed against the Popish rites and ceremonies which Laud was then trying to intro- duce into the Church. Two Puritan divines, Deverish and Norman, were the chief clerical leaders of the movement party in Bridgwater; but their young lay ally was its real leader, and by his genius and activity the powerful local influence of the Stawells and Wyndhams, both ultra- royalist families, was thrown into the shade, while a com- manding position was obtained for the new opinions.[2]

The aspect of affairs at court was lowering. Charles had not only married a French woman and a Papist—

---

[1] Scrap-book of the Rev. Mr. Jones of Bridgwater.

[2] Laud's Diary, 34; Laud's Remains, ii. 67; Clarendon, vi. 41; His- tory and Life, 6-8.

causes of deep offence to a people jealous of the slightest appearance of foreign influence in their councils—but had entered into illegal and insulting engagements with the wily minister who then directed the policy of Versailles. As the price of Henrietta Maria's hand, Richelieu had demanded that the young Queen and her court should have full right to the exercise of her religion— that the children issuing from the marriage should be under the complete control of their mother and her advisers until the age of thirteen—and that for the future all English Catholics should enjoy perfect freedom from the operation of laws against opinion, and be allowed to perform the services of their Church.[1] These stipulations, granted by Charles rather than forego the honour of an alliance with the blood of St. Louis, were agreed to in a series of secret articles; but their purport was soon generally known, and this treason to the law of the land and the strong Protestant instincts of the people alarmed and enraged the whole country. Nor was the popular mistrust unjustified by events:—the children of this unhappy alliance were so ill-trained in early life as eventually to forsake the religion of their country, and with that lapse to forfeit the splendid inheritance of their race. But seeing Popery openly enthroned at Whitehall, the people resented every appearance of an inclination towards Rome in the clergy—whether that inclination shewed itself in the lofty character of their spiritual pretensions, in the pomp and circumstance of their way of life, or in the boldness of their hostility to freedom of thought. On all these points Laud was ob-

---

[1] Hardwicke Papers, i. 523-561; Cabala, 320; Prynne, 72.

noxious to the more ardent Reformers ; and Charles himself was scarcely less hateful. His stock was bad. The
general disgust created by his father's claim to govern
England—not by the semi-divine right of genius like
the first and last of the Tudor sovereigns, but by the
ultra-divine right of royal birth—was not allayed by
any act of manly sincerity or generous explanation of his
own policy. Questions of finance also arose to embar-
rass parties and embitter the contest about principles of
government in Church and State. Ireland and Scotland were even less tranquil than the supreme country,
though from different causes. Beyond the Tweed, the
religious question alone occupied the field of contro-
versy. By law, Charles was not head of the Church in
Scotland, and his attempts—aided by his complaisant
Archbishop of Canterbury—to bring its clergy under
control, to rob them of their spiritual rights, to meddle
with their ecclesiastical government, and to impose on
their unwilling congregations his own favourite ritual,
put his own power in peril and alienated from his person
the friends to whom he might otherwise have looked in
the worst extremities of his fortune.[1] In Ireland the
elements of discontent were more numerous, but they
nearly all had their origin in the religious disabilities imposed on the Catholic masses. When pressed for money,
Charles had sold certain graces or indulgences to a body of
men in the western counties of the island for 120,000*l*.,
though well aware that the very word "indulgence"
would have a startling and papistical sound in English
ears. For this sum he consented to remove from the

---

[1] Bibliotheca Regia, 125-138; Laud's Troubles, 101; Balfour, ii. 224.

purchasers all penal laws enacted against their creed, to allow them a right to practise at the bar, and to exercise other functions at that time prohibited by statute.   To the original infamy of this illegal sale, Charles added the still deeper infamy of taking the money and then refusing to fulfil the contract.   When the poor dupes of his kingly word complained, he sent his stern lieutenant Strafford into Ireland with orders to repress the discontent with a strong arm, to assimilate the Irish to the English Church, and finally to over-ride the ancient constitution and make the King's power absolute at least across St. George's Channel.   Strafford succeeded in this task as only a man of genius, without conscience, can succeed.   Attacking the Catholics in their opinions, their liberties and their properties at the same time, he confounded every measure taken in their defence ; and by harassing suits and galling disabilities, invented by a faculty which seemed infinite in its resources and carried out with a vigour which knew no pause and counted no obstacle, he achieved such a success with the higher classes and in the rich towns as intoxicated his royal master.   The old nobles of the country were brought over, some by threats, others by cajolery, still more by fashion, policy and personal ambition.   But the deputy's fierce and unscrupulous course of conversion fired the vindictive passions of the multitude, and the natural dread lest this rigorous policy should spread, arrayed against him the whole liberal and constitutional party in England.[1]

The armed revolt against Charles began in his native

---

[1] Clarendon, 1-212; Strafford Papers, i. 421-521 ; ii. 36-98.

land. Harassed by Laud's agents, the Scotch Presbyterians took an oath and covenant to maintain their religious independence at all hazards; and when the King
threatened them with the punishment due to rebels,
instead of stealing back to their homes to escape the
royal wrath, they flew to arms, boldly crossed the border into England, and offered to put the issues of their
quarrel to the ordeal of battle. The court raged with
passion and insulted pride. But its contortions were as
vain as they were undignified, for the reforming House
of Commons made the cause of the Scotch Covenanters
their own, and the royalist policy received its first sudden and serious check. Strafford was impeached. Laud
was lodged in the Tower. Finch the lord-keeper and
secretary Windebank were driven into exile. Concessions were obtained for the English people; and in the
northern kingdom Charles was stript of his most coveted
prerogative.[1]

In the heat of his resentment against the Scots, the
King had summoned the two Houses to meet again
after a separation of many years; the step had created
an immense sensation in the country; and the most
liberal men of the middle and upper ranks were returned
for nearly all the large towns. Blake was sent up as
member for Bridgwater; and now he first met with Vane,
Hampden, Cromwell and other leaders of the reform
party. His legislative labours were, however, of the
briefest duration—this meeting of the House being that
which is known in history as the Short Parliament.
Charles wanted money to fight the Covenanters; but

---

[1] Balfour, ii. 366; Clarendon, i. 339-364.

when he asked for it in his usual peremptory manner, the House replied with presenting a long list of grievances, and insisted that before any money-bills were laid on the table, an inquiry should be made into the state of the nation, especially in regard to the attempted innovations in religion, interference with the rights of private property and invasion of the privileges of Parliament. Neither threats nor cajoleries could overcome their resistance; and after a vain trial of his strength on the constitutional ground, Charles suddenly dissolved the House in a fit of anger.[1] Events, however, soon compelled him to issue writs for a new election; and before the year was out, the Long Parliament, fated to see and to survive so many governments, was sitting at Westminster. Of this famous assembly Blake was not a member until 1645, when he was returned for Taunton in the room of Sir William Portman, his seat for Bridgwater being occupied by Colonel Wyndham, governor of the castle, and a strenuous opponent of the popular party.[2]

The noise of armament had not yet died away beyond the Tweed when it arose in the sister country. There, a long-cherished hatred of the Saxon race embittered the quarrel about lands and religions. Under the powerful rule of Strafford, the ancient Celtic population had been made to feel its inferiority in a thousand galling forms; for that statesman had always treated the country as a conquered province of the empire, subject to no law but that of the sword, and capable of no rights

---

[1] Commons Journals, April 17 to May 4; Heath, 12-15; Laud's Troubles, 78.

[2] Parliamentary History, ix. 39.

but such as the prince, his master, might bestow and revoke at pleasure. Yet in spite of his agent's tyranny, and his own often-proved bad faith, the person and government of the King continued popular in Ireland :— that very tendency towards papistical rites and doctrines which rendered him so suspicious in other parts of his dominions won for him the confidence and affection of his ignorant Catholic subjects. In his name, and as they pretended with his approval, they flew to arms. Treachery of a confederate caused the failure of an attempt to seize Dublin Castle ; but the insurrection spread into the remotest districts, and in one week from the outbreak, the entire open country and the chief towns in Longford, Leitrim, Cavan, Donegal, Derry, Monaghan, and other counties were possessed by the rebel hordes. With a confusion of purposes only possible in Ireland, the leaders declared by proclamation that their object in rising was to support the King against the popular members of the House of Commons, who, they said, had invaded the royal prerogative, intercepted the favours granted by the Crown to its subjects in Ireland, and designed to root out the Catholic faith from that part of the empire. The King's cause was adopted as their own, and their blind fury was directed against the very men who had recently brought their great oppressor to the scaffold. Under the drunkenness of unexpected success, their followers committed atrocities at which nature and history shudder. The English settlers, whether of ancient or of modern standing, were cast into prison, their goods and lands seized and divided, their children torn from them, their women ravished before

D

their eyes, and their whole body, the grace, the soul, the sustaining element of the country, was treated with every barbarity which hate could devise and victorious passion inflict. In this outburst of popular insanity, more than forty thousand Protestant settlers were butchered in cold blood.[1]

Preparations were instantly made to check these atrocities. But who was to command the forces sent against the rebels? Those rebels openly declared that they had the King's sanction for what they had done :— a most unhappy declaration for the man in whose interests they professed to devastate and murder, as it rendered it impossible for the two Houses to entrust him with the means of action, and he found himself compelled either to admit that the rising had taken place at his instigation, or to transfer to his new Parliament the general conduct of the war. He chose the latter evil, and in one day his enemies became masters of a fleet and an army. That day the contest began in earnest. After he had ceded all control of the forces necessary to suppress the rebellion, Charles, alarmed at the false position in which he had placed himself, made an effort to get his creature Sir John Pennington appointed chief admiral in the Irish seas, a post of supreme importance at that moment; but as Parliament had reason to suspect that officer of an intention to employ the force under his command against the national movement, they refused to accept

---

[1] Carte's Ormond, iii. 30-47; Nalson, 543-557; Clanricarde's Memoirs, 6-38 ; Borlase's Reduction of Ireland, 230-233 ; Clarendon, i. 423.

the nomination, and sent the Earl of Warwick as their vice-admiral into those waters.[1]

Soon after this event, Charles raised the royal standard at Nottingham, and called the loyal gentry of England to his aid. The two parties now in presence of each other, arming to dispute possession of the realm, and determine the principles on which it should be governed then and afterwards, were as distinct in character as in cause. On the King's side, notwithstanding his personal meanness, a large majority of the old families was arrayed; men of high birth and gentle nurture; brave by nature and from long habit loyal to the regal office; and attached by ancient tradition or private interest to the forms of monarchy and episcopacy; but at the same time devoid of strong convictions, of that sustained mental energy so needful in revolutions, and for the greater part of high moral character. On the other hand, instead of the gay heart and lust of pleasure which so universally marked the Cavalier, the Roundhead was distinguished by a grave demeanour, an austere life, a fiery enthusiasm and fixed beliefs. Between such opponents the contest could not have been prolonged beyond a single summer had they commenced it in equal numbers and with equal means. But their condition as soldiers was as various as their opinions. The royalists rode into the camp almost ready for the field. Many of them had been long familiar with the use of arms; and nearly all had been accustomed to a country life, to hunting, sporting and the exercises which best prepare men for the hardships of a camp and the terrors of a

---

[1] Rushworth, iv. 752; Clarendon, iii. 262.

battle-field. Their enemies were in a great measure
students, small farmers, and city tradesmen. To their
hands, books and implements of trade or husbandry
were more familiar than guns and broadswords. Devotion, courage, enthusiasm they could bring to the contest, but they had the whole art and practice of war to
learn from its very rudiments.[1]

Charles quitted Nottingham for the west of England
at the head of six thousand men, and such was the
enthusiasm for his cause in those opening days of the
great conflict, that by the time he had reached Shrews-
bury his army had increased to nearly twenty thousand.
This vast accession of strength induced him to turn his
face towards London, the head-quarters of his most active and powerful enemies, in the hope of being able
to crush them all at a single blow; but he had scarcely
quitted his halting place when the Earl of Essex was descried hovering with a considerable force on his flank and
rear, ready to cut off his stragglers, intercept supplies,
and enclose him between two fires, should he advance on
the capital. He was forced to retreat or to give battle,
and chose the latter in full confidence of victory. Six
thousand men were slain in this encounter: Essex, somewhat worsted, retired towards Coventry, and the King
advanced his head-quarters to Oxford, whence he sent out
flying squadrons of horse under Prince Rupert to spread
terror and consternation to the suburbs of London.
For a few days the city was distracted with false reports,
and the popular leaders evinced a desire to treat; but

---

[1] Com. Jour. v. 327-385; Granville Penn's Memorials of Admiral
Penn, i. 79; Clarendon, iii. 263, 331.

unfortunately for the royal cause, while the terms of
an understanding were being discussed under cover of
an armistice, Ruthen, the King's Swedish general, made
an unexpected attack on Brentford, and carried it by
assault. The cry of treachery was then raised. London
flew to arms. The trained bands marched out and encamped on the common before the captured town. By
rapid marches Essex brought up his army from the midland counties; and instead of seizing Whitehall and the
Tower, as he intended, Charles was compelled to throw
himself behind the Thames; flying like a fugitive across
the bridge at Kingston toward Reading and Oxford, in
the latter of which cities he resolved to pass the winter
months after fortifying with hasty works and strong
garrisons all the more important places in the immediate
vicinity.[1]

Meanwhile Blake was on the alert in Somersetshire.
Taking the King's hasty dissolution of the Short Parliament as a signal for action, he began, with the aid of
his young and fiery brother Samuel, to count his friends,
to prepare arms and horses, to concoct watchwords and
to keep a keen eye on the movements of the King's partisans. His was one of the first troops in the field, and
both the horse and foot played a conspicuous part in the
first action of any importance in the west of England,
when Sir John Horner routed the newly raised forces
of the Marquis of Hertford at Wells. From that date he
was in almost every action of importance in the western
counties, fighting his way gradually into military notice.

---

[1] Com. Jour. v. 423-439; May, 168, et seq.; Rushworth, v. 33, et
seq.; Whitelocke, 65, 66.

He distinguished himself in the sharp encounter at Bodmin; and gained the confidence of Sir William Waller by his conduct on the fiercely disputed field of Lansdown. Detached from the army to strengthen the garrison at Bristol, he missed the disastrous defeat at Roundway Down. Blake's attention was not, however, confined to the war. His knowledge of business, his activity, and his severe integrity pointed him out for other employments, and he was made one of the Committee for seizing and sequestrating the Estates of Delinquents in Somerset :—a thankless office, the duties of which he nevertheless discharged for several years without giving rise to a single accusation of partiality or making for himself one personal enemy. But the camp was his true sphere of action; his superiority to the men about him lay in the marvellous fertility, energy and comprehensiveness of his military genius. Before the field of action was as yet occupied by large armies, he scoured the country with his intrepid dragoons, rousing the spirit of his friends, carrying terror to the hearths of his enemies, and levying contributions of money and horses on all towns and hamlets known to be disaffected to the national cause. In the royalist camp Prince Rupert could alone be compared with him as a partisan soldier; and that brilliant cavalry officer, fated to be foiled so often on land and sea by Blake, soon made the acquaintance of his redoubtable enemy at the siege of Bristol.[1]

Rupert's youth had been passed like that of a hero of romance. The son of a Bohemian king and an English

---

[1] Elegiac Enumeration, 5 ; Declaration and Ordinance of Parliament, March 31, 1643; History and Life, 8, 9.

princess, he was connected in blood with half the reign-
ing families in Europe, and his long pedigree stretched
back through Charlemagne to Attila. Yet as a boy
he had known nothing of the free grace of boyhood.
Storms raged round his cradle from his birth. In an
ante-chamber of the Hradschin he was one day snatched
up by his nurse while sleeping in the midst of flashing
fires and booming artillery; Austrian and Bavarian
troops were thundering at the gates of Prague; and in
the hurry of mortal fear the menial dropt her royal
charge on the floor, where he was found by a chamber-
lain of the palace, and flung into the last carriage that
followed the unhappy court on its way to Breslau.
Army after army rose to avenge the dethronement of
his mother, the famous Queen of Hearts, but they
struggled in vain against the more prosperous fortunes
of the southern Germans. Rupert and his brother
Maurice wandered from court to court, but dread of the
imperial arms silenced every sentiment of pity in the
royal palaces of Europe; and Holland alone, in its pride
of liberty and power, dared to offer an asylum to the unhappy fugitives. There Rupert passed his early youth.
A hard student at the University of Leyden, a hunter
and hawker over the flat fields of the Zuyder Zee, the
crowned hero of many a courtly tournament, a volunteer
at the siege of Rhynberg,—he was already at the age of
fifteen a man of the world and a soldier who had won
his spurs in actual service. A brief visit to England,
where Laud proposed to make him a bishop, the Queen
to marry him to a rich heiress, and the King, his uncle,
to send him out as viceroy to Madagascar,—led to an

insane enterprise of his own for the recovery of his father's family dominions on the Rhine. Defeated and taken prisoner, he passed three heavy years in the fortress of Linz, varied only by a love-affair with the young Countess of Kuffstein, whom he abandoned for ever the moment he obtained his freedom. His temper soured and his passions inflamed by adversity, he next turned soldier of fortune, repaired to England, where his uncle's growing troubles promised a wide field for the exercise of his military talents, and was immediately named master of the royal horse. The Cavaliers were companions after his own heart. No sooner did he meet the high-spirited gentry of England than he became their leader. Brave, active, impetuous, no foe could withstand the vigour of his onset or escape the celerity of his pursuit. Within three months of his arrival he had already made his name a word of terror in the country. But if his daring spirit and indomitable activity made him a dangerous enemy,—it is nevertheless certain that his cold heart, his lust of money, his ruthless cruelty, his contempt of law, made him a still more fatal friend. In spite of his valour, his vigilance and his success, history must denounce the King's warlike nephew as the real evil genius of his cause.[1]

From his camp at Oxford, Charles ruled about a third of the territory of England. Wales and the whole border land adhered steadfastly to his banner; and his dashing master of the horse, after taking the important town of Cirencester by surprise, proposed to consolidate the royal

---

[1] Lansdowne Mss. 817; Clarendon, iii. 255-436; Howell's Letters, 91; Warburton's Rupert and the Cavaliers, i. 17-113.

power in the west by the capture of Bristol and the line of fortresses along the Severn. With his uncle's consent, he first tried to reduce the city by treachery, but the faithless citizens who would have made themselves his accomplices and instruments were betrayed to the proper authorities, and received the reward of their intended treason; whereupon he advanced at the head of fourteen thousand foot and six thousand horse, and summoned Colonel Fiennes, the commander, to yield the place to the King's officers.[1] Though torn with factions, like most other towns at that time, Bristol was capable of a long, if not a permanent defence. The regular troops within its walls counted in cavalry and infantry not less than two thousand men; many of the citizens were armed; the store of provisions was abundant and of excellent quality; shot and powder were also plentiful; and a powerful park of brass ordnance was distributed among the forts and works. The lines, it is true, were incomplete. In many places the breastworks had not been carried to the proper elevation, and the ditch at some points required greater width and depth to render it defensible. But the castle within the town was a hold of some strength, and the minor forts along the line—one of the most important of which, Prior's Hill, was entrusted by Fiennes to Captain Blake—offered several centres of support to the garrison in their offensive operations against the enemy. Had the chief command been in the hands of an able and resolute soldier, the city would not have fallen, or if so, not ingloriously.[2]

---

[1] Rushworth, iii. part ii. 154; Mercury, August 3, p. 74; Heath, 46.

[2] Seyer, ii. 300-416; Cromwell's Letters, i. 297; Warburton, ii. 236.

On Sunday morning, July 23, Rupert and Maurice sat
down before the place with their whole army, supported
by a not inconsiderable train of artillery, and from their
head-quarters at Clifton — a charming suburb even at
that early time, — they summoned the garrison to surrender. This summons leading to no result, they spent
that day and the night following it in reconnoitring the
position, in exchanging a few shots with the outposts and
driving in foraging parties of horse. Next day the two
commanders prepared for more serious work; Fiennes
ordered the citizens, unless actually engaged in the defence, to keep within doors, leaving the streets free for
the soldiers to act; Rupert drew out his entire force in
two lines, and marched them in order of battle within
view of the forts, hoping to intimidate the besieged by
his immense military superiority. But this display of
his means of offence failing of its expected effect on the
spirits of the garrison, he fixed his lines and began to
erect batteries opposite to the various forts. Lord Grandison and a body of cavalry took possession of a rising
ground, covered by a thick hedge, over against Prior's
Hill, where Blake was stationed with a small body of
men,—and the labourers commenced a rude breastwork,
on which, under cover of the darkness, they planted their
field pieces unseen. At midnight two cannon-shots from
Grandison's position lit up the sky and broke the silence
with their rolling echoes. Blake quickly answered from
Prior's Hill with a discharge of musketry and grape-shot.
On the instant lights were observed moving along the beleaguering lines, and a nocturnal cannonade commenced,
spread rapidly to adjacent parts, and continued for about

an hour. Next day grand preparations were made by the royalists to storm the rude works; and when all was ready they advanced to the assault in six lines, the officers and soldiers wearing green boughs as a means of recognition in the hurry and disorder of the expected sack. The men in the first line bore fagots on their backs, those in the second drove carts laden with earth to fill the ditch, the third line was armed with muskets, the fourth bore long pikes with wild-fire at the points, the fifth carried hand-grenades, the sixth was armed like the third with muskets. The charge was made with Rupert's usual intrepidity. Parts of the shallow ditch were filled, the works were scaled in several places at the same moment, and Cavalier and Roundhead met hand to hand in single encounters; but after a fierce and long-continued struggle, the assailants were repulsed with loss at every point. While the infantry were advancing to storm, a squadron of royal horse was ordered to sweep round the outer lines, make an unexpected appearance before Frome Gate, cut down the sentries, and advance at a brisk pace on the rear of the garrison then engaged with the main body of the royal infantry. But this attempt also failed. The guard at Frome Gate was on the alert, and a hot fire from behind their sheltered positions soon put the horsemen to rout. The fighting went on simultaneously at the forts. Two demi-cannon had been directed by Lord Grandison with some effect against the old walls at Prior's Hill; but Blake's vigorous fire kept the assailants at bay, and when night came down, and the combatants had time to count their losses, besides the usual casualties, Grandison had to deplore the death of his chief cannoneer; Blake, the mutilation of one of his three guns, and serious damage to his works.[1]

The little garrison of Prior's Hill had slight breathing time allowed them. Before three o'clock in the morning, the grey dawn was streaked with bursting lights, and the sleep of the tired soldiers was broken by the cracking muskets of the Cornish division. The prince was already awake in his tent; and on catching the first signal, drew out his troops, and disposed some squadrons of horse under cover of the rising grounds,— ready to second the infantry in case of need, to check sallies, and enter the lines as soon as the foot had forced a passage. His design was to break the curtain between Prior's Hill and the next position, a small redoubt, strengthened by two fortified houses; but finding his flank terribly confused and torn by Blake's steady and well-directed fire, he sent Grandison with a body of picked men to storm that post, while he advanced with the main body against the intervening curtain:—the attack on Prior's Hill thus became the key to the entire operations of that day. Dividing his force, Grandison sent fifty musqueteers to begin the alarm on the line a little to the right of Blake's position, and another fifty to make a similar demonstration on the left. Within gunshot of Prior's Hill the highway entered Bristol through the rude lines, the point of intersection being covered by a spur with a low breastwork, and barricaded by a gate of strong timbers. While the garrison at the Hill was distracted with the movements of the musqueteers, Colonel Lunsford, at the head of three hundred men,

---

[1] Mercury, August 3, 74; Rupert Ms. in Warburton, ii. 237-246.

fell on the curtain,—but after a sharp struggle was driven back with loss. Major Sandars was then sent forward with two hundred and fifty men to storm the spur, and bravely rushing through the steady fire from the works up to the very gate, there came to a pike and pistol contest with its defenders. Nine hand-grenades were thrown into the works. Captain Fawcett fastened a petard to the timbers of the gate, but the explosion only shattered a few bars, without opening a practicable breach. After an hour and a half lost in fighting a series of skirmishes, in which he saw Captain Howell and many of his most gallant comrades fall in vain, Grandison seemed to be convinced that so long as Prior's Hill remained in Blake's hands, the curtain could not be forced at that point; and he consequently drew out his whole strength against the real key of the position. Elated by their success, the little garrison prepared to give the foe a warm welcome. The royalists, led on by their impetuous and exasperated chief, rushed into the shallow ditch surrounding the fort again and again, but always to retire in confusion and with loss. Finding his ammunition about to fail, Blake ordered his men to hurl huge stones on the assailants below, while the best marksmen kept up a steady and destructive fire from the embrasures. Lunsford at one moment placed a ladder against the wall and mounted as high as the palisades, but was then forced back. Lieutenant Ellis gained the line, but was instantly shot through the heart. Again the whole body advanced to an assault; again the heroic garrison repulsed them with slaughter. As the royalists retired in confusion, Blake, feeling, with the untaught instinct of military genius, that the decisive moment had come, led down the drawbridge, and sallied out at the head of his little troop. Rage and shame seized the royalist officers on seeing their men turn from the fire of a handful of rebels, and mounting a horse that stood near, Grandison shouted to them to follow him. At the sound of his voice the fugitives rallied once more, and were led a third time to the assault. At the ditch they met the Roundheads sallying out, Blake in front, and instantly the struggle was renewed, pistol and pike, sword and musket. Grandison was shot in the leg and disabled Colonel Owen advanced to take his place; he received the contents of a musket in his head. Hotly pressed in front, their leaders both put out of action, without plan or directing mind, the royalists at last fell back in disorder to their old position; and having completely swept the line, and cleared the hill, so far as they came within range of his fire, Blake retired with his exhausted troops to their little fort in triumph.[1]

At other points the fortunes of the day had been less favourable to the Roundheads. Between Brandon Hill and Windmill Fort, where the curtain was incomplete and the defence weakest, Colonel Washington broke over with his regiment of horse; and the defenders falling back rapidly, he advanced at a brisk pace through the suburbs up to Frome Gate :— but being unsupported by the prince, his ardour exposed them to the danger of being enclosed and cut off to the last man. From the windows and roofs of houses a flanking fire galled and

---

[1] Rupert Ms. in Warburton, ii. 247-249; Clarendon, iii. 10.

thinned his ranks; some of his bravest officers fell at his side. Rupert himself hesitated to enter the broken line, and kept his troop waiting in a meadow at the foot of Brandon Hill, out of range from its guns. Had Fiennes made a vigorous movement at this time, he might have captured or cut to pieces the whole squadron, and seriously damaged the reputation of Rupert's redoubtable cavalry. But the governor's heart failed him as soon as the enemy appeared before Frome Gate. To the astonishment of the Cavaliers he made signs for a parley; and before midnight, had already agreed to surrender the city next morning at nine o'clock, on condition that the inhabitants should not be plundered, and that the garrison should depart without their arms. Blake's indignation at this strange conduct in his superior officer was loudly and fiercely expressed. At first he could not believe that a man, who had evinced no want of courage in the House of Commons, could give up the second city in the empire after a few hours of not very serious fighting, — and for his own part he refused to admit the terms of capitulation, and threatened to hold his little stronghold to the last man. In the confusion of his preparation for departure on the morrow, Fiennes forgot to acquaint the commanders of Prior's Hill and Brandon Hill forts with the nature of the important act which he had just concluded; and this negligence afterwards became a serious charge against him, as putting in peril many valuable lives. When, therefore, at sunrise a body of royalists appeared before the ditch to take possession of the little fort which they had vainly assailed the previous day, Blake replied to their summons with a volley of musketry that sent them back in reeling and broken columns. On hearing that the redoubtable commander at Prior's Hill refused to admit the articles of surrender, Rupert declared that he would hang him on the spot:—how different might have been his own career had he but carried this threat into execution. Twenty-four hours longer Blake still held his post and kept the Cavaliers at bay; but then learning, from sources on which he could rely, the exact nature of the agreement with Fiennes, and that the Roundhead garrison was already on its march, he reluctantly quitted the position he had shewn himself so well able to defend. The timid governor was afterwards brought before a court-martial at St. Alban's, where he was tried for cowardice, convicted and sentenced to death,—but his life was spared by the lord general Essex. Blake did not appear as a witness against him on the trial.[1]

The loss of Bristol was but one of a series of misfortunes. Ten days previous to the capitulation, Waller had been worsted at Lansdown Heath; a fortnight before that disaster, the Fairfaxes had fought and lost a great battle on Adderton Moor, and were then shut up in Hull. Even Cromwell's genius failed to keep down the Lincolnshire royalists; Gainsborough was taken by their partisans; Lincoln itself had to be abandoned. Hopton had encountered and dispersed the Roundheads at Stratton in Cornwall. With the exception of London, the Associated Eastern Counties, and a few isolated towns, the whole country appeared to be finally reduced

---

[1] Elegiac Enumeration, 5; Mercury, August 3, 74; State Trials, iv 186-298; Clarendon, vi. 41; Rupert Ms. in Warburton, ii. 247-249.

to obedience. Liberty was in its last throes, and one more decisive victory might have put an end to constitutions and parliaments in England for many years.[1] With no fear of meeting an enemy by the way, Charles passed from Oxford to Bristol, where he called a council to deliberate on the next movement. Rupert and the war-party advised the King to march on London and finish the war by one bold and brilliant stroke. But more timorous councils prevailed, and it was first resolved to reduce Gloucester, the only city of any importance in the west still faithful to the national cause:—a fatal determination for the King, as it gave the Roundheads time to recover from the alarm of so many disasters. Rising to the height of the occasion, the London train-bands once more marched, with Essex and his levies, against the victorious Cavaliers. Charles burnt his huts and raised the siege of Gloucester at their approach, and the battle of Newbury, though undecisive, restored in some degree the equality of the two powers.[2]

Meantime Blake received new employments from the Parliament. He was named one of the Somerset Committee for Ways and Means, and appointed, as a reward for his exploits at Bristol, Lieut.-Colonel to Popham's regiment, the finest militia in the country, a body fifteen hundred strong, well equipped, and firmly attached to Roundhead principles. With a part of this force, in which his brother Samuel had command of a company, Blake made a rapid dash into Bridgwater, in the hope of

---

[1] Rushworth, v. 271-285; Whitelocke, 70; Cromwell's Letters, i. 216-7.

[2] May, iii. 140; Parl. Hist. xii. 329; Somers Tracts, v. 296.

E

surprising the castle and securing the town for the good
old cause.   Riding in by the old stone bridge on which
he had so often played as a child, he stationed his men
on the Corn-hill and market-place, and made the *Swan*
his head-quarters. But Wyndham was on the alert. The
guns of the castle, forty in number, were prepared for
action ; the royalist garrison was at least equal in strength
with his own regiment ; and under the energetic influence
of the Luttrels, Trevelyans, and other county families,
instigated and supported by a majority of the clergy,
the townsmen themselves evinced no great eagerness to
throw off the Cavalier yoke.   Without ordnance, field-
stores, or other necessary supplies, Blake did not venture
to sit down and lose his time before the castle; so he
called in his scouts and patrols, and gave marching orders for the south coast, where the regiment had been
already destined for service in the defence of Lyme.   A
painful domestic incident marked his departure from his
native town.   Samuel, his younger brother, a gallant
but imprudent officer, strayed from head-quarters : at
a small village ale-house,—the *Shoulder of Mutton*, at
Pawlett, some four miles down the river,—he heard it
said that a captain of array and one of his followers
were crossing the river at Combwich passage to beat up
recruits for the King's service.   This intelligence he
ought to have carried at once to his brother, instead of
which his zeal and rashness induced him to mount his
horse and ride after the two officers.   At Streachill he
came up with them, a quarrel ensued, and he was killed
in the fray, leaving behind him a widow and two young
children.   Blake was terribly shocked, but he bore the

misfortune in the true spirit of a Roundhead. "When the news came to Bridgwater," says one who lived in his family and often heard the circumstance referred to, "the officers of the regiment were seen to cabal together in little companies, five or six at a place, and talk of it very seriously, none of them being forward to tell Colonel Blake what they were talking about. At last he asked one of them very earnestly, and the gentleman replied with some emotion, *Your brother Sam is killed*, explaining how it came to pass. The colonel, having heard him out, said, *Sam had no business there.* And, as if he took no further notice of it, turned from the Corn-hill or market-place into the *Swan* Inn, of chief note in that town, and shutting himself in a room gave way to the calls of nature and brotherly love, saying, *Died Abner as a fool dieth!*" The same writer adds: " But the sorrow of heroic minds, as it is more powerful than that of the general, so it is sooner spent; and collecting his own great soul within itself, and remembering the duty and resignation to the Divine will, he was in a short time composed both in thought and look, and leaving the *Swan* room, conversed with his officers on the Corn-hill about their march to the south coast. After this gush of grief, he was never known to bewail his brother's untimely death, or let it dwell in his memory." But this sorrow was the more profound because it found no vent in words: to the end of his great career he never ceased to think with kindness and regret of poor Sam,—the only one of his brothers who resembled him in the dauntless intrepidity of his nature; and to the orphan children thus suddenly committed to his charge he became the best of fathers. The oldest boy, Robert, evinced at an early age a longing for the sea; he entered the navy, and served with distinction in the fleets of his uncle; the younger, Samuel, shewed a more pacific disposition. It was to the young seaman, Captain Robert Blake, that the great admiral bequeathed, as the true heir to his naval glories, the gold chain bestowed on him by Parliament for his eminent services to the Commonwealth.[1]

After the fall of Bristol the royal army, increased by new levies, separated into two grand divisions. Rupert and the King turned northward, Maurice went into the west with orders to reduce the few towns on the southwest coast still holding out for Parliament. Lord Carnarvon led the advanced guard of this latter army, a powerful squadron of horse, and in a few weeks swept the country from the Severn to the sea. Dorchester struck without a blow. Weymouth, Corfe Castle and Portland Island fell into Cavalier hands; and these great losses were followed by those of Barnstaple, Dartmouth and Exeter. The natural strength of Plymouth still set the land-forces at defiance,—but with the exception of two or three insignificant places like Poole and Lyme, this was the only centre of influence still retained by the Roundheads. Maurice, flushed with the glories of a triumphant march, tried the effect of a sudden storm at Plymouth; but failing in this attempt, he left a detachment of his army to blockade the impregnable fortress, and with a force of nearly twenty thousand men moved

---

[1] Office-copy of Blake's will, March 13, 1655; Ordinance for raising money, August 3, 1643; History and Life, 12, 13.

along the coast, intending to punish the petty garrisons
of Lyme and Poole, on his way towards London.[1]

Lyme was at that date a little fishing town with nine
hundred or a thousand inhabitants. Built in a narrow
valley, at the dip between two hills, it was overlooked
from the heights on three sides, and the cliffs commanded the whole inner line of the bay. Three narrow
lanes, leading towards Charmouth, Axminster and Sidmouth, cut by a few irregular streets, formed the heart
of the town. Generally the houses were built of soft
stone and covered with thatch, the better sort having curious old gables and balconies opening out pleasantly to
the sea. The church, dedicated to St. Michael, stood on
a rising ground on the left, but every part of the grave-
yard, roof and steeple was overlooked from the brow of
Colway hill. As a port Lyme was of slight importance,
the water being shallow and the shore dangerous. Only
vessels of the smallest tonnage could run in for shelter
behind its ancient Cobb,—a low sea-wall built out
four or five hundred yards from the town to break
the tremendous force of the Atlantic waves,—yet as no
other place of refuge offered itself for several leagues
along that stormy coast, its roadstead sometimes swarmed
with small vessels, the property of London merchants,
and therefore good prize for the expectant royalists.
The town-defences consisted of a dry ditch, a few earthworks hastily thrown up and three small batteries,—
Davies' fort, standing a little above Church Cliffs on a
high ground looking towards Uplyme, but which has
long since fallen into the sea—Gun Cliff and the fort at

---

[1] Clarendon, iii. 131, 249; Warburton, ii. 302-307.

Cobb Gate, two low batteries on the sea-shore, covering
the bay, but of little use against an enemy making his
attack from the hills.   Into this cluster of poor cottages
Blake threw himself with part of Popham's regiment to
protect the ships from marauding Cavaliers.   Colonel
Ceely, civil governor of the town, had won distinction
for himself in many daring sallies against flying corps of
royalists; but when it became known that Maurice was
bringing down the great army from Devonshire, he gave
up the entire direction and responsibility of the defence
to Blake, — whose hold of this obscure and unfortifie
town became one of the most remarkable events of the
war.[1]

As the Prince came down from the hills of Somerset,
Blake counted his forces, and found the number did not
exceed five hundred men.   The town, though its spirit
was good, afforded little aid, for its whole population fell
short of a thousand souls; but with the assistance of
Colonel Weir, Captain Pyne and Governor Ceely, a body
of volunteers, some of them from Charmouth and other
neighbouring villages, was drilled for service.   Earth
works, hastily thrown up, connected the points of the defence from Davies' fort, on the High Cliff, along the slopes
beyond the town to Holme Bush Fields near the Cobb
Two large houses, standing on opposite sides of the
valley, about a mile from the line — Colway House, an
ancient residence of the Cobham family, and Haye, a
substantial farm, were occupied as outposts.   Foraging
parties were sent out in all directions, with orders to

---

[1] Ms. of Siege of Lyme ; plan of siege in Roberts Mss.

bring back fodder, cattle and other necessaries, for all of which receipts were duly given.[1]

Blake's comrades were still working at the rude de- fences when the glittering array of the royal army sud- denly appeared above the brow of Uplyme Hill. The vast expanse of bright sea, the green slopes of that secluded valley, broken to the view by clumps of trees, orchards and corn-fields, and the white houses of the town as they lay, serene and picturesque, in the morn- ing sun, touched some chords of sentiment even in the grim bosom of civil war, and the Cavalier host rent the air with a loud shout of surprise and admiration. It was not until evening that Maurice descended into the valley, drove the outposts from Haye and Colway House, and summoned Blake and Ceely to surrender.[2]

The extreme weakness of the place was well known to the enemy; so that when the Prince found his summons answered with a haughty defiance, he impetuously called to his trumpeters to sound a general charge. The in- fantry sent a shower of hand-grenades into the town, and in the disorder caused by their explosion, a power- ful squadron of horse rode down on the lines, expecting to carry them sword in hand at the first onset. But the tactics which had baffled the royalists at Prior's Hill pre- vailed again at Lyme; after a fierce struggle between pike and sabre, the horse, unable to force an entrance, drew off, and retired up the valley. The foot then ad- vanced in deep columns to storm; again and again they

---

[1] Chute House Mss. In these accounts I find " a good fat bullock" valued at three pounds; a truss of hay "at a very small value," four shillings.   [2] Lyme Ms.

advanced; but always to fall back with loss of men and character before that unwavering and deadly fire. Furious at this sudden check to his career of arms, Maurice rode down to the scene of confusion, rallied the broken ranks, and gave the word to charge once more; but the men refused to obey the word, until he wheeled round his cavalry and drove them on by a few pistol-shots in their rear. It was all in vain. Volleys of case-shot met them in front from an enemy protected by cover from their fire; and as their ranks thinned, the line staggered, broke, and the men turned and fled beyond hope of recal that day. The Prince then changed his plan. Convinced by the firmness of the first day's resistance, that, contemptible as Lyme might seem to the King and his council, he must either sit down to the labours of a regular siege, or march away with his great army, leaving this vigilant enemy in his rear and with the stain of discomfiture on his hitherto victorious banner. Between these two courses there was indeed no choice; so he drew off his forces to a short distance, took up his own residence at Colway House, and threw up a few works on which to plant his siege artillery. More than eight weeks that fine army lay on the slopes over Lyme, baffled by an enemy with only a handful of men, and mud-works for ramparts! At Oxford, the affair was an inexplicable marvel and mystery. Every hour the court expected to hear that the " little vile fishing town," as Clarendon contemptuously calls it, had fallen, and that Maurice had marched away to enterprises of greater moment; but every post brought word to the wondering council, that Colonel Blake still held out, and that his spirited

defence was rousing and rallying the dispersed adherents
of Parliament in those parts. While the western division of the royalists was wasting its time and strength in
an obscure corner,—neither port, nor fortress, nor highway,—the most important towns and castles lay open to
the enemy, and some of them actually fell into their
hands. Lyme itself remained unshaken. Day after day,
week after week, storm, stratagem, blockade, failed to
make any apparent impression on the little garrison.
Maurice felt the bitter humiliation of his position; unable to account to his uncle and his brother for the delay
of its capture, he sacrificed the lives of his men like a
wanton prodigal to secure success. How often would
the thought occur to him—if Rupert had only hung that
Captain Blake at Bristol! In London the press was
filled with the wonders of this remarkable defence; and
Roundhead writers used it as a set-off against their own
prolonged failures at Latham House. Yet the Cavaliers
fought before the breastworks at Lyme with the most
resolute gallantry, and some of the best blood in the west
of England flowed into those shallow trenches. After
the siege was raised, and the royalists had time to count
up and compare their losses, they found to their surprise and horror that more men of gentle blood had died
under Blake's fire at Lyme, than had fallen in all the
other sieges and skirmishes in the western counties since
the opening of the war.[1]

Within the town, all was activity, confidence, enthusiasm. The volunteers from Uplyme, Charmouth, and
the villages along the sea-coast, raised the effective

---

[1] Lyme Ms.

force of the garrison to nearly a thousand men; many
of them rude of speech, unused to arms, unbroken by
discipline, but hardy, fearless and devoted to the good
cause. After a week's service in that fierce school
under that steady command, they stood fire like veteran
soldiers; and they brought into the camp a spirit of disinterestedness quite unusual in men of the sword. Under
pressure of the defence, they served without pay, and
lived on short commons; many of them had no shirts of
other linen, few wore shoes and stockings, and still fewer
could boast of a full suit of clothes. Yet no murmur
was ever heard:—each man felt some portion of the
greatness of the issues then at stake, and ordinary sufferings seemed as nothing when borne in the name of freedom and of God. Nor was this martial ardour confined
to the hardier sex; women not only tended the sick
and waited on the wounded, but wrought at the ditch
and barricades, loaded the bandoliers with powder and
shot, and even learned to handle the musket with effect.
One heroine stood in the ranks during the whole time
of a furious attempt to storm, and fired sixteen rounds
of shot at the enemy's columns.[1]

Possessed of a regular siege train, Maurice had an
immense superiority in the more distant fighting. His
batteries, placed on the cliffs and slopes above the line of
defence, gradually silenced the little forts in the town.
Cobb Gate was destroyed by a battery erected at Holms
Bush, which battery also swept the bay, and prevented
the arrival of vessels, except under cover of night. A
powerful battery was erected on Colway Hill to act

---

[1] Lyme Ms.

against Davies' fort—the key of the defence,—but the
earth-wall on that side being hastily strengthened six or
eight feet, the cannon-shots spent their force on them
to no purpose. In the narrow streets and lanes of the
town, destruction went on slowly but certainly. Hand-
grenades were picked up in every yard; many houses
had been rendered untenable; those on the hill-side
near the road to Sidmouth had been utterly destroyed;
the vessels in the harbour suffered much from the land
batteries; but not an inch of the line had been won—
not an opening into the town had been effected. About
seven at night on May 6th a grand attack was made by
surprise. Six days the Royalists had lain quiet in their
tents, and the town-people had been employed in securing their fishing-boats from the rage of a tempest;
the soldiers, a little off guard, were at supper—and the
approach of the storming party—three separate columns,
supported by musqueteers,—was concealed by a thick
fog. Roused, however, by the enemy's signals, the
Roundheads flew to arms, and met their assailants with
valour and impetuosity superior to their own. Some
companies of Royalists, fighting as if they had resolved
to take the place that night at all costs, forced their
way through the rude works, and pressed on with shouts
towards the market square; but the defenders closed
behind them, and cut off from their comrades in the
narrow alleys of an unknown town, the enemy in front,
flank and rear, they perished almost to a man. The assailants having failed in their onset, the fog and darkness
came in aid of the defence; and in less than an hour
after the signal to storm the breastwork had been given,

the Cavaliers were driven off from every part of the crescent, leaving behind them a huge assortment of pikes,
muskets, hand-grenades and ladders. A hundred men lay
dead in the trenches. By death, wounds, and desertion,
Maurice lost between four and five hundred men that
night. Colonel Blewett, one of the best soldiers in the
royal camp, fell, pierced with three balls, while gallantly
leading his column across the works. The day he joined
the camp before Lyme, the generals told him it was a
mere breakfast matter, and that they would carry the town
before they dined!   Captain Pawlett and many other
officers were left dead in the fields. Next morning,
Maurice sent to beg the body of his friend Blewett, and
Blake at once consented to restore it if his men should
not be disturbed while searching for the body, and pick-
ing up the other spoil.   He would not, he said, in such
a case make conditions, but he would appeal to the
Prince's magnanimity to set at liberty a Mr. Harvey,
Ceely's brother-in-law, who had been seized when going
about his usual affairs, and was then a prisoner in the
camp.   Blewett's corpse was found, washed and put
into a new shroud and coffin; but Maurice refused to
restore Mr. Harvey, and told them they might keep the
late colonel if they pleased. Indignant at this reply,
Blake had the coffin carried to the line, opposite the
entry on Holme Bush, where he signalled the heralds
to come for it. " Have you," said he, scornfully, as
the men approached, " have you any command to pay
for the shroud and coffin?" They answered, " No."
Curling his fine black whiskers with his finger, as was
his habit when in anger, he added with superb dis-

dain — "Nevertheless, take them: we are not so poor
but we can give them to you."[1]

In the meantime, having the sea still open at night,
Blake was urgent in his appeals to Parliament for succour. Provisions and ammunition were both failing;
some of his most active partisans had fallen at his side
in the daily encounters, and his little garrison was rapidly losing its strength by death, wounds and sickness.
But to the Cavaliers he still presented the same resolute
front. Late one night his scouts brought word that
early next morning the enemy intended a surprise;
against this plot he resolved to use counter-plot; therefore, when the assailants, moving with great caution,
came to the works, they found them more deserted than
they had dared to hope; the few men on guard fled
before them into the town, and Cavaliers to the number
of four hundred followed them into the net of close and
intricate alleys where Blake had laid his ambush. Not
a single man escaped. Cut off from their friends and
enclosed in a ring of fire, poured on them from the cover
of windows, doors, and parapets, as well as from the
soldiers in the streets, they struggled gallantly to gain
some open space, but after a great part of their body
had fallen in heaps, choking the way and rendering it
still more difficult to advance or retreat, the rest laid
down their arms and were made prisoners of war. A
parley took place shortly after this signal disaster, when
Blake told one of the royalist generals that he did not
wish for advantage of position: the officer, then standing on the low breastwork, pointed out its weakness to

---

[1] Lyme Ms.

his notice, and spoke with the confidence of a soldier of its speedy capture. " Here," said the commander of the garrison characteristically, "you see how weak our works are; they are not things wherein we trust; therefore tell the Prince that if he wishes to come into the town with his army to fight, we will pull down ten or twelve yards, so that he may come in with ten men abreast, and we will fight him." The Royalists replied that they would come into the town when they could do so to their own advantage :—which did not happen in Blake's time.[1]

The twenty-third of May found the two commanders anxiously counting up the store of bread and powder. Indeed the crisis was at hand; in two weeks more the last sack of flour would be consumed, and if no relief came in by sea the heroic garrison would be starved out, and either forced to surrender or cut their way through the beleaguering hosts. But with the fortune that attends the brave, they descried on that very evening a sail rounding Portland Point; and when the next morning dawned the fleet of the Earl of Warwick was seen in the offing, lying as near to the shore as the dangerous form of the coast would allow. He had brought by order of Parliament a small relief of provisions and some military stores. The sailors sent on land with these supplies were so shocked to see the naked and deplorable condition of the little garrison of whose prowess they had heard so much, that they immediately returned to the ships and spread the touching details of the story among their comrades. These noble fellows at once

---

[1] Lyme Ms.

made a collection of all the articles they could spare; and many a man that day gave up his best shoes, his warmest shirt, and more than half his ration to the defenders of Lyme. They contributed from their scanty stores, thirty pair of boots, a hundred pair of shoes, a hundred and sixty pair of stockings, a heap of old clothes, a good round number of shirts, and a considerable quantity of bread and fish. Nor was this the largest part of their generous sacrifice:—they proposed to the commissariat to give up for the same uses a fourth of their daily allowance of bread for the next four months, in all nine thousand pounds weight. While these arrangements were being made in their favour on board, the garrison was fighting in the streets. Blake was at the head of a sallying party about to issue from the gate, when Captain Southern, sent by Maurice to make another desperate effort to carry the town by assault before Warwick could send re-inforcements on shore, began the attack. The shock was brief but terrific. Colonel Weir, Blake's most active and efficient officer, was shot in the abdomen; Captain Pyne, his gallant master of the horse, received a wound which soon proved mortal; Blake himself was hurt in the foot, enough to make him limp ever after. Sixty Cavalier corpses strewed the ground; among them Captain Southern, who for a freak had that day dressed himself in Lord Pawlett's armour —a man most hateful to the people of Lyme, and afterwards heavily mulcted for his share in these transactions for the express benefit of the town.[1]

Few had done so much for the defence as Captain

---

[1] Harl. Mss. 368; Com. Jour. August 5, 1648.

Pyne; and Blake, true to the Roundhead idea, ordered a solemn funeral to be performed in his honour. Unfortunately the death-bell, tolling from St. Michael's Tower, and the usual volleys fired at a soldier's grave, informed the Cavaliers, who from Black Venne and Colway Hill could look down into the very churchyard, that another mournful act of the drama was in progress and the attention of men drawn off from the defence; and as the people in their mourning attire turned slowly from the chancel where they had paid the last duties to their old companion in arms, a cry of attack was raised along the streets, and a cannonade, louder, fiercer and better sustained than on any former occasion commenced from all the batteries. After thundering at the works until noon, tearing away the earth-walls in several places, bursting through roofs and knocking down chimneys, the foot advanced with their scaling-ladders, hand-grenades and long pikes. Three points were assailed at once, from Charmouth road, from Uplyme and from the high grounds above Holme Bush. The outraged Roundheads met the attacking parties with the fury of demons. That day blood flowed down the steep gutters, and both the rivulet and the town-water were died crimson. The royalist gentry held their ground resolutely; but their ardour was no longer seconded by that of the common soldiers, and they were three times driven back with shame and loss to their entrenchments. Yet their repulses were dearly bought, and in the diary of the defence this day was marked as that on which the town suffered most severely in the lives of its garrison.[1]

---

[1] Lyme Ms.

When all was still again, Blake went on board the fleet and arranged with Warwick the details of an operation for the ensuing day. In pursuance of this scheme three hundred men were secretly landed from the ships; the fleet then weighed anchor, and stood away eastward towards Charmouth, making feints of a wish to throw a body of men on shore at some favourable point. Maurice, anxiously watching this movement from the heights, concluded that the Earl had taken part of the garrison on board with the intention of throwing them on his rear or flank, and he sent his cavalry and a few hundred foot along the brow of the cliffs, to wait on this suspicious movement, and, if possible, prevent a landing. By firing a few broadsides towards the cliffs, Warwick drew this force to the east of Seatown, seven or eight miles from Lyme, where he commenced a more steady cannonade, and made appear as if he designed to send a body of men towards Chideock Castle. This movement induced the Royalists to throw up a breastwork. Meanwhile, as Blake had foreseen, the Prince resolved to make a grand and final attempt to carry the works by storm. Three thousand men were chosen for this forlorn hope; arranged in three deep columns, and ordered to support and succeed each other in the attack. By the accession of three hundred seamen Blake could now muster about twelve hundred men, and as Maurice's formidable cavalry was away among the hills beyond Seatown, the two forces were nearer equal than they had been in any previous encounter; with the advantages for Lyme of concentration, narrow streets, houses, every one of which was a little fortress, and the works in advance, such as they

F

were. At six in the evening, while there were still three good hours of daylight, the first shots were ex·changed, and until past eight the slope leading to Up·lyme was like a battle-field, and the firing so swift and fierce as to give the town an appearance of being wrap¹ in flames. Some houses were set on fire and destroyed, others were battered down with shot; but the sight of burning thatch and falling rafters only served to inflame still more the courage of the people. A full third of the town was already in ruins, and even had he succeeded Maurice would have gained nothing at Lyme but glory and a heap of stones.[1] The first column fought for half an hour with much gallantry; it then retired, and the second column occupied its post. By half-past seven it was also broken, and the last column advanced with tre-mendous shouts on the now almost exhausted garrison· Falling back a little, so as to recover breath under the cross fire from the nearest houses, the defenders there made a vigorous stand, and in half an hour the result was no longer doubtful. Blake then gave his final orders. Advancing from all sides, as if quickened with new life, his officers appeared on both flanks of the enemy, while he pressed them steadily in front. A little after eight o'clock the column was cut through, and the soldiers fled in disorder to their entrenched quarters. Stragglers continued to fire their pieces at intervals until night-fall; but the battle was already over. That day cost King Charles five hundred of his bravest followers.

Maurice had made his last effort,—and it had failed Cannonades were repeated again and again, but the

---

[1] Mayor's Accounts in Roberts Mss.   [2] Lyme Ms.

crisis was now past; for Essex was moving westward with a large army, and the Prince felt that his position before Lyme was no longer tenable. As a parting salute he fired into the town a quantity of red-hot balls and bars of twisted lead. Poor Maurice! His rage, though vain, was not unnatural : for his fortunes and his military reputation were both broken on the rocky beach at Lyme. The loss of the Cavaliers in men amounted to two thousand :—more than had fallen in the conquest of both the two western capitals, Exeter and Bristol. Their loss in time, material, moral influence, and military cha-racter were still more considerable and more irrepa-rable.[1]

---

[1] Lyme Ms.; Elegiac Enumeration, 6.   Other particulars will be found in Clarendon, iii. 363, 376, 398; the True Informant, No. 43; the Spie, No. 19; Exact and true Relation of relieving the resolute Governor of Lyme, 2-5; Colonel Weir's Diurnal, April 20 to May 23; Letter of the Earl of Warwick to Speaker of the House of Lords, 2-4; the Kingdom's Weekly Intelligencer, No. 58.

CHAPTER III.

1645-1649.

Taunton.

THE long detention of the royal army in the valley of
Lyme enabled Essex to march by slow stages from London to Dorset, without meeting an enemy, but with the advantage of being able to recruit his forces and strengthen
the interests of his party by the way. This commander,
though without great military talents, barren in conception as he was slow in execution, had yet the good
fortune to be every where popular. His name was a
pledge of order. A regiment of raw levies is seldom
kept under the strong curb of discipline, but the legions
of Essex contrasted most favourably with Goring's crew
and Maurice's marauders. Many of those who had
hitherto been neutral in the quarrel, and comparatively indifferent to the issue, so that it should come
to a speedy end and relieve their houses from pillage
and their women from insult, received him with open
arms. Hundreds flocked to his camp, anxious to serve
under so chivalrous a leader, the knight without fear
and without reproach. Thus, while the Royalists were
wasting their strength to no purpose in an obscure corner of Dorsetshire, their enemies, recently broken and
dispersed almost beyond hope, were rapidly gaining in
moral and material power. Alarmed for his own safety,

Maurice had watched the movements of this new army
with great anxiety; and as soon as he heard of the dexterous turn which restored Weymouth to the Roundheads without the loss of a single man, he drew to his
tents a great part of the Taunton garrison, and aban-
doning to the enemy all the trophies of his former march,
fled away with his reduced, but still magnificent army
towards Exeter.[1]

This retreat of the Cavaliers enabled Blake, now
advanced to the full rank of Colonel, to take the field
with his heroic regiment and such other troops as could
be hastily drawn together. Already his fame had become a spell in the west. Rivalling Rupert in the rapidity and brilliancy of his execution, his plans were laid
with a caution and sagacity, and were followed out with
a steadiness of purpose, quite unknown to the royal Cavalier. Essex, moving in the wake of Maurice, took
the road towards Cornwall, in the hope of cutting up
the western division of the grand army,—but leaving
nearly all the important towns of Somerset and Devon
in the king's hands, and separating his devoted troops
from their natural base of operations. A fatal error!
Every step westward led him deeper into a country
unknown to him, with inhabitants either neutral or
unfriendly, and of which all the strong places were possessed by the Royalists. With the exception of Plymouth, still held in a state of blockade, all the great fortresses owned the King: Poole, Lyme, and Weymouth,
had been maintained or recovered by parliamentary
officers, but between the sea-coast and the head waters

---

[1] Rushworth, v. 683-4, 701; Clarendon, iii. 376, 385, 439.

of the Severn, they had not a single town or castle of real military importance. The Cavaliers had powerful garrisons at Bath, Bristol, Exeter, Bridgwater, Langport and Ilchester,—as also in such strongholds as Ninney Castle, Chideock House, Dunster Castle, Corfe Castle, Portland Island, Farley Castle, and the Scilly Islands. Essex, on his part, possessed no more of the country than his patrols covered with their muskets. Still he pressed on. Naturally brave, but with scarcely any other quality of a great general, he could not see his enemy in full retreat without the wish to hang on his rear and compel him to hazard daily skirmishes. At Oxford this imprudence of his was soon understood, and Charles proposed to march down into the far west with all the forces at his disposal, place him there between two fires, and compel him to fight a pitched battle at a great disadvantage.

Affairs were in this position, when Blake, now master of his own movements, conceived one of those bold and happy thoughts, which, with little waste of life or cost of material, produce results equal in importance to the gain or loss of a great battle. His idea was to break the formidable line of royal fortresses in the midst,—to cut off the supplies and interrupt the most direct means of communication between the Royalist camps,—to cover, at least for some days, the rear of Essex, now entangled in the Cornish hills, unable to force a battle or to retreat,—and, finally, to secure for himself and for the good cause a new and commanding centre of operations. These objects were all to be achieved by the capture of Taunton. A glance at any old map will

shew how favourably that town was placed for his purpose—were it only in his possession! It was surrounded
by castles and garrisons. It stood on and controlled the
great western highway. All letters, levies, stores and
ammunition sent from Charles to Maurice, or from the
generals and officers in the west to the King and to each
other, had to pass through it. With the exception of
cross-country roads, out of the way and almost impracticable for cavalry and artillery, there was no other route
between Oxford, Bristol, and Exeter. In other respects,
Taunton was at that time of singular importance to the
Roundheads. The inhabitants—rich, brave, devoted,
numerous—were for the most part well affected to their
cause. The farmers, artisans and peasants of the neighbouring hamlets were many of them Puritans in religion.
A large pile of arms, seized in Roundhead houses by
Sir William Portman, the borough member, was laid
up there, together with ten thousand pounds in ready
money extorted during the late successes from rich and
poor of the same party. Unwalled itself and surrounded
at no great distance by strong fortresses and garrisons;
Bridgwater and Langport, both within an hour or so
of hard riding, Dunster and Ilchester also within easy
reach,—and no enemy nearer than the exhausted little
troop at Lyme,—the Cavalier generals had never imagined that Taunton was in danger. But Blake, who had
private friends in the place, was informed of the state
of public feeling, of the exact strength of the garrison,
of the irresolute character of the military governor;
and notwithstanding the hazardous nature of such an
attempt with the poverty of force at his command, the

prize being one of supreme importance in that stage of
the war, he resolved to try the effect of a sudden and
impetuous attack.   His men were inured to danger, and
had never known defeat.   His Taunton friends assured
him that he had nothing to fear from the inhabitants,
and that Colonel Reeves's garrison was unequal to the
defence of so large a town.   Blake foresaw that his great
difficulty would lie, not in seizing the position, but in
holding it afterwards against so many enemies.   He
trusted in God and the justice of his cause!   But he
also considered the human means and instruments of
successful defence.   Taunton was not like Lyme.   No
aid could come to it by sea; on every side it was shut
in by hills; every road from it led to a royal stronghold.
Yet once master of the town, he did not despair of being
able to maintain himself long enough to give Essex time
to create a diversion in the west; and at the moment this
seemed sufficient.   Joining his flying corps, therefore,
with the regiment of Sir Robert Pye—afterwards governor of Leicester, when Rupert stormed that unhappy
town,—he suddenly appeared before the gates of Taunton, summoned the garrison to surrender, and offered
them in that case honourable terms.   Startled at this
unexpected apparition, unaware of the exact strength
of his assailants, and not willing to throw himself on
popular support, Colonel Reeves asked for a parley, in
which he agreed to give up his post, on condition of
being allowed to march away with his men to Bridgwater.   As soon as the humbled Royalists had marched
out in silence at the east gate of the town, Blake and
Pye entered with their respective corps, amidst the peal

of St. Mary's silvery bells and the uproarious joy of the
Puritan people. A demi-culverin, ten small pieces of
ordnance, two tons of match, eight barrels of gunpowder, a considerable stock of swords, pistols, pikes and
other arms, with a magazine of provisions, were found
in the castle. A great quantity of household furniture
—carried by force from the dwellings of suspected persons—was also among the spoils of this bloodless victory, and was no doubt now restored to its former owners.
Not a single incident had occurred to dash the glory
of this brilliant capture. When the news of it arrived
in London, patriotic citizens lighted fires in honour of
Colonel Blake, and Parliament hastened to appoint him
governor of the town which he had so gallantly assailed
and so unexpectedly won.[1]

Blake took Taunton on the eighth of July 1644; on
the second of the same month Cromwell had defeated
Prince Rupert at Marston Moor. Intelligence of these
events reached the court about the same time at Bath,
whither Charles had already moved in order to be nearer
the scene of operations between Maurice and Essex.
Two such disasters convinced the Royalist generals that
they must either act with more vigour or be content to
see the west of England, now the stronghold of their
power, torn from their hands. Exeter still held out
for the Queen, then a guest within its walls; all the
active inland towns and garrisons, Taunton alone excepted, were with the King; and the Roundhead army

[1] Elegiac Enumeration, 6, 7; Whitelocke, 95; Sprigge's England's
Recovery, Introduction; Toulmin's History of Taunton (ed. Savage), 412;
Oldmixon, i. 257; Clarendon, iii. 439; History and Life, 14-16; Parl. Hist.
ix. 39.

under Essex had failed to establish for itself a decided
superiority in the field. Under these circumstances it
appeared to the royal generals that there was time
—and only just time—to strike such a blow as would
recover for them the entire west of England. A few
rapid marches, undertaken with a clear purpose, had
already brought the army from Oxford, across the Cots-
wold Hills, to Cirencester and Bath; at Bristol Lord
Hopton had been previously required to concentrate a
large body of troops, blindly devoted to the King, from
the Welsh borders; and as this ever-increasing army
continued its westward march, Blake, who had long ago
seen that the object of the movement was to overwhelm
the imprudent Earl of Essex, prepared to dispute its
passage along the great highway, aware that the interruption of his line of march would compel the King
either to throw himself on Taunton with his whole power
or make a detour through the hills over almost impassable roads in order to avoid it. In either case he
knew that a certain number of days must be lost to the
Royalists, and during these precious days a man of any
military genius would have been able to reduce Exeter
or force Prince Maurice to fight a decisive battle. But
unfortunately Essex was not a Cromwell! Much discussion and some differences occurred in the royal camp
as to the course to be pursued in consequence of the
attitude assumed by Blake. The Cavalier gentry of
Somerset and Devon burned with rage at the idea of
one of the fairest towns in the two counties being held
by rebels; the more ardent generals expressed nothing
but indignation at what they called the insult which

Blake had offered to the royal army in throwing himself with a mere handful of adventurers into a position
that every soldier knew must be untenable; and they
urged the King to advance from Bristol by the great
highway, and punish the obstinate rebel who had foiled
the great army before Lyme. But the very name of
that obscure little town suggested the strongest reasons
for avoiding Taunton. Charles's object was an immediate concentration of his two remaining armies on
the borders of Cornwall, so that by a decisive victory
over Essex he might be able to relieve Exeter and
reduce Plymouth to obedience. If he attempted to
force his way through Taunton, it was impossible for
any one to tell how long he might be detained there,
whilst the number of days to be lost in going over
the Quantock Hills and round by north Devon to
Exeter could be reckoned with the greatest certainty.
The Royalists, therefore, leaving Blake in undisputed
possession of his prize, took the cross-country roads, and
in due time arrived at Exeter. The King's plan succeeded to a miracle. Joining Maurice at Liskeard, he
found they had no need to risk a battle in order to con-
quer. Led by false statements into a country of which
he knew absolutely nothing, Essex saw his army waste
away hourly by sickness, desertion and the enemy's fire,
with no hope of action or of escape. Shut up in a
narrow gorge by the sea-shore, land-locked on all sides,
with a hostile population about him, provisions failing
and a mutinous spirit spreading in the ranks, he at last
determined to quit the country which he could no longer
hold with honour, leaving his deserted followers, many

of whom had taken up arms for his sake, to the clemency of an incensed sovereign! He embarked with a single attendant, secretly, and in the night. Next day the army was without a leader, and nothing remained but to surrender at discretion. This was a terrible and an unexpected calamity for the poor burgesses of Taunton. Of that great Roundhead army, not a single battalion kept the field to divide with them the attention of the victorious Royalists. One man alone appeared undismayed by an event which laid the West of England once more at the King's feet. But Blake prepared, not only to defend his post against the foes who would soon be disengaged from other tasks, and swarming round it in the hope of booty, but also continued as before to carry fire and sword, levies and requisitions, into the enemy's quarters. Hanging, with a mere handful of intrepid men, on the left flank of the royal army, he had harassed their westward march, cut off their stragglers, intercepted their supplies; and by sudden and frequent visits to the weaker sort of Royalist towns, had kept the district in such a state of alarm, as, even after the flight of Essex, prevented Charles from settling the country in his own interest. His unfailing good fortune had raised the spirits of his followers to the height at which danger becomes a mere excitement. Undaunted by the presence of two armies, unchecked by the numerous castles and fortified houses, their bold excursions were extended to the very gates of Exeter; and in the midst of their rejoicings for the victory in Cornwall, the court ladies were suddenly alarmed by the appearance of a squadron of Roundhead horse under the walls of that city. From these sallies Blake seldom returned without bringing back arms, ammunition and prisoners. Nor was Taunton itself neglected. Though determined to keep as wide a space of country open round it as vigour and vigilance could clear, he did not overlook the fact that, isolated as he was from his Roundhead friends, it would be impossible to hold the open country much longer against the Cavalier forces which occupied the western towns; such parts, therefore, of the ancient fortifications as admitted of hasty repair, were strengthened and restored.[1]

Little time was allowed the garrison for preparation. Flushed with their successes in Cornwall, the returning Cavaliers swept the country from the gates of Plymouth to the suburbs of Taunton, without encountering a single hostile band. Charles himself, too elated to think of a petty town in Somerset, was bent on a rapid and victorious march on London, whither he now summoned all his subjects by common proclamation to attend him and compel the two Houses to make peace —peace on his own terms. But although the town was undisturbed by the grand army, parties of horse and foot from Exeter, Bridgwater and Dunster Castle, Irish rebels, wild men from the Cornish mines, and yet more detested foreign mercenaries, prowled like beasts of prey about the beautiful hamlets near Taunton,—not daring to approach too near the rude lines, or engage in an open assault, but committing acts of rapine and cruelty on unarmed persons met with in the highways. Sir

---

[1] Elegiac Enumeration, 7; Rushworth, v. 685; Oldmixon, i. 278; History and Life, 18 ; Clarendon, iii. 386-418.

Francis Doddington, a brave but brutal soldier at the head of a marauding party from Bridgwater Castle, made himself conspicuous by these outrages. One day he met a clergyman on the road a short distance from Taunton, to whom he shouted in his rude voice—" Who art thou for, priest?" The clergyman answered calmly —"For God and His Gospel." Doddington drew a pistol and shot him through the heart. While the Royalists were yet at Exeter, a council had been held to consider what course should be taken in face of the recent capture of Taunton, and the consequent interruption of the great western highway. Many of the local magnates, indignant that the finest town between Bristol and Exeter should be held by a handful of rebels, urged the King to march at once in that direction; but the royal generals, still anxious to gain time, resolved to proceed through Honiton and Chard towards London, leaving the task of reducing Taunton to Colonel Wyndham, the governor of Bridgwater, and Blake's old political rival in his native town. Wyndham was proud of this employment, believing that it would enable him to triumph over a local as well as a public enemy. Suddenly appearing before the town with a small force drawn from Bridgwater, he wrote a letter to the burgesses in very menacing terms, threatening the town with fire and sword, if it were not immediately surrendered. Blake's answer was brief and emphatic:—" These are to let you know," he wrote, " that as we neither fear your menaces nor accept your proffers, we wish you for time to come to desist from all overtures of the like nature unto us, who are resolved to the last drop of our blood to main-

tain the quarrel we have undertaken; and I doubt not
but the same God who hath hitherto protected us will
bless us with an issue answerable to the justness of our
cause; however, to Him alone shall we stand or fall."—
As threats had produced no effect, Wyndham sent a
second trumpeter to his old neighbour and townsman,
almost entreating him to accept terms of surrender; for,
as he said, the town was unwalled — the place inconsiderable—and an attempt to defend it against the royal
forces, now masters of the West, could only lead to an
unnecessary waste of Christian blood. Blake referred
to his former answer as expressing all that he had to say
in return:—and from that moment the siege may be
considered as begun.[1]

In itself, and apart from the important influence which
it exercised over the course of the war, Blake's defence
of Taunton was one of the most interesting acts in that
great drama. Abounding in deeds of individual heroism
—exhibiting in its master-mind a rare combination of
civil and military genius,—the spectacle of an unwalled
town, in an inland district, with no single advantage of
site, surrounded by powerful castles and garrisons, and
invested by an enemy brave, watchful, numerous, and
well provided with artillery, successfully resisting storm,
strait, and blockade for several months, thus paralysing
the King's power, and affording Cromwell time to re-
model the army, naturally arrested the attention of
military writers at that time, and French authors of this
class bestowed on Taunton the name of the modern

---

[1] Elegiac Enumeration, 8; Toulmin, 413, 414; Clarendon, iii. 419;
Oldmixon, i. 278; Whitelocke, 96, 116.

Saguntum—a name well won, though, unlike and happier than its ancient rival, Taunton did not fall in order to save the cause for which it fought.[1]

In some respects Taunton was a more defensible place than Lyme. It lacked the vast advantage of a sea communication, but then it was not surrounded by heights commanding its streets and public buildings. The nearest hills were far beyond the range of cannon. The only rising ground for a mile or more was that on which the castle stood near the centre of the town : consequently the enemy's powerful artillery inspired but little terror. The character of the country also favoured defensive operations, for the fields were small, the hedges thick and high, and the roads narrow and circuitous. Only three entrances led into the town—the north road from Minehead and Dunster, crossing the river Tone under the castle-guns by means of an old wooden bridge —and the great highway, entering from Bridgwater and Bristol at East Reach, and passing out at the West Gate for Exeter and Plymouth. The castle and the river covered the first; a sort of stone blockhouse, honoured with the name of the New Castle, flanked West Gate. East Gate had no other defence than a narrow passage closed up with a solid oak door. Walls there were none. On every side the town was open, except so far as garden walls, high hedges, and outhouses might afford a slight covering from the enemy. The town itself consisted then, as it does now, of three principal streets, corresponding with the three roads into and through it, East Street, North Street, and High Street, meeting in a

---

[1] History and Life, 23 ; M. Larrey's History of England.

triangular space near the castle gates, and occupied by the market and the bull-ring. Part of this space was covered with sheds and shambles; in the centre stood an ancient stone cross, and facing it were the low picturesque fronts of the Townhall and the famous Inn then and long afterwards known as the *White Hart.* In the angle formed by the junction of East Street and North Street rose the high and graceful tower of St. Mary Magdalen. With one exception all the streets were strait and winding. The houses were mostly built of brick or stone, with peaked gables, tile roofs and bow windows. The castle, a structure of the Saxon time, and a hold of importance during the wars of the two Roses, was then partly in ruins; but its position was good; the walls, gates, and old drawbridges remained, and a double moat, fed by a brook from the hamlet of Chedford, strengthened in some degree its outworks. But what would these wretched defences avail against a hostile force? asked many a terrified burgess when the enemy was reported to be near. Blake carried on his preparations with a vigour which left little time for either thought or fear. Strong barricades were thrown across the roads. Breastworks were raised at the gates; and at East Gate, where he believed that the principal fighting would take place, he planted some of his artillery, and garrisoned the alms-houses on one side and the dwellings on the other with his best musqueteers. Still, when every thing had been done, the situation seemed dreary in the extreme. In the earlier periods of the war Taunton had changed hands as Royalists or Roundheads happened to be in greater force in the neighbourhood. Hopton had placed there a Royalist garrison. These men fled at the approach of Waller, who left a body of troops to secure the place for Parliament. Hertford drove these Roundheads away, and left the government to his friends. Reeves in his turn had surrendered without a blow. Blake was the first man who had ever thought of holding the town against a superior force. The Cavaliers believed him mad. For, as they knew, he had no base of operations in his daring attempt, no flanks on which to lean for support, no source of supplies but the chances of an occasional forage, and no hope of relief until a new army could be created, drilled, disciplined, and led to victory by some of the parliamentary generals. How terrible the present evil—how vague and distant the hope of aid from London![1]

On receiving Blake's brief answer to his entreaty, Colonel Wyndham advanced along the road from Bridgwater to make a demonstration in the meadows on the east, hoping to intimidate the inhabitants, and afford to the Royalists in the town an opportunity of rising against the garrison. But a party issuing from East Gate, and falling unexpectedly on his line, obliged him to face about and defend himself, which he did at first with some firmness, though in the end he was forced to retire with loss from his awkward position. Unwilling, after this encounter, to risk an assault, his troops tore up the roads and barricaded them with fruit-trees,—cut

---

[1] The points of this description are derived from a careful comparison of existing ruins and the traditions of the town with old maps, assisted by several members of the Somerset Archæological Society, and by two local octogenarians, Mr. Kinglake and Mr. Downing Blake.

off communications with the distant Roundheads,—and stopped all market-carts on their way to the town with produce. For several months this blockade continued; sometimes it was strict, at others loose and ineffectual; but altogether without producing a material change in the position of the two forces. Wyndham indeed had much to gain by delay. The entire district—Lyme, Poole, Weymouth, and Plymouth excepted—was occupied by his friends. He had Bridgwater and Ilchester to fall back on in case of need, either to rest his men or to recruit his strength. The other Roundhead towns were all of them closely invested: though, being in every case open to the sea, they were not in immediate peril. Yet they were too well guarded to be able to send relief or create any diversion in favour of Taunton. Day by day Blake saw the stock of provisions dwindle. Of course no effort was spared to bring in new supplies— every week or two a vigorous sally was made by part of the garrison, which for a moment broke the cordon, and enabled the farmers and gardeners to carry in fresh garden stuff, corn and cattle. Nevertheless, hemmed round as he was by so many strongholds, it was impossible to enlarge the radius very much or preserve it long; and in spite of every effort to increase the store, joined with a most careful husbandry of his means, want of food soon became a serious question for the besieged. Even hope of succour from without was for a time denied. Lord Goring, with a large army of Royalists, lay at Salisbury, ready to oppose the march of any relief-party from Kent or Middlesex, and the parliamentary chiefs began to fear that Blake would ultimately be starved out of his commanding position, and forced to give up without a blow one of the finest towns in the west of England. But help came to him in the hour of need. A gallant German officer, named Vandruske, passing with a body of horse on the flank of Goring's dissolute army, rode rapidly down the vales of Wiltshire, Dorsetshire and Somerset, and falling unexpectedly on Wyndham's line, cut it in a trice and rode triumphantly into the town. In the panic thus created among the Royalists, Blake sallied forth at the head of his disposable force, attacked the beleaguering regiments, routed them at the first onset, and chased them in their flight to the gates of Bridgwater, in the castle of which town they found the first shelter from Vandruske's fiery dragoons. The great roads opened up by this brilliant action, Blake, attended by Vandruske's horsemen, made a circuit of the country, rousing his friends from the torpor of despair, and striking his exulting foes with a sense of the sudden vicissitudes of war. For a few days the action of the Royalists in those parts seemed paralysed. The garrisons retired behind their ramparts, leaving the open country at the energetic Roundheads' mercy; every town in Somerset and Devon was disturbed more or less by these excursions; and Goring's force was suddenly ordered down to Weymouth, lest the siege of that place should be interrupted by them.[1]

The spirits of the Roundheads rapidly revived with success. The Weymouth garrison, driven by surprise from the upper town and the forts, still held out in the lower town, and shortly after Goring's arrival with his

---

[1] Whitelocke, 107; Clarendon, iv. 9, 10; Sprigge, 14.

full strength of horse, foot, dragoons and artillery, the place, to use the words of the Royalist writer, " was re-taken by that contemptible number of rebels, who had been beaten into the lower town, and who were looked upon as prisoners at mercy." Baffled in his expectations at Weymouth, Goring retired with ten thousand men and a large park of ordnance into Somerset, raising wonder and horror along his line of march. War had made the country familiar with the ordinary license of the camp. Exactions of money—levies of corn, horses and men—arbitrary arrests—drum-head trials—and sum-mary punishments, were every-day events. But Goring's army—known to the common people by the oppro-brious name of Goring's crew—pillaged without legal forms, insulted women, and burnt the property they could not carry off. Houses and villages were deserted at their approach. Drunkenness and debauchery marked their course; shame, misery and desolation followed in their track. The less warlike of the population, women, children, old men and ministers of religion, fled before them as before a consuming fire; and with such valuables as they could snatch up in the hurry of departure from their homesteads, threw themselves into Taunton. Of the clergy who thus flew to Blake for protection against Goring's crew, was one who proved singularly useful during the long and trying defence :—Thomas Welman, vicar of Luppit near Honiton. Educated at Oxford, where he was distinguished for learning, piety and gentle manners, he married a Honiton lady, and settled in a quiet country hamlet to the work of his Christian ministry, among a people who soon became attached to him by the strongest ties of gratitude and love. The rapine, cruelty and profligacy of the Cavaliers roused his mild nature; he fled from the pleasant place in which his lot had been cast; and during the hottest period of the siege of Taunton, his indignant denunciation of the shame and ruin he had seen that beleaguering host commit in the valleys of Devonshire, served to inflame and sanctify the patriot ardour of the garrison and people.[1]

As time wore on, every hour developed still more strikingly the vast importance of the blow struck by Blake at Taunton. It had hitherto prevented the concentration of the royal armies. It had thrown a new subject of discord into the King's council. It had created a thousand local jealousies, discontents and suspicions. Lord Goring, general of the horse, quarreled with Lord Hopton, master of the ordnance, about the command. Sir Richard Grenville, Sir John Berkeley, and other West-of-England men, loudly expressed their discontent at what they called the meanness which permitted such an enemy to remain master of Taunton; and in a critical moment, Grenville obstinately refused to obey the orders of his superior officers, when those orders directed him to leave the trenches before that town without first taking it. Meanwhile the New Model was perfected; and under the Self-denying ordinance, the command in chief of the Roundhead army was transferred from Essex to Fairfax, with Cromwell for his general of the horse. Cromwell soon joined Sir William Waller; and the combined forces of the two generals

---

[1] Clarendon, iv. 12, 13; Palmer's Nonconformist Memorial, i. 378.

making a feint as if they would fall on Goring, the out-
witted Royalist drew off to Exeter, leaving the road
open for Vandruske and his dragoons to regain the main
body of Roundhead cavalry. These indications of a
change of fortune called the Prince of Wales into the
west, where he summoned the Commissioners for Somerset to Bristol, to advise with him in person on the state
of that county. They complained bitterly of the riot
and insolence of Goring's soldiers, and mourned in spirit
over the obstinate defence and troublesome sallies of
the Taunton garrison; which, they said, kept the whole
country for thirty miles round in a state of alarm, and
rendered it difficult to raise either men or money for
the royal cause in Somerset. On all sides, it was urged
that the most important operation for the western armies would be the reduction of that town. Messages
were therefore sent to Goring, and at his request two of
the prince's council, the Lords Capel and Colepepper,
went to Wells to consult with him on the aspect of
affairs; when after long consultations, Goring drew up
in writing a plan of action. Leaving the greater part
of his horse and two hundred foot on the borders of
Wiltshire and Dorset to observe the motions of the
enemy,—but so conveniently placed as to be able to retire towards his main body, should Cromwell or Waller
advance in too great strength,—he proposed to move
with his infantry and artillery, a few select squadrons
of horse, and as many of the flying corps as could be
drawn together on a sudden, into the vale of Taunton,
and either capture the heroic town or burn it to ashes.
Prince Charles approved of and adopted this plan. Or-

ders were thereupon sent to Sir Richard Grenville to appear in the trenches before Taunton with his regiments, consisting of eight hundred horse, two thousand two hundred foot, and a large body of pioneers, — orders which he obeyed with the most ardent zeal. The Commissioners of Somerset were instructed to repair to the camp, and encourage by their presence the labours of the besiegers, as well as use their great local influence with the citizens. Magazines of stores and ammunition were prepared; and in a few days Grenville had already occupied all the roads leading out of Taunton,—put an end to the free intercourse between town and country,—and drawn his line within a few hundred yards of the suburbs. Through the beautiful vale then occupied by his soldiers, the highways skirted orchards and cornfields, winding and twisting even more than is usual with English country-roads; so that, although Blake had converted the high steeple of St. Mary Magdalen into a watch-tower, the distance plainly visible to the eye was slight, and he had to rely chiefly on his scouts for information as to the enemy's movements.

Since the defeat of Wyndham, that officer had lain still at Bridgwater or Bristol; no enemy had been descried from the castle-turrets; no warlike clangour had been heard from the silvery bells of St. Mary's church. But the fiery Grenville soon made his presence known to the inhabitants; with dogged valour he was fighting his way to the very gate at East Reach, when a sudden movement by Waller forced Goring to turn his force eastward. In expectation of a pitched battle, the commander-in-chief ordered Grenville to quit his trenches, and repair with his whole force towards Shaftesbury. Grenville refused to obey these orders. The Prince of Wales interfered; but the obstinate knight answered that his men would not stir a yard, and that he himself had solemnly promised the Commissioners of Cornwall and Devon not to advance beyond Taunton until he could advance through it. At the same time, however, he declared his conviction that in a few days the place must fall under the weight of his assaults, when he said he would joyfully push forward to the rendezvous of the royal army. Two or three skirmishes occurred between Goring and Waller, but without result. Goring again complained to the Prince that without that important re-inforcement he dared not risk a battle; Grenville answered, that with six hundred men more he would undertake to deliver Taunton into the Prince's hands in six days. Perplexed by these quarrels, without the character and authority necessary to overrule both officers for the common good, the Prince of Wales called a council to determine which would be the best course to pursue under such painful circumstances. Rupert was present and took a principal share in the debate. Taunton still held out:— Grenville would not quit the trenches even at the positive command of the King's son, his own future sovereign, until it fell:—Goring could not fight a decisive battle without the four thousand men then occupied in the siege. These were the fixed facts of the case. Rupert urged that a combined attempt should be made to expel Blake; arguing that the possession of Taunton by the Roundheads was the chief obstacle to the raising of men and money in that rich and populous county; that

the siege employed one of the best of the royal armies;
that in the event of its reduction, not only would Grenville's force be released for other services, but volunteers
would come in, and new levies could be made at pleasure.   In this way it was thought possible to pacify the
four western counties, raise an army for Goring to carry
into Kent and Sussex, and another for the Prince to
march with towards his father's camp.   The six days
mentioned by Grenville was considered enough to effect
the important capture; and the least sanguine officer in
the royal army professed to believe that it could not hold
out more than ten days or a fortnight against the combined armies of Goring and Grenville.   The council,
therefore, resolved to compel it to make immediate submission at any cost of men and material that might be
found necessary for the purpose.[1]

An immediate concentration of troops took place.
Colonel Wyndham repaired to the camp with his regiment.   Sir John Berkeley made his appearance there.
Sir Joseph Wagstaffe brought down from Wells the
main body of Goring's foot, and the whole of his great
park of artillery.   The forces thus gathered before Taunton were of superior appointment and overwhelming
numbers.   The very day of their arrival, Grenville advanced his lines within musket-shot of the town, occu-
pying the entire circuit of the suburbs; and then set out
to inspect Wellington House, an outpost five miles distant, into which Blake had thrown a small garrison.
From a window of this house he was marked by a mus-
queteer, and shot in the thigh; the wound was consi-

---

[1] Clarendon, iv. 14-17; Cromwell's Letters and Speeches, i. 270.

dered mortal, and he was immediately carried away by his servants to Exeter. Sir John Berkeley, who had served some weeks in the leaguer before Lyme, and was therefore supposed to know something of Blake's tactics, succeeded to the command. The six days, however, passed, and the town still held on. Week followed week, but no one could tell with certainty how many days longer it would defy storm and stratagem. Some progress the besiegers undoubtedly made. The little garrison at Wellington House was overpowered, after an heroic resistance, by superior numbers, and in their rage the Cavaliers set fire to the house and destroyed it utterly. The investing lines were gradually drawn closer round the town; the suburbs, especially that of East Reach, were pillaged and burnt. Many houses in the outer circuit of streets and lanes were battered down with the incessant play of cannon; and now and then for a few hours the Royalists occupied advanced positions within the shelter of ruined cottages and gardens. But the heart of the town remained inviolate. The castle, churchyard and market-place never once saw the enemy. Berkeley hoped to see a profound moral effect produced on the garrison and inhabitants by the storm and conflagration of Wellington House:—Blake better understood the moral effect of such wanton barbarity, and as soon as he heard of it, he ordered the joy-bells of St. Mary's to ring out a merry peal! In the outer streets—especially in East Street and just outside East Gate—there were daily battles. Blake planted a few pieces of cannon at East Gate, in front of which the street widens considerably and the road falls about twenty feet: the houses, almost reaching to each other across the narrow gateway, served his men for ramparts; the doors, balconies, and chimneys for embrasures. Every day the Cavaliers stormed up the outer street. When cannon and musket could be used no longer with effect, the pike and pistol had to decide. Without regular walls and with insufficient artillery, Blake had few advantages of position to set off against the tremendous disparity of men; and gallant and unyielding as the little garrison proved itself, he saw its ranks grow thinner daily, as his brave companions fell under the enemy's fire, while the prospect of relief still appeared distant and uncertain. But what distressed both people and garrison beyond the loss of their houses and gardens, the fatigue of nightly watches, and the destruction of daily conflicts, was the terrible scarcity of provisions. Bread already sold for fourteen pence a pound and beer at eighteen pence a quart—more than twenty times their market value! Other articles of food were equally dear. The rations of the soldiers were reduced to the lowest limit; and in spite of public care and private charity, it is probable that many of the poorer inhabitants died of starvation. Berkeley was well aware that famine fought his battles in the town; for, as in every other place where there were men, there were adherents of both parties within its gates; and in his despair of being able to win his way pike in hand, he sent to invite the garrison to surrender to the King rather than die the lingering death of hunger. Blake replied to this request, that he had not yet eaten his boots, and that he should not dream of giving up the contest while he had so excellent a dinner to fall back on! Tradition says, that at this time only one animal, a hog, was left alive in the town—and that more than half starved: in the afternoon Blake, feeling that in their tragic state of mind a laugh would do the defenders as much good as a dinner, amused them by having this hog carried to all the posts and whipped, so that its screams, heard in many places, might make the enemy suppose that fresh supplies had somehow been obtained. But while assuming this defying attitude towards the Cavaliers, he wrote frequent and most urgent letters to London for relief. He assured the Houses that if succour did not speedily arrive, they must be put to the last straits for bread and powder. He said he had hitherto met with scorn every offer of a parley: he had still a barrel or two of powder; and as for food, the garrison had re-solved to eat their horses. But he begged the Houses to consider their distress; and, in conclusion, he said he committed himself and his cause to God, in the con-fident hope that He would relieve them in His own good time. Parliament answered this appeal by an assurance that aid should soon be sent. Meanwhile, house by house and street by street, the town was burned, razed, and destroyed by cannon-shots. Hand-grenades and fire-arrows were thrown into it from every post. Not a day passed without a fire; sometimes eight or ten houses were burning at the same moment; and in the midst of all the fear, horror, and confusion inci-dent to such disasters, Blake and his little garrison had to meet the storming parties of an enemy, brave, exas-perated, and ten times their own strength. But every

inch of ground was gallantly defended. A broad belt of
ruined cottages and gardens was gradually formed between the besiegers and the besieged, and on the heaps
of broken walls and burnt rafters the obstinate contest
was renewed from day to day.[1]

The rage of the Royalists at this prolonged resistance
knew no bounds :—and in the pages of Clarendon their
loud wail and gnashing of teeth are still almost audible.
Blake could not be conquered, and the royal army
could not march away, leaving an enemy so redoubtable,
so popular, so full of resources in its rear.   The Prince
of Wales left Bristol for Bridgwater to be nearer the
scene of action, and to encourage his officers and men
by hopes of royal favour. At the castle of that town,
Commissioners for the western counties waited on him ;
and after long consultations it was resolved to raise and
arm an additional eight thousand men in those parts,
and to bring the whole weight of Royalist power in the
west to bear on Taunton, which, it was now considered
certain, must, from want of bread and powder, fall
within a month.   These things were all arranged, says
Clarendon, " so that in order to the taking that place
and to the raising an army speedily, all things stood so
fair that more could not be wished."   Yet Taunton did
not fall !   And all this time that famous Model Army,
fated to break and humble the proud chivalry of England
in almost every encounter, was being slowly created and
organised by the genius of Cromwell. At length this force,
reformed and re-officered under clauses of the Self-deny-

---

[1] Elegiac Enumeration, 9 ; Toulmin, 415, 423 ; History and Life,
19, 20 ; Clarendon, iv. 16-20.

ing ordinance, was fit to take the field. But opinions
were divided as to the course to be followed. Cromwell
wished to face towards Oxford, where the King lay entrenched, and fight a great battle there while the Royalists
of the west were occupied in Somerset; urging in defence of this plan, that as the King himself, the chief
army of the Cavaliers, and the best part of their artillery lay there, one defeat would put an end to the war,
and the reduction of a few towns and fortresses would
then become a mere question of time and detail. On
the other side it was urged that the issue of battle was
uncertain, even should it be found possible to force the
King to engage in open field; that Taunton was the
key of the four western counties; that its fall after so
glorious a defence would produce a great moral effect
in the country; and that, moreover, its heroic garrison
had a right to expect the first relief that could be despatched into those parts. The humane considerations
overruled the military; and the word for Taunton being
given, the soldiers started with a burst of enthusiasm
which shortened the journey several days. For an
entire week the army refused to take an hour's repose;
and they were already among the Cavalier tents in
Dorsetshire before the Cavalier generals had heard of
their departure from the neighbourhood of London.[1]

But at Blandford, two expresses, riding post-haste
from Westminster, overtook the army on its march,
bringing an unexpected and unwelcome order to turn
round towards Oxford, sending on a mere relief-party to

---

[1] Sprigge, 13-15; Toulmin, 415, 416; Clarendon, iv. 22.

Taunton. The reason for this sudden change of purpose, was the receipt of intelligence that Charles had taken the field, at the pressing solicitation of Prince Rupert, and was then on his way to the north, leaving Oxford with only a small garrison, which the Roundheads in that city promised to attack and overpower if the new army would advance against it. Fairfax at once obeyed; first detaching four regiments under the command of Colonel Welden, with instructions to recruit his strength on the way—enlisting all volunteers and carrying down all the flying corps willing to join in the relief—and to send word by trusty messengers to apprise Blake of his approach, and concert with him the signals to be used in announcing that fact. At Dorchester six companies of foot joined his party; every town through which he passed afforded volunteers; and the whole garrison of Lyme, now freed from the enemy, turned out to the assistance of their old commander. By forced marches, Welden crossed the Chard Hills into Somerset at the head of two thousand horse and three thousand foot, to encounter an army more than thrice his strength. Berkeley had notice of the approach of this party, and tried by a stratagem to induce Blake to make a premature sally, during which he had hopes of being able to cut him off and enter the town by surprise. From the watch-tower on St. Mary's steeple Blake received intelligence that a large body of cavalry was approaching the Cavalier lines from the Chard road, as if to attack them; personal observation, however, soon convinced him that these were Royalist soldiers bearing down on the besiegers, and surmising the real fact—that it was a feint to tempt him out of his impregnable position, he stood still, waiting the development of this curious manœuvre. As the clouds of dust cleared off, he could see masses of foot and cavalry moving forward, and as they drew near Berkeley's tent the Royalists faced round to engage them. For more than an hour the battle seemed to rage with great violence, when the attacking party wavered and fled. But the ruse had failed. Convinced at last that Blake would not accept the bait, Sir John recalled his flying squadrons, formed them in deep columns for assault, and rushed towards the ruins which separated the real combatants. Vast quantities of hand-grenades were thrown into the houses, and two long and fine streets were that day consumed to ashes. Never had the Cavaliers fought more gallantly. Pike in hand, they cleared the outworks, passed the gate, and stormed the slight timber barricades in East Street; but the besieged fell back only to concentrate their strength and recruit their stock of powder. Resisting with passive courage until the enemy began to shew signs of weakness, Blake then gave the word for his reserves, drawn up in the bull-ring, to advance at a pike charge, while the musqueteers stationed in and behind the houses in East Street, opened up a sharper fire, and after a tremendous struggle the streets were again cleared and the Cavaliers driven back to their entrenchments, leaving behind them hundreds of their comrades, killed, wounded, and prisoners.[1]

---

[1] Rushworth, i. second part, 29; Sprigge, 16-18; Clarendon, iv. 37, 51; Toulmin, 418.

While the Cavaliers were suffering from the effects of this severe repulse, the boom of artillery was heard among the Blagdon Hills, in the direction of the road from Chard, by which Welden's party was known to be advancing. Blake counted the echoes carefully, and when the firing ceased, finding that altogether ten guns had been discharged, he knew by the signals previously arranged with the scouts, that the army of relief had left Chard and was come within ten miles of Taunton. The intelligence of this long-expected succour being at hand soon spread in the town, reviving hope in the brave and rousing despair from its apathy. Blake made his dispositions to co-operate with the relief party in an attack on the still superior forces of the enemy,—and his companions in toil and danger retired to rest that night with a conviction that the morrow's sun would go down on an entirely altered aspect of things. High as their hearts beat for the contest, proud and calm as their leader looked in that crisis of their fate, they could not forget that Berkeley's army was large enough to spare a division superior to that commanded by Welden to watch and check his movements, and yet maintain the siege in all its rigour. If they knew no fear, they had little cause to exult. At length the morning dawned, Sunday morning May 11th; the troops were mustering in the bull-ring and in the court of the castle, when news was brought that the Cavaliers were already in full retreat on the roads towards Ilchester and Bridgwater, having struck their tents in the night and abandoned their entrenchments before sunrise. Trusty scouts were sent off in every direction to watch Berkeley's movements;

from the church-tower the long lines of the Cavaliers could be seen in full retreat; the patrols sent word to their commander that the camp was almost deserted; and that in their haste to get away, arms, ammunition and camp-furniture to a great value had been left behind. Assured by his various intelligence that the retreat was not a mere feint to draw him into a snare, Blake sounded his trumpet for a sortie, and passing through East Gate he fell on the stragglers and rear-guard, put them to rout, seized a pile of arms, cleared the orchards and meadows lying between the Chard and Bridgwater highways, and would have pursued the fugitives farther, only that they had taken the precaution to make the roads in their rear impassable for cavalry by cutting down the trees and throwing them across for barricades. Their retirement from the works after so long and fierce a siege produced a powerful reaction on the inhabitants, and the pious people flew to St. Mary's to return thanks for so unexpected a mercy. Welman took for his text the words of Malachi—" I am the Lord: I change not: therefore ye sons of Jacob are not consumed." And the fervid preacher exhorted them to continue to put their trust in the Lord of Hosts. He assured them that their cause was the cause of heaven, and that all the powers of earth could not prevail against it. The miraculous retreat of the royal army,—since, in the opinion of its own commanders, it was equal to twice the number of Roundheads then arrayed against it,—gave point and meaning to the preacher's words; and just as the congregation had risen to his own height of enthusiasm, several persons ran into the church gasping out—Deliverance! Deliverance! A squadron of Welden's horse had galloped unopposed to the very works at East Gate and exchanged greetings with the defenders. The people rose to their feet at these magic words; some embraced their friends and children; others ran about wildly in the extravagance of their joy; many rushed for the doors, anxious to get ocular demonstration of this good news. But Welman called to them in a loud voice to pause, and having recovered silence in the sacred edifice, he motioned them with a solemn gesture to kneel down and join with him in giving thanks where thanks were most due for so great and unexpected a mercy. The main body of Colonel Welden's corps arrived at four o'clock in the afternoon, when the aspect of Taunton and its heroic defenders filled the rough soldiers, inured as they were to sieges and battles, with wonder and pity. More than a third part of the houses had been burnt or battered down with artillery,—and both garrison and inhabitants were dying of hunger in the streets. Harassed as they were by the march over hilly and broken roads, the relief party refused to touch a morsel of the still remaining provision; and after effecting the first object of their visit, returned that very night towards Chard.[1]

Parliament learned in due time of the relief of Taunton. Bonfires were made in London in celebration of the happy event. A day of general thanksgiving was appointed. Letters of thanks were sent to Fairfax for

---

[1] Mercurius Civicus, 103; Welden to Fairfax, May 11; Sprigge, 18, 19; Toulmin, 419, 420; History and Life, 21, 22.

having despatched the relief corps ; Welden and his officers received their share of the nation's gratitude for
their successful expedition; and governor, garrison and
people were all lauded in high terms for their zeal, courage, and sacrifices in maintaining a town without walls
or other military defences, and already exhausted by a
long siege and blockade, for fifty days against such
overwhelming numbers. Two thousand pounds were
voted to the soldiers, and five hundred pounds were sent
to Blake, as a testimonial to his genius and devotion to
the national cause. To the inhabitants of the town and
neighbourhood the 11th of May was ever afterwards a
day sacred to happy memories, celebrated in anniversary
sermons and in popular ballads. To the Roundhead
party throughout the country, Taunton, even in the
depths of its material desolation, was a watchword and
an omen of eventual triumph.[1]

But its sufferings were not yet ended. At the first
movement of the new model army, the court called
Goring's forces from the west ; but finding Fairfax
march towards Devon and Somerset instead of on Oxford, as they had expected, a new and bolder policy was
adopted. Charles despatched Goring to the scene of his
former license, to cover the leaguer before Taunton and
crush the new model, whilst he himself, considering Oxford strong enough to resist assault, resolved to make a
rapid march northward—join his forces with those of
Rupert and Maurice, raise the siege of Chester, then
sorely pressed by the Roundheads, and if possible regain

---

[1] Clarendon, iv. 36; Walker's Sufferings of the Clergy, 18; Whitelocke, 146.

some of his lost ground in the great county of York.
But this division of the central and western armies proved
fatal to the King. Covetous of the glory of reducing
Taunton, and burning to flush his libertine soul with the
spoil of a city famous for the wealth of its citizens and
the beauty of its women, Goring led back his division
into Somerset, after making a terrible oath that he would
reduce that haughty town or lay his bones in its trenches.
Fairfax turned his flank in obedience to the fresh orders
from London, and, to the consternation of King and
court, suddenly appeared under the walls of Oxford.
This movement recalled the royal expedition from the
north, and the two grand armies were once more and
for the last time in presence of each other.[1]

Goring's crew overran Somerset. Rape, robbery
and murder again became daily and nightly incidents.
Falling on Colonel Welden with superior forces, he drove
him into narrow passes in the hills, from which a more
skilful general would have made it difficult, if not impossible, for him to retreat without serious loss. But
Goring's orders were so imperfectly given, that Colonel
Thornhill and Sir William Courtney, whom he had sent
by different routes to cut off the Roundheads unexpectedly at Petherton Bridge, not aware of the double
nature of the expedition, fell on each other, and with such
ardour, that both officers were hurt, one of them made a
prisoner, and many persons killed on both sides before the
blunder was discovered! While they were fighting with
each other, Welden escaped into Taunton. Goring fol-

---

[1] Elegiac Enumeration, 10; Fairfax Correspondence, iii. 217-228;
Carlyle's Cromwell, i. 277; Clarendon, iv. 43.

lowed in his rear, and once more the unhappy town was
invested on all sides—Dunster Castle, Langport, Ilchester
and Bridgwater affording the enemy so many strong rallying points. But no fresh attempts were made to carry it
by storm. The Royalists acted on the defensive only;
patrolling the country, checking sorties, and trusting to
the effect of famine. Goring boasted in his letters to
the Prince of Wales that he could take the place in less
time now that Welden's party had added so much to
the physical wants of the garrison. All depended on the
strictness of his blockade. Blake knew this, and his
only chance of an indefinite prolongation of the defence
lay in being able, by frequent sallies, to break the lines
and open up temporary communications with the country.
Nearly every day foraging parties went out in search of
corn and fodder; sometimes these adventurers were cut
off, more frequently they escaped the vigilance of the
Cavalier patrols; but such as returned almost invariably
brought in prisoners or provisions. The spirit of the
garrison now rose with every encounter. They had
learned to regard that mixed host of Irish, Cornish, and
German mercenaries, so cowardly in the field, so brave
in the ale-house and farmyard, with a contempt equal to
their hate. The governor's sarcastic humour fed this
feeling. One day, by way of insult, Goring sent a poor
fellow into the town, dressed in rags, with a tattered
drum, to demand an exchange of prisoners. Blake expressed a superb contempt for the miserable insulter—
not by hanging the poor drummer, or by harsher treatment of his prisoners, as the Cavalier general would
have done under like circumstances, but by dressing the

man in a new suit of clothes and setting all the prisoners free without ransom or conditions!

In the valleys, Welden's horse did excellent service :— but the courage of the colonel sometimes led him into unnecessary dangers. One day, making a sortie with his cavalry, he was received so firmly by Goring that his charge was broken, and his whole troop put in peril. Happily Blake, from his watch-tower, saw the danger; and with characteristic rapidity sounded his trumpets for a sortie, formed two squadrons of his veteran horse in the market-place, rode at their head through East Reach, fell on the flank of the Cavaliers, and threw the whole body into momentary confusion. Welden seized the moment to disengage his men, and draw them off towards the town. Blake brought up the rear, disputing every inch of ground, and retiring in perfect order, and with his face towards the enemy. The example of these brilliant episodes incited persons at a distance to acts of almost romantic daring. A party from the garrison at Lyme undertook to find or force their way through the Cavalier camps, and carry a small supply of powder to their former chief,—a feat which they performed with the utmost gallantry and success. As a reward, Blake invited them to witness a grand sortie, which proved to be the most murderous conflict that had yet taken place before Taunton, four hundred Cavalier corpses being picked up in the trenches after the battle. This victory was of immense and immediate importance to the be- sieged, as Goring drew off his men to a greater distance, enlarging the Roundhead quarters five or six miles,— and the Londoners, once more roused to activity by the glorious news from Somerset, formed an association for the special purpose of sending down relief to Taunton. Members of the Common Council, private merchants, traders and gentry commenced a subscription, and in a few days four thousand pounds were already raised. Parliament also promised speedy and effectual aid, and Colonel Massey distributed handbills in the taverns and workshops, calling on volunteers to join him in the expedition. Such was the alacrity of the patriotic citizens, that before Massey was prepared to march with the government aid, they had already equipped at their own expense a thousand horsemen.[1]

While Goring was thus employed in the vale of Taunton, the Cavalier cause was being decided on the field of Naseby. With that battle the war was almost at an end. Fairfax turned westward to raise the siege of Taunton, crush Goring's crew, and recover the great strongholds of Somerset and Devon for Parliament. On the second of July he met Massey at the head of three thousand new levies, specially designed for that service, at Blandford; and the following day, heedless of the oath which bound him never again to quit the leaguer before Taunton so long as the Roundheads occupied it, Goring burnt his tents and drew off to Langport, whither Fairfax followed him, and routed his troops in two or three brief but destructive encounters. The march of the Roundheads through the West was brilliant and victorious. Bristol was carried by storm. Bridgwater, Langport and Ilchester, keys of the western counties,

---

[1] Elegiac Enumeration, 9; Toulmin, 424; Sprigge, 54; Whitelocke, 144, 146; History and Life, 23, 24; Clarendon, iv. 51, 52.

were also carried by storm. Finally, Taunton was freed
from its enemies; and all the neighbouring towns, castles and strongholds,—Dunster Castle alone excepted,
—were soon in friendly hands. The last part of the
siege had lasted five weeks—the former more than seven;
but reckoning from the date when Blake seized the town
to that of Goring's final retreat, there was exactly a
year as the duration of this marvellous and successful
defence. One of the King's best armies had been occupied and destroyed by it. Some of the bravest of his
captains had lost their reputation or their lives in its
trenches. Grenville, Digby, Berkeley, Hopton, Wyndham, Goring, and many others had retired from it foiled
and dishonoured. Major-general Digby, brother of the
famous Sir Kenelm, received there a mortal wound,
and the last attempt to blockade the town cost the
lives of fourteen hundred Cavaliers.[1]

The town itself presented a most deplorable aspect.
For many miles round, the country, once like a rich and
cultivated garden, interspersed with orchards, nursery-
grounds, and water meadows, was a dreary desert. The
corn had been cut down green—fruit-trees destroyed in
mere wantonness—barns and mills emptied of their contents—farm-houses ransacked and burnt—the peasants
and farmers driven with insult and violence from their
homesteads. The relieving army noticed with horror
that between St. Nicholas and Taunton they marched
for half a day without seeing a single human creature
or one human habitation standing, in the most populous

---

[1] Somers Tracts, v. 236; Fairfax Corresp. iii. 235; Clarendon, iv. 65;
Toulmin, 428; History and Life, 23-25; Carlyle's Cromwell, i. 293-316.

and wealthy district of provincial England! In the immediate suburbs of the devoted town the work of destruction had been done completely : — there all was black, grim and ugly ruin. The streets of the town proper had all suffered, more or less, up to the walls of the church on one side, and to those of the castle on another. A third of the entire number of houses in the town had either been burnt by means of wild-fire and red-hot balls, or battered down by the artillery. Blake had the proud satisfaction to feel that he had kept his ground ; but towards the end of his year of hard fighting, he was master of little more than a heap of rubbish.

After the retirement of Goring, his first care was to diminish the number of mouths to be fed daily, by sending Welden's corps to the lord general's camp ; his next was to provide for a regular supply of fresh provisions from a distance, until the ravages of the fierce soldiery could be restored in his own neighbourhood, and the lands so terribly wasted could be again brought into culture. Nor were the heroic sufferings of the people forgotten at head-quarters. The two Houses issued warrants for a general collection in behalf of the ruined citizens, and the money raised under their warrants was chiefly employed in rebuilding the burnt and battered houses. For several months Blake's genius and energy were devoted to the relief of the inevitable distress, in aiding each man to recover his former position, and in forwarding the interests of his party in Somerset.[1]

One of his negociations during the autumn was with the celebrated club-men or peace-makers. These men,

---

[1] Fairfax Corresp. iii. 219, 220 ; History and Life, 20-24.

instigated by the royalist gentry, had risen in arms under pretence of self-protection from the marauders of both parties, though in reality they desired and intended to serve the King; Goring, however, whose disorderly followers were supposed to be glanced at in their declaration, issued a severe order against them from Exeter, which greatly incensed many of those who had expressed themselves to the intriguers favourable to the royal cause. Blake saw as clearly as Goring the inconvenience of having a third party in the field, of uncertain good faith, without leaders and without flag, and he therefore tried to win them over to his own cause, and induce them to combine with the parliamentary forces. To this end he proposed a form of submission for them to sign and send to Fairfax, in which they were to thank God for having freed those parts of " the plundering and dissolute army, which consisted of many Papists, Irish rebels, and outlandish commanders, officers and soldiers, whose common practice was to rob and destroy the inhabitants,"— to assert their fixed resolution to protect themselves from violence and rapacity,— to express their readiness to join with Fairfax for the purpose of putting a speedy end to the war,—and to offer to submit themselves to the laws, orders and commands of Parliament. But the club-men refused to subscribe such terms. " Our intentions," they replied, " are to go in a middle way; to preserve our persons and estates from violence and plunder; to join with neither; and not to oppose either side, until, by the answer to our petition, we see who are the enemies of that happy peace which we really desire." On his part, Fairfax refused to treat with this anomalous body; and his lieutenant-general soon afterwards gave them a terrible chastisement near Hambledon Hill.[1]

Early in the following spring, Dunster Castle still holding out against the victorious Roundheads, Blake, no longer fearing for the safety of Taunton, took the field with his recruited corps, joined by volunteer parties from neighbouring garrisons, in the hope of carrying that fortress by storm. Built on the crest of a hill, of very difficult ascent for troops, and defended by a body of men resolute in their attachment to the royal cause, it had hitherto resisted every attack, and was generally thought impregnable to the military science of that age. It was indeed a virgin fortress, and is often spoken of in the old writers as the strongest castle in the west of England. Blake appeared under its walls about the middle of April; and the demand to surrender being answered by a stern defiance, he gave instant orders to his trumpeters to sound a charge. The battle was continued for some days; but as the progress towards victory was too slow for his Roundhead zeal, Blake secretly prepared a mine, which he sprung at a favourable moment, throwing huge masses of the solid masonry into mid air, and making wide rents in the walls, through which the assailants stormed with an impetuosity that nothing could resist. That sun-down saw the red cross of England floating from the highest tower of Dunster Castle.[2]

Though elected by the burgesses to represent them

---

[1] Public Acts and Orders, Sept. 20, 1645; King's Tracts, 234, art. 13; Carlyle's Cromwell, i. 289-291.

[2] Elegiac Enumeration, 11; Oldmixon, i. 303; History and Life, 26.

in Parliament, instead of Sir William Portman, expelled
for disloyalty to the House, Blake continued to reside at
Taunton, and to busy himself with the pacific duties of
his government.   Unlike so many of the selfish officers
who had hitherto been his rivals in glory and public service, when the King's cause was lost, and the King himself was become a prisoner, he made no attempt to throw
himself into the centre of intrigues or to use his great
influence in the West for his personal advancement.
With a true Roundhead contempt for wealth and the
dazzling prizes laid open to the ambition of genius in
troubled times, he remained at his post, doing his duty,
humbly and faithfully, at a distance from Westminster ;
while other men with less than half his claims were asking and obtaining the highest honours and rewards from
a grateful and lavish country.   A sincere Republican, it
was his wish to see the nation settled on the solid basis
of a religious commonwealth ; but though his principles
were stern, his practical politics were all essentially moderate.   That, at any period after the sword was drawn
and blood had actually been shed in the quarrel, he
would willingly have treated with the King, as King, is
doubtful ; but after Charles's refusal of the terms offered
for his acceptance while he was still with the Scottish
army, it is certain that Blake no longer entertained a
thought of maintaining the monarchy in his person.
The whole town of which he was representative and
governor, he at its head, prayed the House never to
make peace or receive proposals from the perjured sovereign, but to continue the war even to an end, so as
to obtain a firm and lasting settlement of religion and

public quiet—pledging themselves to support Parliament in this course of action to the last drop of their blood. Yet this patriotic zeal did not blind him to the suggestions of justice and true policy. The proceedings of the army-chiefs after Charles fell into their hands gave him great annoyance. Like Algernon Sidney, the younger Vane, and other of the wiser or more moderate men, he wished to see the King deposed and banished. He deprecated even the appearance of illegality and violence; and when he found the party of which Cromwell was the inspiring genius bent on his trial and execution, he loudly expressed his discontent with their proceedings, and under the influence of his humane convictions, declared openly that he would as freely venture his life to save the King as ever he had done to serve the Parliament.[1]

The influence, moderation, and military genius of Blake rendered him at this critical period an object of continual jealousy and suspicion to the friends of Cromwell. Before they dared to bring the King to trial, they took the precaution to lessen his power, by disbanding the principal part of those forces which had performed so many prodigies of valour at Lyme and Taunton. Care was taken to conceal from public notice the real motives for this measure; and the order was accompanied by an expression of gratitude and thanks from the House for his eminent services, and by another donation of five hundred pounds. Still, it was known to some and suspected by many, that these flatteries

---

[1] Parl. Hist. ix. 39; Lords Jour. viii. 423; Humble Petition of the Town of Taunton, Feb. 9, 1647.

were paid with a view to disarm suspicion on the part
of their object.   Blake obeyed the orders without a
word of remonstrance.   Others felt and resented the
intrigue and the slight, though he did not : — and it was
not long afterwards referred to by one of the most distinguished naval commanders of that age, as affording a
sort of excuse and justification of his own treachery to
the national cause.   But the governor of Taunton had
no share in such feelings.   He never attempted to conceal his thoughts from friend or foe—for he had no fear
and no ambition.   He considered Cromwell violent and
illogical in his desire to put the King to death, and he
stated that as his deliberate opinion.   But he never professed to think the question of what should be done
with the faithless King other than one of mere policy
and detail.   In the idea of founding in England a grea
religious commonwealth, he concurred with all his soul
What else was left ?   He had seen monarchy, in what was
then considered its best form, produce only falsehood
tyranny, spiritual intolerance and moral debauchery
—he wished therefore to try the experiment of a demo-
cracy founded on religious principles.   Yet, overriding
all his private theories and desires, there reigned in his
heart the strong sense of patriotic devotion.   Covetous
of glory, but free from the lower vices which often
grow up in the neighbourhood of that noble passion, his
thought by day, his dream by night, was how he could
still be useful to his beloved country, and to those great
Protestant and liberal principles for which she had sac-
crificed her domestic peace, and poured out her best
blood in torrents.   An opening for a new and glorious

career soon offered itself at sea, and the appointment of the hero of Taunton to the chief naval command—whether, as has often been conjectured, the motive had its origin in Cromwell's wish to remove so powerful and incorruptible an officer from the scene of his own intrigues, or in the general belief of the parliamentary chiefs that his executive genius, dauntless valour, and unvarying good forture would be as conspicuously displayed in his naval as in his military exploits,—it was one of the most important events in that age, and opened a new and most brilliant era in the history of the British navy.[1]

---

[1] Navy Mss. No. 69, State-Paper Office; History and Life, 28; Batten's Declaration (in Granville Penn, i. 268).

CHAPTER IV.

Naval Command.

IN the earlier period of the Revolution the navy had occupied an almost neutral attitude. For three years the Earl of Warwick acted as lord admiral under the commission issued by Parliament in its own and the King's name jointly; but, with the exception of a not very strict blockade of Ireland, varied by a few skirmishes of no political or naval importance, the fleet had had little more to do in those eventful times than to ride in the English Channel, watch the movements in foreign ports, and guard our shores against the surreptitious arrival of arms, levies, and munitions of war from France and Holland. The state of public opinion in the coast towns had placed nearly all those important stations in the hands of Parliament from the outset; so that of all the famous sieges, storms, and blockades which make the historical romance of the civil war, there was scarcely one in which the fleet had been required to take a prominent part. On the whole this was a happy circumstance. Standing apart from the scene of strife, the seamen were not swayed by the violent and bitter passions which ruled their less fortunate brethren in camp and city. Not that they were indifferent to the quarrel. High church and despotic doctrines were as little popu-

lar in the navy as in the army. But, mixing less frequently and fiercely in the actual conflict, they were
less blinded by passion, and took a clearer and more moderate view of the nature and course of events than the
generals and soldiers. As time wore on, and the nicer
shades of opinion came out in stronger relief, some differences in religion assisted in dividing the two great
arms of the public force. The army became Independent—the navy remained Presbyterian ; and these words
involve two entire systems of ideas and of policy. When
Warwick surrendered his command under a clause of
the Self-denying ordinance, the affairs of the Admiralty
were put in commission, and he was rewarded for his services by a seat at the new Navy Board, a post which he
retained four years, notwithstanding the many changes
which occurred in the other members. Admiral Batten
succeeded to the command vacated by the Earl ; and so
long as the King lived, this able officer discharged the
duties of his high station to the perfect satisfaction of
Parliament. On occasion of the Queen running into
Bridlington, a small port on the east coast of Yorkshire,
with arms, money and stores from Holland, to support
the failing cause of her unfortunate husband, to the infinite horror of the Royalists he did not hesitate to follow
the Dutch ship into the port, while, by a hot fire on the
town, he compelled her majesty to quit her house in the
night and take shelter in a place protected from the fury
of his guns. He made foreigners, as well as Cavaliers,
respect the flag of the Parliament—distinguished himself in the blockade of Ireland, and captured a Swedish
fleet which had refused to lower its topsails in token of

his supremacy in the narrow seas. For his good services he received the nation's thanks on more than one occasion.[1]

But the time was now at hand when neutrality was no longer possible. Every great branch of the public force was compelled to choose a side; and as the army grew more and more outrageous in its pretensions, murmurs began to arise in the fleet in regard to the conduct of those on shore. Flushed with its recent victory, the nation seemed as if about to divide against itself. The sudden rise and successful career of the Independents was a source of fierce and deeply-seated jealousies in the navy; and the series of events, as questionable in their character as they proved in their consequences, which led to the purchase of the captive King from the Scotch army, his unceremonious arrest by the soldiers at Holdenby, and his subsequent imprisonment at Carisbrook Castle, gave rise to the most dangerous explosions of discontent in the Downs. Charles was surprised and seized on the 4th of June; and, eight days after this event, the Earl of Warwick found it necessary to write to Batten, urging him to be on his guard in such distempered times, lest the mariners should be seduced from their duty, and the vessels under his command be surprised into some act of disobedience. He took care to remind the admiral that Parliament had raised the seamen's wages above the rates paid in former times; and expressed a hope that his old comrades would remain faithful to the two Houses. But as the mutinous spirit rather increased than abated, Batten himself fell under suspicion of fo-

---

[1] Whitelocke, April 9, 1645; Granville Penn, i. 74, 243.

menting this evil spirit in his men. He was therefore
called to London. Colonel Rainsborough, an Independent, and one of the army faction, was appointed vice-
admiral. But this new commander was unequal to the
work of restoring order, for the mutinous spirit of the
navy was continually fomented by the royalist intriguers
of Kent, and he no sooner arrived at his post than he
was seized and displaced by the officers under his command. At the same time the mutineers declared for King,
Parliament and Covenant, and sent a message to the
Earl of Warwick, offering to obey his orders if he would
come on board, and agree with them in the terms of their
present declaration. Unprovided with means to punish
this act of usurpation, the Houses reluctantly concurred
in the nomination of Warwick ; and at the earnest solicitation of the Lord Mayor and Aldermen of London,
whose commerce and supplies were threatened by the
revolters, Batten was also restored to his rank as vice-
admiral :—the latter an act of grace which Parliament
had instant and serious cause to lament. Already a
traitor in his heart, Batten went back to the fleet with
his commission in his hand, and, in the absence of Warwick, who had not yet gone on board, took possession of
the supreme authority, when calling his partisans together,
he informed them of his resolution to declare for King
Charles, and requested their advice as to whether he
should drop down the Channel to Cowes, and take the
royal prisoner on board, or stand over for Holland to
consult with the Prince of Wales. Unfortunately for
the object of their sympathy, they adopted the latter
course, and eleven vessels, carrying altogether 291 guns

and 1260 men, renounced their comrades and their obedience, and sailed for the Dutch coast.[1]

This important defection raised once more the
drooping hopes of the Cavaliers. Prince Charles received Batten with open arms, though he had fired on his
royal mother a few years earlier at Bridlington,—and
conferred on him the honours of knighthood. Under
the erroneous impression that the whole fleet would
follow Sir William Batten's example, the Prince of
Wales and his brother James, Duke of York, went
on board the revolted ships and sailed towards the
Downs, where Warwick was then lying, having already
joined his forces in the river with the fleet from Portsmouth, making altogether nineteen ships and three
ketches, a force about equal in men and guns to that
under the two princes. On heaving in sight of the
Roundhead squadron, Charles sent a messenger commanding the Earl to lower his standard and repair to
the royal presence; orders which he of course firmly but
respectfully declined to obey. The temper of his men
was good, and Parliament being assured that they would
fight with alacrity against the revolted ships, a formal
resolution was passed authorising and requiring him to
attack and capture them in spite of their having royal
commanders on board. The two divisions of the fleet
dodged each other for several months without coming
to an engagement. On both sides there was a want of
energy, promptitude and well-defined purpose; and on
that of the Cavaliers loud and fierce dissensions in addition. The common sailors again mutinied against their

---

[1] Granville Penn, i. 247-261; Parl. Hist. xvii. 185, 190.

officers: Batten, Gordon, and Lord Willoughby quitted
the service in disgust; and the better sort of seamen,
deserting from the enemy's ships, daily returned to their
former stations. Some of the repentant crews contrived
to carry back their vessels; and it soon became apparent that, under such weak and purposeless leaders, the
remnant of debauched, quarrelsome and insubordinate
seamen at Helvoetsluys could afford little more than a
momentary alarm to the country. Nor in all probability would they have ever again required the attention
of a great fleet, had not a new commander appeared,
whose iron will and contempt of law and right as between man and man, nation and nation, gave him advantages over captains who contended in the names of
liberty and civilisation, and with the weapons which
befit those sacred words.[1]

Long before the battle of Naseby put an end to the
war on a grand scale, Prince Rupert, distrustful of the
final issue, had endeavoured to secure some part of the
spoil which passed through his hands for his own future
use; but one or two vessels which he had freighted with
this plunder fell into the hands of Parliament. After
the fall of Bristol and his disgrace with his uncle, this
adventurer and his brother Maurice were ordered to quit
the country. At first Rupert retired to Holland. From
that state he went to France, where the romantic Queen
Regent received him as a knight of chivalry might
have been received in olden times by the Queen of
Beauty. She offered him any post in her service which

---

[1] Rushworth, iii. 1255; Granville Penn, i. 261-277; Carte's Coll.
188; Clarendon, iv. 364-460.

he would himself select. He obtained from her a troop of horse and a regiment of foot. He was made a Field-marshal, and placed at the head of all the English then serving in the French army:—not an inconsiderable body, as the Cavaliers who fled to the Continent nearly all turned soldiers of fortune. Under Gassion and Rauzau he had already served in the Low Countries with some distinction, when the defection of Batten and the arrival of the revolted fleet in Holland threw a fresh lure in the way of his ambition, calling him once more to the side of his royal relatives.[1]

The affairs of the Stuarts were then at the lowest ebb. The exiles starving in their retreat—the Marquis of Ormonde unable to make way against the Roundheads and clamouring loudly for succour in Ireland—ships without stores and ammunition—officers without a plan—men mutinous, disorganised and without pay,—such was the aspect of affairs when Rupert returned to his cousins and proposed to take the supreme command at sea. On being allowed to name his own terms, he pledged himself to restore discipline, to supply the more pressing wants of the royal court, to carry assistance to the lord-lieutenant of Ireland, and to harass the naval power of Parliament. In return he asked to be invested with the same powers at sea which he had formerly enjoyed on land; that is, to be free from any and every sort of control. The Prince of Wales, poor, wasteful and inexperienced, consented. From that moment Rupert became a corsair in the very worst sense of the word. One of his largest ships he sold to the Dutch,

---

[1] Mercurius Civicus, 17; Rupert Ms. in Warburton, iii. 236-7.

and with the money he bought stores, powder and shot. Once out at sea, he threw off every restraint imposed on men by natural and international laws. With him every ship that he could take was an enemy — every argosy a prize. No flag afforded its bearer protection against this predatory warfare. Not only were the unoffending merchants of England spoiled of their goods, but French, Spanish, Swedish ships were also attacked, captured and sold by this pirate. On these robberies the court of the exiles depended for their daily bread. If Charles found a speculative merchant willing to risk the discount of a bill, he drew on Rupert for the amount, and sent a frigate out to inform him of the date and sum of the transaction. When his sailors murmured at the long arrear of their pay, the freebooter bade them go out and catch a ship for themselves, the first that should heave in sight. In this manner, states with which England was at peace, powers which the young princes were trying to enlist in their father's cause, were insulted and wronged without regard to consequences near or remote. No country suffered more in its commerce from the marauder than that very Holland from which he had sailed, and which still afforded protection to his own parents and to the sons of his sovereign![1]

Against such a commander and such a system the Council of State soon saw that the slow-paced genius of the Earl of Warwick and the naval officers of his school would avail but little. While the Earl lay in the narrow seas with a powerful fleet, the Prince sallied out from Helvoetsluys with two ships and captured as

---

[1] Clarendon, iv. 467; Warburton, iii. 255-270, 275, n.

many prizes as enabled him to fit out the remainder of his vessels. When passing down the Channel to his destination on the Munster coast, his men shewed some disposition to go over to their countrymen; but he excited a change in his own favour by audaciously riding down on the hostile fleet and opening through its line of guard a passage to the south. To this boldness, energy and rapidity of action, it became necessary for Parliament to oppose qualities similar in kind. But with the exception of Blake, there was perhaps no man in England, having any knowledge, however slight, of sea affairs, equal to the Prince in personal courage, fertility of resource and brilliancy of execution. Blake was therefore called from his pacific government at Taunton to assume the chief command at sea, in conjunction with Colonel Deane and Colonel Popham—the latter a brother of his old friend and fellow-soldier of the same name—under the title, invented for the occasion, of Generals and Admirals at Sea, or as they came afterwards to be usually styled—Generals of the Fleet.[1]

The tasks which the three Generals took upon themselves were at once varied and onerous. When they went on board it was well known that the navy was in about the same condition as that in which Cromwell had found the old army. Abuses existed every where, in the Admiralty offices, in the dock-yards, in the ports and naval stations, on board the ships,—and many of these were of long standing and most flagrant character. To provide the Generals with full powers to examine

---

[1] Lansdowne Mss. 155, 98.

into and correct these abuses they were also appointed
Commissioners of the Navy, with seats at the Admiralty
Board. The mandates under which they acted required
them to employ all available means to achieve these
three ends:—1. to completely re-organise the naval
power, so as to rid that great arm of the public service
of all doubtful and disloyal elements; 2. to disperse,
capture or destroy the revolted ships, and drive the
Princes, Rupert and Maurice, from the high seas; 3.
to co-operate with the Land Forces in a new and more
efficient attempt, then in course of preparation by Cromwell, to put down the Irish rebels.[1]

The new system began with a change of flag. From
the accession of the Stuarts the Union Jack had streamed
from the topmasts of every vessel engaged in the service
of the State; but the King's removal having dissolved the
necessary legal connexion of the two countries, all ships
at sea in actual service were henceforth ordered to carry
only the red cross on a white ground. When the new
Commissioners came to examine the details of the actual
state of the navy, they found the disorder greater than
was feared. Few of the vessels were sea worthy. The
dock-yards were ill-managed. Stores and arms were
systematically stolen. The wages of the common sailors
were not regularly paid; and when vessels came into
port the poor men had commonly to wait some weeks
before they could obtain their money. No proper care
was taken of the rations. Often the biscuit was mouldy,
the beer sour, the meat rank. The system of forced

[1] Com. Jour. Feb. 12, 1649; Rupert Ms. in Warburton, iii. 282.

impressment was bitterly complained of; while in the neglect to provide hospitals for the wounded and asylums for the infirm, the dictates of sound policy and the calls of humanity had been equally spurned. In all these matters Blake became a reformer the very day he became an admiral. His letters, still preserved in the Admiralty papers, shew how minute and constant was his care for the comfort and welfare of his men: in these documents his kindness of heart seems more conspicuous than even his naval genius. Fearless himself, he was remarkably tender of the lives, the health, and even the comforts of others. He would at any time weaken the force under his command in order to send a frigate home with a few wounded men, if he found they could not be treated with sufficient care on board in the midst of daily-renewed battles. The minutest details engaged his attention, when the comfort of his men was concerned, even in the crisis of a great campaign. No wonder that he was adored by them! A curious instance of his popularity occurred shortly after his nomination to the command. The watermen of the Thames had by ancient usage a right to priority of impressment for the service; but this usage, like many others, had fallen into abeyance, with the full consent of all parties; the dangers and disorders of the service having few attractions for men who possessed other means of obtaining a livelihood. But no sooner was the new system understood than the overseers of the watermen petitioned Blake to restore their old privilege, on the grounds—that the watermen on the river were all well-affected to the Commonwealth, that they were the proper raw material out of which to make expert seamen, and that this priority was an ancient right of their order.[1]

The first measures adopted by the new commanders in fitting out the fleet give evidence of the energy and character about to become the distinguishing marks of the service. They went down and purged each ship of the idle, the vicious and the disaffected;[2] good and true men were alone retained, and it was to fill the places of the discharged sailors that the watermen of the Thames put in their claim. The ablest captains of the service were sought out and employed, without regard to age, interest or personal consideration. No incompetent noble or honourable person was allowed to occupy the place of a better seaman. Merit alone found favour with the new generals; and Penn, Jordan, Ascue, Stayner and Lawson, next after Blake himself the most famous captains of the Commonwealth, were all appointed to important commands. Although Blake was but one of three Commissioners, there is every reason to believe that he took the lead in their deliberations; and that the general features of the campaign, which had to be adapted to the particular character of the enemy to be encountered, and the other exigences of the service, were the work of his brain. These were the chief dispositions of the naval force :—
Deane was stationed with a squadron in the Downs, having instructions to cruise between Portsmouth and Dover and keep the trade of the narrow seas free from

---

[1] Humble Petition of Watermen, with General Blake's Answer, April 6, 1649, in the Deptford Mss. in the Tower; Minutes of Council of State in Granville Penn, i. 288, 289.

[2] Blake and Deane to Com. of Admiralty, April 3, Dept. Mss.

interruption; Popham, with a second squadron, was to lie off Plymouth Sound, check the depredations of the Scilly pirates, and guard the southern entrance to the Channel; Sir George Ascue, with a third squadron, was to cruise in and near the bay of Dublin, hinder the Irish rebels from communicating with their English partisans, and keep St. George's Channel open; Blake reserved to himself the especial task of chasing, fighting and destroying the pirate fleet under Prince Rupert.[1] Before going on board the flag-ship, he took the precaution to supply himself with jacks, standards and studding sails for giving chase.[2]

On the eighteenth of April (1649) at the age of fifty, Blake set his foot on deck for the first time as a commander, and from that moment to the hour of his death no man in England ever thought of contending with him for the first place as a seaman. Envy, jealousy and hatred dogged the steps of every other officer in the fleet; but of him, both then and afterwards, every man spoke well. The common sailors regarded him with an enthusiasm which bordered on idolatry; the veteran admirals, against whom he fought in so many brilliant and destructive battles, considered him the perfect model of a knightly foe; the country gentlemen in England, while they abhorred his political principles and affected to contemn his religious opinions, allowed that his whole course of action was frank and noble; and even the coarse and malignant writers of the Restoration spared

---

[1] Navy Mss., No. 69, in the State-Paper Office.
[2] Blake and Deane to Admiralty, May 12, Dept. Mss.

his memory the abuse which they heaped so plentifully on men like Vane, Hampden and Sidney.[1]

After cruising about for some time in the narrow seas, doing much damage to commerce, Rupert attacked and captured the *Robert* frigate; and the blockade of Kinsale having been raised by orders from London, he made for that harbour with the intention of there co-operating with the Marquis of Ormonde, and establishing for himself a convenient station whence he might sally out on his marauding expeditions and shelter his prizes from the pursuit of Blake.[2] The town and castle of Kinsale being in the hands of Irish rebels, who still made some show of loyalty to the King, Rupert had no difficulty in there disposing of the stores and merchandise which his formidable industry enabled him to bring in. Certain of his best ships were always out on the search for unarmed traders, and the harbour of Kinsale was soon filled with the prizes of all nations. Lately without a shilling in his coffers, the royal buccaneer was now flush of money; the most daring spirits in the south of Ireland flew to the standard of a man who had set up so profitable a system; and neither men, money nor stores were wanting to equip the captured vessels and get them ready for service. The seceded fleet again became a formidable power in those waters; and the daring outlaws began to plough the deep with all the confidence of prowess and success. Affairs in Ireland took what appeared to the court a happy turn; and even the cautious Marquis of Ormonde sent to invite the exiles into that

---

[1] Heath's Chronicle, 402.

[2] Blake to Admiralty, May 12, Dept. Mss.

country, assuring them at the same time that with the assistance of the squadron then at Kinsale, the greater part of that kingdom would soon be brought into obedience,—that large armies could then be raised,—that the Scots might be cajoled or coerced into a league,—and that a vast material power could be suddenly hurled from those shores against England. The exiled court leaped with joy at a prospect of renewing the war. But Charles was too poor and his credit too low to raise money for the expenses of an outfit:—Rupert coolly and characteristically sent out a frigate, caught a Dutch trader, sold her for ten thousand pounds, and despatched the money to his cousin at the Hague![1]

As soon as the arrangements for his new model were in progress, Blake passed down the Channel with the fourth division to check these growing disorders at Kinsale. Nor was it long before the Cavaliers had good reason to know that a new system had begun with the new general. Their fleet, returning from a cruising expedition, encountered a violent storm, and the frigate *Charles*, separated from the other vessels, got involved in a dense fog, which prevented a good look-out being kept. Before the captain had time to tack about and make off, he was assailed by the *Constant Warwick* and the *Leopard*, part of Blake's squadron, and after a sharp action was compelled to surrender. Pushing forward this success, Blake followed the returning fleet to their pirate hold and shut them up safely within it,—as Ascue in an earlier part of the summer had endeavoured to do, but without success. The arrival of this new force at

---

[1] Rupert Ms. in Warburton, iii. 275 n., 288 ; Clarendon, v. 3.

Kinsale disconcerted the vast plans of the Cavaliers.
Charles did not dare to sail for the Irish coast; Rupert
had no opportunity of sending out his predatory bands;
and the sources of supply cut off by the strict blockade,
his mass of acquired capital soon grew less. Though he
had more than half Ireland at his back, his prospects
were not pleasant. He saw that he could only escape
from his perilous position by cutting through the guard-
ships; and even if he got away from Kinsale and from
the enemy, he knew of no other harbour in which he
could seek refuge from pursuit or carry on the sale of
his prizes. This position was the more annoying to
him, as the fine weather being come, and his fleet
careened and ready for a summer voyage, he had raised
an extraordinary levy of men; but instead of sweeping
the coasts and rivers of their mercantile marine, as he
had hoped, he was now forced to act on the defensive,
and erect batteries on the shore to prevent the enemy
from sending fire-ships into the harbour and burning his
ships. Worst of all, his men began to murmur and
desert. Blake offered them lower pay and none of that
license which they had enjoyed at Kinsale; yet his personal popularity was already so great in the navy, that
they went over to him at every convenient opportunity.
To strike terror into the hearts of his men, Rupert one
day seized ten of them, on the plea that he suspected
them of a desire to escape, and mercilessly strung them
up at the yard-arm. Harassed by these causes of discontent and impatient of a prolonged inactivity, he wished
to risk an engagement with his wary adversary; but in
a case of so much moment, he listened to the counsel of

K

his more experienced naval officers, who told him it would be rushing on destruction to attack Blake in his present position, until they had prepared some fire-ships, and crowded their decks with an overpowering body of soldiers and marines.   The town of Kinsale being open to the country, Rupert himself went overland to the various port-towns on the coast, and engaged as many men as could be prevailed on to accept high pay and hard service; but when he returned to Kinsale with these recruits, the courage of his captains had been so much cowed by the activity of Blake, that they still voted in the council of war, that it was unwise to hazard a trial of strength with such an enemy, and that consequently the only course was to secure their ships in the harbour until the hostile fleet was driven by bad weather to quit their station and return to Bristol Channel or the Downs. Infinitely chagrined at this turn of opinion, Rupert, compelled by the failure of his funds, disbanded his new levies, stowed away the useless barques, and kept only the flag-ships and four frigates to wait on them, ready for active service :—and so the summer of 1649 passed away.[1]

Meanwhile, the approach of the victorious Roundheads by land, storming their way from Dublin southward, under the command of Cromwell, warned Rupert that, in spite of his batteries and castles, his hold was growing insecure.   As dangers thickened round him, his mind became a prey to jealousy and distrust; he accused the governor of Cork of a desire to betray him

---

[1] History and Life, 29, 30; Elegiac Enumeration, 12; Rupert Ms. in Warburton, iii. 290-295.

to the enemy; he shot an ensign and all his company on suspecting them of an intention to afford a passage to Blake through the line of guard-ships; in his nervous agitation he conceived doubts of the fidelity of the Cavalier governor of Kinsale castle, and actually took it by surprise as a precaution against an imaginary act of bad faith. As the winter neared and the strong winds of the north-east set in, Blake was forced to ride out at a greater distance from the mouth of the harbour; it being an extremely dangerous lee-shore, and entirely without safe anchorage. Thereupon Rupert prepared for his long-expected day of escape. The greater part of his ships he was unable at the last moment to man, and they were reluctantly left behind as a prey to the enemy; the castle he gave up to the Marquis of Ormonde, then retreating towards Cork before the parliamentary army; and when he came to reckon up the effective force with which he had to begin life anew, he found that his whole fleet consisted of only seven sail of all rates. With this force, aided by the elements, he had the good fortune to escape from Kinsale. Continued storms had made it impossible for Blake to keep his fleet together off that terrible coast; many of his ships were driven to the nearest ports for shelter; and towards the end of October, a violent gale having still further weakened the blockading squadron, and scattered the few remaining vessels widely about the offing, Rupert seized an opportunity to steal away unobserved, and once out at sea, spread his sails for Portugal.[1]

[1] Carlyle's Cromwell, ii. 181, 224; Rupert Ms. in Warburton, iii 297-299.

His duties at Kinsale being ended by the Prince's flight, Blake repaired to Ross—where Cromwell was negociating the surrender of that important town under the threat of such an assault as had already overwhelmed Tredah and Wexford with sudden ruin,—to co-operate with the land forces in effecting a final reduction of the island to obedience. By agreement with Cromwell, who desired him to act with Admiral Deane, now on the Irish coast, Lord Broghill and Sir William Fenton as a Commissioner for the general management of affairs in those parts, he returned to the Cove of Cork. Cork city, after these successes, returned to its duty, and repelled the attempt of Lord Inchiquin to re-establish it as one of the head-quarters of the Cavalier-Catholic interest. But Blake was soon called away from these more pacific duties to go in chase of his old and formidable adversaries. With their characteristic impartiality, the corsair princes, when they had escaped from the Irish seas, levied black mail on all nations. In standing across for the Continent, Maurice encountered a Malaga trader, which struck at his first summons, and was of course seized; shortly afterwards Rupert met with two English merchant-men, bound from London to San Lucar in Spain, and after a desperate struggle mastered and manned them for further service. While scudding along the shore towards the Tagus, in which river the King of Portugal, in his horror of Puritans and patriots, had given him a promise of protection against his pursuers, a vessel from Brazil, freighted for Lisbon with the property of Portuguese traders, stood across his line of sail, when he instantly gave chase, overtook, captured and condemned her as a prize, on the absurd plea that she had not struck her colours to him at the first summons! Though other nations suffered from these outrageous piracies, the chief losses, of course, fell on the mercantile men of England; and as the Council of State received from the London and Bristol traders most urgent complaints of the insecurity of the narrow seas, they took on the 4th of December the very unusual resolution to fit out a winter fleet, and invited Blake to assume the command and go in pursuit of the pestilent marauders.[1]

By the middle of January 1650, a small force, consisting of five ships, the *Tiger, John, Tenth Whelp, Signet,* and *Constant Warwick,* carrying altogether only one hundred and fourteen guns, was got ready for sea; and as soon as he could obtain his final instructions, Blake went on board the *Tiger.* These instructions directed him " to pursue, seize, surprise, scatter, fight with and destroy" the ships of the revolted fleet and to suppress pirates and protect lawful traders in the exercise of their calling. If any foreign prince or power joined with or assisted the corsair princes, he was required not to spare the revolters on that account; and in case the foreign power assisted the revolters by force of arms, he was to fight with them, and by God's help destroy them. He was to prevent any injury to the foreign prisoners who might fall into his hands; but to send them at his convenience to England, there to await the decision of

---

[1] Cromwell to Council of State (Carlyle, ii. 237); Carte, ii. 91; Rupert Ms. in Warburton, iii. 299, 300; Minutes of Council of State, Dec. 4, 1649.

Parliament. If any vessel or vessels belonging to the revolted fleet should be sold by their commander to a foreign power or the subject of a foreign power, he was directed to demand, attack, capture or destroy them wherever found, as a part of the English navy which the revolters had no right to sell. In the next place he was instructed that time out of mind the lordship of the seas had belonged to England; and this ancient right he was directed to maintain as far as in him lay; to cause the ships of all nations to strike their flags in his presence; and in case of refusal to seize and send them in as prisoners, unless they should offer such obedience and reparation as he might judge sufficient. It was submitted to his prudence, however, not to proceed so far in these demands as to force hostilities with any superior fleet, until the particular object of his voyage had been accomplished; but in all cases he was to keep for future use a strict account of any that refused to acknowledge his dominion of the sea. Towards foreign powers at peace with England he was directed to avoid every cause of offence and to offer to renew ancient leagues of trade and friendship with them, unless such States should join with and protect the revolters; in which case he was instructed to assail the said powers to destroy their fleets and to capture their merchant vessels, and send them as prizes into the most convenient English ports. Lastly, as the turn of event could not be foreseen, and the means of communication with London would be slow and uncertain, he was invested with a wide discretionary power in the disposal of his fleet. The final clause contained the essential spirit of his instructions—"You are to order and dispose of the said fleet and the ships under your command *as may be most advantageous for the public,* and for obtaining the ends for which the fleet is set forth; *making it your special care* in discharge of that great trust committed to you, *that the* COMMONWEALTH *receive no detriment.*"[1]

To the five ships first equipped for this service eight others were added early in the spring, four men-of-war —*Resolution, St. Andrew, Phœnix* and *Satisfaction*—and four merchant-men—*Hercules, America, Great Lewis* and *Merchant*—under the command of Admiral Popham, who also carried out some additional instructions to his colleague. In the meantime Rupert had sailed into the Tagus and received the most cordial and flattering welcome from John of Braganza, King of Portugal, who assured him that he would protect him in that river against all his enemies. A friendly salute from the forts along the coast welcomed the fugitives with royal honours. The first night the princes anchored in Weyrs Bay, near the river mouth; next day they stood higher up the stream, fixing their station at San Katherina, until Rupert should find leisure to present himself at court in due form. His reception was enough to turn a steadier brain than his; for King John sent some of his proudest nobles to attend the fugitive Prince from Belleisle to the palace, where he confirmed in person and in the warmest manner the promises of protection which he had previously made through his envoy. The fleet then anchored under the guns of Belleisle, and the officers sold the goods taken in their prizes to

---

[1] Thurlow, i. 134-136; List of Fleet in the Admiralty Office.

the Portuguese merchants; which done, they sailed to Lisbon, where they employed the seamen during the winter months in careening, victualling and fitting out their prizes as men-of-war. At the approach of spring, Rupert, tired of court festivities, went on board and dropped down the river to Belleisle, with the intention of renewing, under more favourable auspices, the profitable piracies of the former year; but before he could get clear of the Tagus, Blake was at its mouth with his little fleet of five ships; and not daring to attempt a passage by force against such a commander, he anchored again under the guns of the fort. Blake now sent an officer to ask the King's permission to attack the revolted ships at their anchorage; this being absolutely refused, he attempted to enter the river without leave, but was induced to desist from this design for the moment on finding the governor of the castle determined to oppose ·his entry by force. On hearing the first shot from Belim Castle, Blake sent a boat to inquire the reason for this show of hostility against a friendly power, there being no war at that time between Portugal and England? The officer simply replied that he had received no orders to allow any other ships to pass. With great moderation, Blake sent his complaint to Lisbon; and some prominent members of the Council, alarmed at the false position in which their King's rash promise to the revolters had placed the country, urged him to make concessions to the powerful Commonwealth even at the last moment, rather than incur the hazards of a naval war. His own fears inclined him to listen to these prudent councils, so that, instead of a haughty reply, he sent one of his courtiers to compliment the new Admiral, and to beg that, for the sake of peace, he would not attempt to enter the river unless foul weather should force him to seek a shelter for his ships. To these civilities he added a supply of provisions. In return, Blake declared that he was anxious not to violate a friendly river. But he urged on the King's attention that he was the minister and representative of a powerful nation; that the fugitive princes possessed no country, nor even a single port of their own into which they could send their captures for legal condemnation, and were therefore incapable of being regarded as a neutral power; that the ships then in their possession were a part of the English navy, which had been armed, equipped and furnished by Parliament in their own ports and manned by their own servants; that, moreover, these princes had acted as pirates and sea-robbers, and by adding the captured ships to their fleet, were growing into a power likely to prove dangerous to the lawful commerce of all nations; finally, that having no place in the world which they could pretend to call their own, they were unable to appeal to the law of nations, or ask the protection of any prince in their revolt and piracy, without thereby creating a cause of war between that prince and the Commonwealth of England.[1]

To this clear statement of the question the King could only oppose his personal feelings and his rash promise. The royal Council was divided in opinion : the Conde de Miro, an expert and sagacious minister, spoke

---

[1] Orders in Council (Granville Penn, i. 298-301); Rupert Ms. in Warburton, iii, 300, 301; Oldmixon, i. 388; Heath, 256.

the sentiments of the more prudent, and his views were shared by all the traders and merchants interested in the commerce and colonies of the country. But the Queen, ardent, prodigal and fascinated, warmly espoused the cause of her brilliant guest; and two violent factions soon arose in the court and city, of which the rallying cries were " peace" and " war" with England. The weather growing foul, Blake entered the river with his fleet and anchored in Weyrs Bay, whence he unceasingly pressed the King and Council for leave to fall on the revolters; but weeks passed on and he could obtain no satisfactory reply to his requests. Duplicity and delay characterised all the proceedings of the court. The Brazil fleet, then fitting out for the summer voyage, was almost ready to set sail; and it soon became apparent to the Admiral that they were trying by their civilities and councils to gain time until this fleet was despatched and out of danger, with the intention of ultimately declaring against him and his purposes. Rupert himself was mystified. He complained that his enemy was allowed to come up the river to San Katherina, only two miles from his own station. His sailors deserted to Blake in spite of every severity; and one of his largest ships, the *Swallow*, of thirty-six guns, was in the very act of escaping when the plot was discovered and defeated. Alarmed at these dangerous symptoms of revolt in his crews, and doubtful whether the Queen would be able to prevail against the Miro or Peace party in the Council, he secretly prepared to defend himself; and, if his worst fears should be realised, to force a passage through the English squadron or perish in the attempt. But these preparations of his did not escape the vigilance of the court, and they created a suspicion in high quarters that, urged by hatred and despair, he was about to commit some act of wanton hostility against his protectors. Fear in some, contempt in others, were thus raised. But the more factious and alarmed the city grew, the safer Rupert felt himself. As a ready means of sowing dissensions in Lisbon, he courted the priests and the populace. Though a Protestant, he did his best to arouse the lowest passions of the Portuguese Catholics against his adopted country. He urged the priests to preach a crusade against England, not only as a point of conscience, but also as a means of increasing their own worldly influence. These men willingly gave their aid and countenance; they harangued against patriots and protested against the shame of a Christian nation treating with rebels, until the people were so incensed that the King could hardly pass down the streets of his capital without hearing the exclamations of their rage and fanaticism. To gain over the mob to his interest, Rupert went among them continually, gave them money and soft speeches, and made a pretence of placing himself and his cause under their protection. These artifices succeeded so far as to compel the Miro party to be extremely wary, and to postpone a final arrangement of the question.[1]

But not content with the success of this appeal to base passions, the fugitive armed an assassin against the life of his formidable enemy. The only plea ever put forth by his partisans in excuse for this attempt at private murder was a false report to the effect that some persons

---

[1] History and Life, 31; Rupert Ms. in Warburton, iii. 302-304.

from the Admiral's fleet went on shore at Belleisle to attack a hunting-party, including Rupert, Maurice, and several other Cavaliers, in which, however, they pretend that the Roundheads got the worst of it, and were glad to retreat; the real truth being that the men were sent on shore in the ordinary way to obtain a supply of fresh water, and while so employed were assailed by Rupert's party, who killed one of their number, dangerously wounded three others, and made five prisoners. Towards evening of the day on which this incident had occurred, a bombshell, placed in a double-headed barrel, with a lock in the middle so contrived that on being opened it would give fire to a quick-match and cause the whole to explode, was sent by Rupert to the Admiral's flag-ship in a Portuguese boat, manned by a trusty sailor and two negroes, the former dressed as a Portuguese tradesman. The men sent on this murderous errand were instructed to say they were oil-merchants come with a present for the seamen. But when the boat arrived at the ship's stern, they found the ports there closed, and while they were rowing round to the transom-port, some of the crew observed and recognised the Englishman as one of Rupert's men whom they had frequently met on shore at Belleisle; and before any mischief could be done he was arrested and the device of which he was to have been the executioner discovered.[1]

Having missed his aim, and doubtful of the King's resolution even more than he feared a change of sentiment in the populace, with failing provisions and wavering men on board, Rupert engaged the governor of the

<hr/>

[1] Rupert Ms. in Warburton, iii. 305; Thurlow, i. 145, 146.

castle to connive at his passage, and prepared to fall down the stream with the first favourable wind. But Blake had friends on board the Prince's ships, and being informed of this design, he towed his vessels in a dead calm to the mouth of the river, which movement compelled Rupert to fall back to his old position. Months were spent in these blockadings and negociations without result. Blake, now strengthened by the arrival of Popham's squadron, represented to the King that his port had been dishonoured, that innocent blood had been shed ; and he demanded in more urgent terms permission to right himself. But instead of complying with this request, the weak-headed monarch at last threw off the mask, put some of the English merchants under arrest, and pronounced for the cause of the two princes. This course of action, while it simplified the state of affairs and left Blake to act as he thought proper, added the whole weight of the Portuguese navy to the force of the revolters. Blake's answer, however, was swift and certain. The Brazil fleet of nine sail coming out of the Tagus, he seized them without ceremony, removed the officers and crew, put trusty men in their places, and thus at a stroke raised his own effective strength from thirteen to twenty-two sail.[1] At the same time he threatened to seize the American fleets on their return, if the revolters were not immediately compelled to quit the Tagus. Hitherto the English Admiral had been so modest in his demeanour, so moderate in his demands, that the King was astounded at what he called the temerity of this act of self-defence ; and in the first outburst

---

[1] Judges' Ms. Reports, March 24, 1650, State-Paper Office.

of his rage he began to arm the coasts and fit out his fleet for service. The Conde de Miro was disgraced and his friends discountenanced. A squadron of thirteen men-of-war was equipped; and, under the command of Vara John, was ordered to join the force under Rupert; but even then they did not consider it prudent to attack the English, who continued to cruise about the river mouth, interrupting all their commerce by sea, and threatening to intercept the richly-freighted vessels then known to be coming home from the Brazils.[1]

Autumn was now deeply advanced. The fleet had been in those unfriendly waters seven months, and although provisions and stores had been supplied by Popham's squadron and by other means, the ships were sea-worn, the stores well nigh exhausted, the men suffering from the effects of long confinement and severe duties; and the storms of winter being now about to set in, the court of Portugal believed it would be impossible for them to stay much longer on that bleak and hostile coast. But Sir Henry Vane was indefatigable at home in preparing the materials of naval war; and in spite of the elements Blake remained in the Portuguese waters to encounter one of the Brazil fleets, consisting of twenty-three sail, just as they were about to enter the Tagus, when a brief but fierce engagement ended in the loss of the admiral, which went down during the cannonade, and three others, which were set on fire and consumed; and the capture of the vice-admiral and eleven large ships, all laden with the most precious cargoes.

---

[1] History and Life, 31, 32; Rupert Ms. in Warburton, iii. 305; Thurlow, i. 155.

Only seven of the smallest barques escaped, and that was by running into the river while the contest was at its height. As soon as the King heard of this great disaster, he went on board the Prince's flag-ship, and ordered him to attack the English with the combined fleets and recover his lost treasures; but the winds kept no terms with the royal thirst for revenge, and the Portuguese pennons floated idly in the river, while the victorious English repaired their losses and counted their magnificent gains by the late engagement. At last, however, a fair wind sprang up, and with provisions already on board for fourteen days—ample time as the courtiers thought to capture or destroy the blockading squadron, Rupert dropped down the river, at the same time hoisting signals for Vara John to follow and join him below Belim with all his disposable force. But the Portuguese commander either could not or would not raise his anchor for several hours, and the revolters were already up with the English squadron before their friends had yet got under sail. Want of concert prevailed throughout. The ships were scattered over a wide expanse of sea, and neither party was able to afford assistance to the other. While moving about the harbour in a thick fog, the Prince suddenly discovered the admiral, with Blake's pennons floating at the maintop, riding within pistol-shot of his stern; and with that fearlessness which concealed so many faults, he gave orders to tack round quickly and run alongside the flag-ship, without firing a single shot or raising the least shout till they were near enough to spring on board. The men of the admiral caught a glimpse of the suspicious craft through the thick atmosphere, and as she passed in silence under their lee, poured into her a broadside that shattered her fore-topmast,—and satisfied with this passing salute, Blake continued his course, and was instantly out of sight. The rest of Rupert's fleet was too far to leeward to give chase or render assistance. Their outfit being exhausted, the allies returned ingloriously to their former station at Belleisle, mutually accusing each other of incapacity. Poor Vara John was deposed from his command, and judged unworthy ever to be again employed in his country's service. Blake and Popham, after despatching all their prizes to England, returned to block up still more completely the mouth of the Tagus.[1]

A second descent of the combined fleets was equally unsuccessful. Without risking a general engagement, which he had no desire to do unless compelled, Blake remained master at sea. Rupert had seen no more service on this new element than himself; but it is curious that the veteran admirals of Portugal should have been foiled in all their attempts to force him either to quit his position or fight a battle. At length the loss of so many vessels, and the continual outcries of his subjects, induced King John to sue for peace on reasonable terms. As necessary preliminaries to a peace, the Conde de Miro was restored to favour and it was intimated to the fugitive princes with well-feigned regrets that the crown of Portugal could no longer protect them against the might of England. As the redoubtable English Admiral was at that moment absent from the

---

[1] Rupert Ms. in Warburton, iii. 307-309; History and Life, 32, 33.

river in search of the dispersed fleets of Brazil, some of which had stopped short at the Azores, while others had run for safety into Spanish ports, it was suggested to them that they might get clear away if they chose; and if they did not depart, they were given to understand that on Blake's return to the blockade, he would be allowed to attack them at their moorings. Rupert therefore again unfurled his corsair banner, slipped his cables, and under a friendly salute, the last he ever found in Portugal, he dropped down the river in search of new fortunes and adventures.[1]

As soon as the princes had quitted Belleisle, Don John despatched an envoy tŏ London to sue for peace and friendship with the English Commonwealth. His former pride was remembered against his present humility, and the Council of State made rather hard conditions. But the envoy granted all the preliminaries demanded. He agreed that the English merchants who had been laid under arrest should be set at liberty ; that they should have all their losses made good to them ; that the King of Portugal should defray a considerable part of the war expenses already incurred. But as the envoy presumed to dispute some dates and details, the haughty Council commanded him to quit the country. However galling to his pride this contemptuous act might be, Don John was obliged to submit. He sent a nobleman of high rank, the Conde de Camera, as his extraordinary ambassador, to deprecate the anger of Parliament. The Conde assented to every proposal made to him by the Council :— but delays again arose through the change

---

[1] Rupert Ms. in Warburton, iii. 313.

from the Parliamentary to the Protectoral form of government, and it was not until January 1653 that the
treaty of peace, trade and friendship was finally ratified
between the two powers. So long as he lived, Don
John gave England but little further trouble.[1]

At the close of the dispute with the court of Lisbon,
the owners of the nine ships seized and detained by
Blake at the mouth of the Tagus were allowed to present a statement of their grievance to the judges of the
Court of Admiralty. Blake's conduct in the matter was
minutely investigated; Admiral Popham was called on
to give evidence as to the facts; and after a full inquiry
the judges decided that the General-at-Sea had acted in
the spirit of his instructions. But they acknowledged
the private losses which the owners might have suffered
by the forcible detention of their ships, and decided
that the same compensation should be awarded to them
for the service, as in cases where ships had been hired
by the State.[2]

---

[1] Elegiac Enumeration, 12, 13; Lords Jour. Dec. 17, 1650 to Jan. 5,
1653; Whitelocke, 486 ; Rupert Ms. in Warburton, iii. 313.

[2] Judges' Ms. Reports, March 24, State-Paper Office.

CHAPTER V.

1650-1651.

Cabalier=Corsairs.

THE intensely piratical character of Rupert's sea-life has, in a great measure, escaped the notice of our historians. Hume merely writes of it in this way : " Prince Rupert, having lost a great part of his squadron on the coast of Spain, made sail towards the West Indies. Everywhere this squadron subsisted by pirateering, sometimes on English, sometimes on Spanish vessels. And Rupert at last returned to France, where he disposed of the remnants of his fleet, together with his prizes." In like manner Lingard gives his reader the impression that the Prince did not turn pirate until after his expulsion from the Tagus. Avoiding any reference to such illicit courses in the text of his work, he remarks in a note : — " Rupert sailed into the Mediterranean and maintained himself by piracy, capturing not only English but Spanish and Genoese ships. All who did not favour him were considered as enemies. Driven from the Mediterranean by the English, he sailed to the West Indies, where he inflicted greater losses on the Spanish than the English trade." Eliot Warburton, the editor of Rupert's letters and journals, says, " There was something very attractive in this sort of adventure, and it required all the native characteristics of gentlemen to

prevent the sea-going Cavaliers from carrying their buc-
caneering to excess. But it was *not* carried to excess;
at least all was done fairly and above board as to an
enemy; no cruelty was practised; fair terms were
offered and honourably kept towards the victims of this
predatory war." This is a fair expression of the views
of our popular historians;—yet it is demonstrable that
from the period of his first offer to go on board the
revolted fleet, he seriously and openly proposed to live
by plunder; intending to establish one or more strongholds, from which he flattered himself that he should
be able to interrupt at his will the rich commerce of the
narrow seas. His first idea was to make his lairs, as many
of the old northern jarls and vikings had done before him,
in the Channel Islands, particularly in the formidable
groups of rocks lying off the land's end, then, as now,
known as the Isles of Scilly. Nature herself might have
formed these islands for a pirate hold. Dangerous
sunken rocks, an extremely intricate channel, a sea
unrivalled for swell and violence, combined to prevent
the approach of frigates or other armed vessels towards
the centre of the group; and, as the ruins still visible
shew, art had come efficiently in aid of nature, for at
every point where it seemed possible to effect a landing,
stood block-houses and batteries connected with each
other by lines and breast-works of the most formidable
character. On St. Mary's Island, even at that time the
wealthiest and most populous of the group, these field-
works were bound together by castles of great strength
and commanding position: Old Town Castle, a strong
pile in the days of Leland; Star Castle, with its ditch

and ramparts, built by Sir John Godolphin in Elizabeth's reign; and the Giant's Castle, standing on the crest of a bold and rugged cliff. Some of the islets were extremely fertile; corn grew in abundance on many of them, and they were all well stocked with rabbits, cranes, swans, herons, and sea-fowl. Into this convenient hold Rupert poured men, money and warlike stores. To ensure them against the risk of their being captured by sudden assault,—for the Dutch were anxious to possess so convenient a port, and their famous Admiral, Tromp, had been seen hovering about under suspicious circumstances,—he gave the command, civil and military, to the gallant Sir John Grenville, then perfectly recovered from his Taunton wound. The islanders, mere children of the sun and sea, willingly joined in the attempt to convert their home into an important magazine and naval station. And to render this extraordinary combination of natural and artificial defences perfect, two thousand picked men were landed there as a garrison, aided by a multitude of Cavalier gentry, whose private fortunes had been wasted in the long wars.[1]

When cruising in the South Channel, before the approach of Blake's squadron had driven him to Kinsale, Rupert had carried the fruits of his terrible industry into this pirate hold. The store-houses on these rocks were filled with the captured merchandise of all nations; but the chief articles stored up were silks, corn, wine,

---

[1] Clarendon, iv. 467; Leland's Itin. iii. 8 ; Camden's Britannia, ii. 1523; Heath's Islands of Scilly, c. iv. (a very good account of these islands drawn up by an officer in the service, and published, with a good chart, in 1750); Kennett's Register, 408 ; Borlase's Scilly Islands, 10-16.

oil, timber, and the precious metals. While in Ireland, apparently engaged in the work of co-operating with the Marquis of Ormonde in the royal cause, he had been chiefly occupied with the task of strengthening this position. On the 3d of March he sent to Sir John Grenville from that country as much corn, salt, iron and steel as the ships could stow. His project of starting in the corsair line was not even decently disguised. In April he wrote to Grenville on the subject nearest his heart:—"You will receive," he says, "if these ships come safe, such provisions as we can spare here, and also some men, which I was feign to send out of my own regiment. They are all armed, and have some [arms] to spare. The officers have formerly served his Majesty. You may trust them. I doubt not ere long to see Scilly a second Venice. It will be for our security and benefit; for if the worst come to the worst, it is but going to Scilly with this fleet, where, after a little while, we may get the King a good subsistence; and, I believe, we shall make a shift to live in spite of all factions."[1]

The exiled family and their chief adherents seem to have entertained no conscientious scruples about this extraordinary system of freebooting. On hearing of a new capture, Charles writes from the Hague to his cousin: "Having already disbursed for the fleet a considerable part of those moneys which we intended for our own support and maintenance, and being now totally destitute of means to pay the debts of our dear brother, the Duke of York, and our own, and to provide for the subsistence of ourselves and family, we are no ways able

---

[1] Fitzroy Ms. in Warburton, iii. 289-295.

to discharge the debts contracted at Helvoetsluys for the fleet; and we intend, therefore, to provide for the satisfaction thereof out of the proceeds of the goods in the ship lately taken, if it prove good prize."—Charles drew on the corsair prince as on an inexhaustible bank; and when Rupert could no longer meet the demand made on him by his royal cousins out of the stolen property at hand, he had recourse to the goods and chattels laid up for future use in his stronghold at Scilly. Mr. Prog, a merchant, who had discounted a bill of 5000*l.* drawn by Charles on Rupert, arrived at Kinsale when it became due to ask for his money; but being somewhat dissatisfied with the prizes offered to him in liquidation of his claim, the prince gave him 533*l.* in gold and silver, and an order on Sir John Grenville, at Scilly, for 10,909 lbs. weight of Ardasse silk, as an equivalent for the remaining 4567*l.* In this way all the business of the exiled court was done. Men who had formerly been colonels of regiments became captains of frigates; those who could not find vessels to command, repaired to Scilly, Jersey or Guernsey, to share in the defence or join predatory parties as volunteers; so that when St. Mary's Island fell at last into Blake's hands, he found as many colonels and captains in the forts and castles as would have sufficed to officer a large army. The court itself was daily busy with these piratical matters. Instead of concerning itself as usual with the affairs of nations, with the progress of intrigues at Madrid, London and Versailles, the royal Council became engrossed with price-lists, trade speculations, and rates of exchange. There was something ludicrous in the gravity with

which the old statesmen of the Stuarts discussed the
market value of hides, sugar, silk, timber and other
articles of commerce.   Clarendon, Cottington and other
of the most reputable members of the party, gave their
sanction to this course of life,—accepting from necessity
that which the Bohemian Princes had adopted from love
of adventure and lawlessness of spirit.   Nor was Charles
himself averse to it.   Sir George Carteret, his deputy-
governor of Jersey and Guernsey, fitted out a fleet of
ten light and fast-sailing frigates, each carrying eight or
ten guns, for the purposes of piracy, with his consent, if
not by his orders,—and this gallant freebooter brought
in and sold numerous prizes in the ports of Jersey, while
Charles himself was present on the island.[1]

In one of his letters to Charles, Prince Rupert gives
some account of his lawless adventures during his flight
from Kinsale :—" Some forty leagues from shore," he
says, " it happened that in the night, by a mistake of a
light, all our fleet [five vessels] except Sir John Men-
nes's [ship] lost me.   Two days after we made early in
the morning seven ships to windward.   We gave chase
to them, and they to us, which proved to be our fleet :
Marshall being come in with a prize, and my brother
having taken another, made up the seven.   At night,
being moonlight, we made two great ships and a small
vessel, which we immediately chased.   In the morning
the *Black Lady*, the *Black Knight*, the *Scott*, and the
Mary overtook them.   The small ketch bore up right
before the wind, and the *Black Knight* gave chase, but
in vain.   The other two, being proved English, did not

---

[1] Whitelocke, January 23, 1649 ; Fitzroy Ms.

alter their course. Our small ships fell to work, which lasted from seven in the morning until ten, about which time their admiral's main-top-yard and main-sail were shot by the board, which stopped her way until my ship came up, to which she struck without a shot of ours: after which the other yielded also. These prizes being considerable, and being fearful of some disaster, having near three hundred prize-men aboard us, it was generally thought fit to secure and sell them with the first convenience to do, which no place was thought more convenient nor safe than Lisbon." The goods captured in these vessels he sold to the Portuguese merchants for 30,000*l.*; the vessels themselves he fitted out as men-of-war. It is true that Blake's vigilance and activity never allowed him the indulgence of a hope of being able to return to the Channel Islands; but it cost the country both much blood and much treasure before they were finally reduced to obedience.[1]

When the news arrived in England that Rupert had quitted Belleisle on a new piratical expedition, the Council of State hastened the preparation of another fleet to go in pursuit of him. The *Fairfax*, then on the stocks at Deptford, was rapidly finished. Penn was called post haste from St. George's Channel, the war being almost at an end in Ireland, and was appointed Vice-admiral of the Straits. The new fleet for the south consisted of eight of the best and fleetest sailers in the navy, commanded by some of the most eminent captains of the age. The flag-ship, *Fairfax*, Vice-admiral Penn, carried 52 guns and 250 men; the *Centurion*, Captain,

---

[1] Borlase, 42; Fitzroy Ms. in Warburton, iii. 295.

afterwards the famous Admiral Sir John Lawson; the *Adventure*, Captain Andrew Ball; the *Foresight*, Captain, afterwards Admiral Howett; the *Pelican*, Captain, afterwards Admiral Sir Joseph Jordan; the *Assurance*, Captain Benjamin Blake, younger brother of the Admiral; and the *Nonsuch*, Captain Mildmay, were all frigates of 36 guns and 150 men each. The other vessel, the *Star*, Captain Sandars, carried 22 guns and 80 men.[1] On the heels of this squadron, a fourth fleet, consisting of the *Triumph*, *Tiger*, *Angel*, *Bonadventure*, *Trades-increase*, *Lion* and *Hopeful Luke*,—carrying in the whole 1226 men and 270 guns[2]—was sent out under the command of Vice-admiral Hall, for the special purpose of acting as convoy for the protection of English merchants in the waters of southern Europe. By these squadrons new and enlarged powers were carried out to Blake. Hitherto he had been required to forward all his prizes to England for condemnation and sale; he was now desired to deal with his prizes as he thought best for the service, sending them home or selling them in foreign ports, and using the money so obtained to revictual and refit his ships as occasion might seem to him to require. His commission was renewed for an indefinite term; and all the naval power of England in those seas, with the single exception of Hall's convoy squadron, was placed at his absolute disposal. This mighty, and for the moment irresponsible power, was wielded by Blake with a wisdom, energy and success that received unqualified admiration in England, and extorted applause from the most rancorous of our enemies abroad. He had literally no in-

---

[1] Navy Lists in Add. Mss. 17,503. [2] Idem.

structions that could in any way control his movements. Translated out of the mere forms of office, the language of the Council of State to their great Commander was briefly this:—Uphold the interests and the honour of England; pursue, capture, or destroy its revolted fleet; protect its trade and its citizens abroad; overawe its rivals and false friends; harass and humble its avowed enemies! In the execution of this task he was bound by no forms of law. The Commonwealth knew that the Kings of the continent were not its friends; for although war had not been declared in words, the courts of France, Spain, Holland, Tuscany, and Portugal, had all favoured the royal fugitives, or pronounced their hatred and disdain of the English people and their Parliament by acts of open or secret hostility. The old ties of amity, the old treaties of commerce which bound England to the nations of Europe, were regarded as all broken and abrogated by recent events; and not knowing when or from what quarter a sudden blow might be struck at its peace and honour, it behoved the man who went abroad as the true representative of his country, to treat with the suspected powers boldly, proudly, energetically, with words of peace and friendliness on his lips, but with his hand occasionally on the hilt of the swift and trenchant sword of the young Commonwealth.[1]

Meanwhile, after their expulsion from the Tagus, the crews of the revolted fleet were beginning a new life. As adversity gathered round him, Rupert grew reckless of even the semblance of legality.—" Misfortune being now no novelty to us," says the manuscript memoir

---

[1] Thurloe, i. 167-8; Granville Penn, i. 309-312.

found among his papers, " we plough the sea for a subsistence; and being destitute of a port, we take the
confines of the Mediterranean Sea for our harbour: poverty and despair being companions, and revenge our
guide." In this spirit the Royalists sailed from Lisbon.
Coasting the shores of Andalusia, they fell in with the
Malaga fleet during a dark night, and any sail being
now regarded as good prize, they fired into them, and
captured two ships. Under cover of night the others
escaped, followed by the *Second Charles*, which vessel,
missing the signal for retreat, parted company, and was
for several days given up as lost. Rupert stood in for
Malaga, intending to enter that roadstead by night and
surprise the ships found lying out. With this design the
frigate *Henry* was sent forward with instructions to take
up, as if by accident, a position between the vessels and
the mole, so that when the Prince fell on them in the
night it might prevent them from retreating into the harbour. But, as was generally the case when one of his
vessels was separated from the flag-ship, some of the
Henry's men deserted as soon as the frigate anchored off
the mole; and these deserters having informed the Spaniards of the intended night attack, a signal from the
batteries warned the ships of their danger, and they rode
safely in while it was yet broad day. Finding his plan
defeated, Rupert adopted a friendly tone towards the
citizens, and not able to drive him away by force, they in
their turn tried to soothe his disappointment by the empty
honours of a royal salute. As nothing could be got by
staying there, the fleet sailed for Veles-Malaga, higher
up the coast, where they had heard that some English

merchant-ships were there lying in apparent security under the protection of a friendly power. On hearing of the appearance of the Bohemian corsair on the coasts of Andalusia, the governor of Veles-Malaga despatched a courier to Madrid for instructions how to act should the Prince make any hostile demonstration in his district; but on the plea that this messenger had not returned when Rupert arrived, he refused to interfere, and six English ships were fired and burnt by him under the guns of the Spanish batteries!

Blake was out at sea, waiting the arrival of a supply of stores sent by the Council of State, when intelligence of this atrocity, committed in a friendly port, reached him. Having already serious causes of complaint against the Spanish court, he wasted no time in the endeavour to communicate with the English Admiralty on this new complication of affairs, though it seemed not unlikely to lead to a war with that mighty empire; but leaving orders for Admiral Penn to cruise about the mouth of the Guadalquiver, and watch the line of coast between Cadiz and Gibraltar, he at once turned his bows towards the rocky entrance of the Mediterranean, and passed the Straits with all his fleet, being the first English Admiral who had ventured into those remote and celebrated waters since the time of the Crusades. The chase now became more exciting. Rupert had sailed from Malaga, no one knew whither. At Motril and at Capo de Gata, Blake could only pick up vague and contradictory rumours. At Capo Palos, near Carthagena, the revolted ships had last been seen in the midst of a tremendous squall; when, fortunately for their personal safety, the two princes separated from their companions and ran out to sea. As the storm abated, they descried a Leghorn trader, and the corsair instinct being strong within them, gave chase, following her to the Barbary shore, where she was at last overtaken and captured. The remainder of the revolted ships ran into Carthagena for shelter; and as soon as the foul weather cleared a little, the English fleet was seen riding before the harbour, cutting off every hope of escape. Blake sent a messenger to inform the governor of the town that enemies to the Commonwealth of England had taken refuge in that port; that he, as Admiral, carried instructions from Parliament to pursue and destroy them; and that, the two nations being then at peace, he hoped to be allowed to execute his orders without interference. The answer to these demands was not satisfactory. The governor pretended he could see no difference between one Englishman and another; he said he had nothing to do with their private quarrels; and he concluded by stating his determination to protect every one flying to his harbour who was not a declared enemy of his royal master. As yet Spain had not learned to comprehend the genius of the young Republic. While professing herself ready to acknowledge the new order of things, she maintained a haughty and suspicious reserve of her real sentiments. Willing enough to see England on doubtful terms with her own enemies, the Dutch and Portuguese — not much offended, in consequence of the late King's behaviour towards the Infanta, at the disasters of the royal house, the court of Madrid, nevertheless, assumed a right to suspend judgment on the course of events—to hold out a

hand to either party as it might suit its pleasure or policy—and when occasion served to treat both Roundheads
and Royalists with indifference and disdain. Nor was
this proud caprice the only thing which Blake found
written in his book of wrongs. Early in that very year
Anthony Ascham had been sent by the Council of State
as their ambassador to Madrid. A suitable residence
not being ready for him when he arrived, he repaired to
an hotel with his servants and Baptista Riva his inter-
preter. Clarendon and Cottington were then in Madrid
prosecuting what appeared to be a hopeless suit in favour of their master; and on hearing that Ascham was
on the road from Cadiz, where he had received great
hospitality from the people, the two lords protested
in bitter and indignant terms to Don Louis de Haro
against his reception at court; and even hinted that,
in their opinion, it would not be safe for him to appear
in Madrid. Whether the royalist lords were guilty
of more than a wicked suggestion to their servants is
a point involved in mystery; what is quite certain is
the fact that Henry Progess, one of their personal atten-
dants, and five other needy Cavaliers, went to Ascham's
hotel the day after his arrival, and finding him alone with
Riva at dinner, rushed in upon the two men, crying—
Welcome, gallants! welcome! and in a moment they
both fell on the floor pierced with many wounds. This
atrocious deed, done in broad day, on the sacred person of an ambassador, in the centre of a great city, and
under the eye of the court, raised a storm of indignation
not only in Spain and England but all over Europe.

Clarendon and Cottington were suspected of being
privy to the murders ; and Don Louis gave them to understand that if the enraged populace of London should
retaliate on his ambassador there, the King would hold
them responsible for the shedding of innocent blood
A special agent was sent to deprecate the wrath of Parliament, and a great parade was made of prosecuting the
assassins.　But Progess, the man whose confession was
of greatest consequence, was kept secreted in the Venetian embassy ; the other scoundrels, though murderers
could not lawfully plead privilege of sanctuary, were allowed to remain in a church to which they ran reeking
with blood ; and after some time the priests organised a
scheme for their escape, which they all effected except
Sparks, who was taken in the act and executed.　These
events made it absolutely necessary for Blake to shew a
strong hand at Carthagena.　Disdaining to notice the
governor's pretended ignorance of the state of things in
England, he bore down on the revolters, mastered the
Roebuck, set fire to another ship, and drove the remainder on shore utterly disabled.　The guns, tackle, furniture, stores and ammunition were saved by the crews, and
after some negotiation these were delivered up by the
Spaniards to the Admiral's agent.　With the exception
of the *Reformation* and the *Swallow*, the two vessels in
which the princes sailed, and the *Marmaduke*, their recent prize, the whole of the revolted fleet was now captured and destroyed ; and that corsair power, only a few
days previous an object of terror to the pacific traders
of all nations, was reduced to so mere a wreck that it

was impossible for it ever again to become a formidable element in the European waters.[1]

Not to leave a remnant behind him, Blake endeavoured to gain some intelligence of Rupert; and put on a false scent, either by design or otherwise, he steered for Majorca, expecting to find him lurking about the ports of that island. But the two brothers, feeling that the game was nearly up, — for three vessels would be unable to attack merchant convoys with certain success, and from the position of royal corsairs making war on a grand scale against all flags and fleets, they had now become petty plunderers of unarmed and unequal vessels, — stood across for Toulon, where they had reason to expect a good reception from the omnipotent Cardinal Richelieu, that statesman being for the moment on doubtful terms with the Commonwealth. A sudden storm, however, separated the *Reformation* from its two fellows; Maurice rode, with his prize, into the great road of Toulon, where he was quietly allowed to sell her cargo; Rupert was driven by bad weather to the east, as far as Sicily, in which island he was compelled to remain part of the winter, entirely uncertain as to his brother's fate. At length, however, he reached Toulon, whither he was quickly followed by the English squadron. Blake instantly sent into the town to protest against the honours and succours granted in a friendly port to fugitives from justice and enemies to the English Parliament. This remonstrance producing no effect, the

---

[1] Heath, 275, 6 ; Rupert Ms. in Warburton, iii. 313-318; Harl. Misc. vi. 236-247; Clarendon, v. 149-156; Thurloe, i. 148-202; Granville Penn, i. 323.

M

Admiral declared that he should consider the permitted sale of a cargo of English goods, piratically seized, in that port as an hostile act; and that unless Chevalier Paul, the French Admiral then commanding in the road, undertook to drive the corsairs from his harbour and restore their plunder to its lawful owners, he should hold himself free to make reprisals on the commerce of France. The Chevalier tried to avoid the necessity for such destructive measures, by hastening the departure of his dangerous guests. With his assistance they re-fitted and prepared for sea, when seizing a favourable opportunity, they escaped from the roadstead, passed through the Balearic Islands and the Straits of Gibraltar, and finally made their way to the West Indies, where they lived by plundering the commerce of Spain and England; and were now and then heard of in Europe for several years after through the tale of some hapless merchant returning from the New World beggared by their depredations. At length the two brothers parted company in a tropical storm. Maurice was never heard of again; but Rupert lived to invent pinchbeck, and to enjoy the amenities of the Restoration.[1]

Nothing is more curious in the history of those times than the off-hand, yet masterly and successful way in which Blake exercised the tremendous powers entrusted to him by the Council of State. Men of office and an-cient routine were startled by his bold and open policy, so far removed from the old turns and tricks of diplo-macy. His logic was brief and simple: in face of any event he asked himself but one question—Is this for the

---

[1] Heath, 276; Rupert Ms. in Warburton, iii. 318 et seqq.

honour and interest of England? Whatever the answer,
that settled the question. If it appeared to him clear
that the thing ought to be done, it was done. There
was no looking right or left, backward or forward, to
antecedents or consequences. Portugal and Spain had
refused either to do justice or to give him formal permission to execute justice for himself; caring little for
their offended majesty and pride, he had taken the matter into his own hands, and had taught them that the
young Commonwealth of England would not be cheated,
like an old and decrepit monarchy, with lying laws and
treacherous formalities. France had now roused his ire,
and powerful as that country was under the great Cardinal's sway, it soon felt the inconvenience of the reprisals
which he never threatened in vain. Months before the
affair of the *Marmaduke* at Toulon, there had been some
slight bickering between the two navies. James, Duke
of York, had issued from the Hague a number of blank
commissions to be filled up by his agents with the names
of persons able and willing to fit out privateers and
harass the coasts and commerce of England, all goods
taken by them being declared beforehand lawful prey.[1]
Under the sanction of these commissions, men who cared
nothing for Roundheads or Cavaliers, Republics or
Monarchies, chartered fleet sailers, and manning them
powerfully, roved about the narrow seas in search of
plunder. Some of their prizes had been carried into
Brest and Havre; and speedy justice not being obtained
for this wrong from the Court of Versailles, Parliament in
its turn had issued letters of marque against French ves-

---

[1] Navy Mss. No. 69, State-Paper Office.

sels. Except in a single case, where he found a French man-of-war lying in wait for English merchants, Blake had hitherto scrupulously avoided every appearance of an intention to carry out these free instructions; but after the authorities at Toulon had openly received the revolters, he felt himself bound to retaliate on every occasion that should now offer itself. On his voyage homeward, he captured four French prizes, — one of them a fine frigate of forty guns, the combat with which reads like an episode in an ancient romance. Meeting the Frenchman in the Straits, Blake signalled for the captain to come on board his flag-ship; and he, considering the visit one of friendship and ceremony, there being no declared war between the two nations, readily answered the invitation. The Admiral, when he entered his cabin, told him he was a prisoner; and asked him if he would give up his sword. Astounded at such a demand, the Frenchman boldly answered—No! Blake felt that an advantage had been gained by a misconception, as the captain probably knew nothing of the Toulon affair or of the English threat of reprisals; and scorning to make a brave officer the victim of a mere mistake, he told him he might go back to his ship, if he wished, and fight it out as long as he was able. The captain thanked him for this handsome offer and retired. After two hours' hard fighting he struck his flag, and being brought once more on board the flag-ship, like a true French knight he made a low bow, kissed his sword affectionately and delivered it to his conqueror.[1]

After an absence of twenty months, during which he

---

[1] Thurloe, i. 134; History and Life, 33; Whitelocke, Jan. 16, 1651.

had completely dispersed and destroyed the revolters, rebuked the pride of Portugal, read a significant lesson to Spain and France, freed the southern and great midland seas from privateers, and left a salutary dread of the young Commonwealth on the shores of Barbary and among the naval powers of Italy, Blake returned to England. For the first time during centuries the fleets of Venice and Genoa had found themselves in the immediate neighbourhood of an English power; and though the name of Blake had not yet grown into the word of terror it became in those distant parts a few years later, the rights and the honour of Englishmen were more respected there from the date of his first memorable cruise in the Mediterranean. At home, however, applause and more substantial rewards awaited him. The Council of State made him a warden of the Cinque Ports. Parliament recorded its special thanks in his favour and voted him a donation of a thousand pounds. The whole country rang with the renown of the man who had revived the traditional glories of the English navy and exercised so perilous a power with such unequalled wisdom, resolution and success.[1]

Blake had little time allowed him for repose. Though the strength of the corsair Prince had been broken, the hold which he had built for himself in the Channel, not only held out against the power of Parliament, but the desperate men whom he had thrown into it continued to harass the peaceful trader.[2] The reduction of this group of rocks, together with the islands of Guernsey and Jersey, was accordingly the naval work

---

[1] Parl. Hist. xix. 459; History and Life, 37.   [2] Whitelocke, 396, 464.

laid out by the Council for the year 1651. The former
colleagues were again named Generals of the Fleet; and
in April Blake and Ascue threatened St. Mary's, the
largest of the Scilly group and the residence of the
governor. On receiving the usual summons to surrender,
Sir John Grenville replied in the tone of a man who was
prepared to impose rather than submit to conditions.
He said he was willing to enter into a treaty; but he
spoke of having a large force at his disposal, not only
sufficient to maintain the islands, but to restore the
exile to the throne of his fathers. Despising this bom-
bast, Blake selected eight hundred men, under the command of Captain Morris, to land at the back of Tresco,
an island lying over against St. Mary's, and of all the
Scilly group next to it in size and military importance.
A garrison of nearly a thousand men, posted behind
a line of breastworks, opposed this attempt; but the
Roundheads threw themselves into the water, waded to
shore, and as soon as the first company could form they
advanced pike in hand to assault the entrenched positions. The Cavaliers fought gallantly, disputing every
inch of ground with pike and pistol after their field-
artillery failed. But having obtained a lodgement in
the outset, Morris held his own stoutly, and when night
put an end to the first day's contest the garrison withdrew to their boats and passed over to St. Mary's, leaving
Blake in possession of all their works, arms, and some
prisoners. At daybreak the Roundheads pushed forward, passed the ridges of high ground, and came down
the south slopes of the island, when one of the most
picturesque and striking scenes in Europe burst on their

sight. Full in front, girt round with rugged rocks and green islets, rose the wealthy and populous St. Mary's, crowned with ramparts and castles ; below them lay the narrow roadstead, shut in by innumerable rocks and points of land like a beautiful alpine lake, in which the pirate pinnaces and caravals were moored. As the light of morning fell on verdant field and barren peak, on busy town and shining water, brightening all with its summer glories, the novelty and beauty of the scene grew absolute. Little time, however, had the Roundheads to spend in admiring wonder. Their chief soon fixed on a jutting point of ground, somewhat in advance of the regular lines, for a battery, which, when finished, would command St. Mary's harbour and roadstead, and effectually prevent the arrival of relief from Jersey or the harbours of Normandy. Erected almost as soon as it was conceived, this battery soon became a source of great annoyance to the garrison. Grenville's position was indeed growing critical. Besides the population, itself larger than the natural means of supply, more than sixteen hundred men were crowded together on that little islet; and as all chance of free communication with their friends on the Continent was for the moment cut off, the Cavaliers saw themselves reduced either to submit to a blockade, certain to end in their destruction, or by a bold and combined effort to dislodge the enemy from Tresco, and again open the passage of the main roadstead. The latter, however, seemed a most desperate adventure. Blake had already landed a considerable force at Tresco and encamped them, as the remains of lines and mud-huts still shew, on a low neck of land facing the harbour; and nothing less than a terrible battle and decisive victory could have enabled the Cavaliers to recover the position which they had so hastily abandoned. Meanwhile, seeing that his batteries produced little or no effect on the castles at that distance, Blake adopted the bold and unexpected resolution to bring his frigates through the intricate and dangerous channels, plant them in the roadstead under the castle guns, and fight a regular battle of artillery between land and sea. This feat has been achieved so often in later times, that it is not easy now to estimate the daring which it then implied. Up to that day it had been considered a fundamental maxim in marine warfare that a ship could not attack a castle or other strong fortification with any hope of success. Blake was the first to perceive and demonstrate the fallacy of this position; and the experiment, afterwards repeated by him in the more brilliant attacks on Porto Ferino and Santa Cruz, was first tried at the siege of St. Mary's. With infinite labour and danger he contrived to get some of his lighter frigates through the rocks and shoals of that intricate channel, and to moor them in the road,—when a furious cannonade began from the castle, still more fiercely answered by broadsides, and raged until dark. Daybreak saw this terrible contest of cannon recommenced:—but the battle was soon decided in favour of the frigates. A practicable breach being made in the castle wall, the command for an immediate assault had been already given by Blake, when Grenville, very much changed in his late opinion as to the impregnable strength of the pirate hold, sent to beg a parley, which ended in an engagement on his part to surrender the islands, garrisons, stores, arms, ammunition, standards, and all other implements and materials of war, on condition that the lives of all the officers, soldiers, and volunteers should be spared ; the common soldiers and sailors being allowed to enter the nation's service, and the gentlemen sent to London to await the final decision of Parliament in their favour. These terms were thought by many to be too favourable to the Royalists,—and that now fallen party began to look up to Blake as the most friendly or most lenient of their conquerors. To prevent the garrison from giving him any further cause of alarm, he sent part of the men into Ireland and the rest to Scotland, to be there incorporated with the armies of the Commonwealth. Sir John Grenville and the corsair gentlemen taken with him, arms in hand, were put on board Sir George Ascue's squadron and carried into Plymouth sound. Acting in the spirit of Blake's articles, Parliament treated Sir John Grenville with extreme leniency. He was even permitted to enjoy his forfeited family estates without molestation. For some years his turbulent soul, rebuked by a Cause equally strong and magnanimous, remained quiet ; but after the death of Cromwell he again appeared on the stage and had a conspicuous part to play in the drama of the Restoration.[1]

---

[1] Borlase's Scilly Islands, 41, 42; Parl. History, xix. 459; Clarendon, vi. 217 ; Kennett, 408; Whitelocke, 465, 467. Original articles, agreed on this xxiii. day of May 1651, between Admiral Blake and Colonel Clerke, Commanders-in-chief of all the forces by sea or land, in and about the islands of Trescoe and Briar, on the one part; and Sir John Grenville, Knt., Governor of the islands of St. Mary's and St. Agnes' in Scilly, on the behalf of His Majesty on the other part, touching the rendition of

The Scilly Islands cleared of their lawless occupants, Blake next addressed his attention to Jersey and Guernsey, the only remaining centres of the corsair-Cavalier power, then commanded by Sir George Carteret as deputy for Lord Jermyn. Carteret, a gallant officer, who had served in the royal navy while the navy was yet called royal, and had received and refused the appointment of Vice-Admiral under the Earl of Warwick, was one of the ablest generals and stanchest Cavaliers whom Blake had yet had to encounter by land or sea; and his prolonged defence of these islands, especially that of Jersey, which he conducted in person, though in the end it was unsuccessful, covered his name with glory—and after the restoration of the Stuarts, when he became co-proprietor of an American province, Charles insisted on calling it New Jersey, in lasting honour of this his famous exploit. The sphere of duty which devolved on him at Jersey was exactly suited to his capacities. Daring as Rupert himself, but cautious as he was brave, his piratical adventures were conducted with forethought, gallantry and success. For more than two years his name had been a terror to the London merchants, and the Council-board at Westminster was kept in a flutter of fear and rage by the letters which arrived almost weekly with accounts of the discomfiture and loss suffered by vessels carrying the national flag at the hands of this terrible freebooter. Whitelocke's journal throws some rays of light on the scene of these disasters, while Blake

those islands, together with all the castles, &c. to the Parliament of England.—A copy of this treaty was formerly in the library of the Society for Propagating the Gospel; its present location I have not been able to ascertain.

was chasing Rupert in the South of Europe. For instance :—On Feb. 21, 1650, "letters that several merchantmen have been taken on the western coast by Jersey pirates;" Feb. 26, " letters that two Dutchmen laded with salt came to anchor within half a league of Dartmouth Castle, and that presently two Jersey pirates came up with them, cut their cables and carried them away." The gunners in the castle fired on the bold marauders, but without effect. Success made them still more daring, and the complaints laid before the Council became more frequent and more vehement. March 1, "letters of Jersey pirates very bold on the western coast;" March 6, " letters of several ships taken by the Jersey pirates;" Mar. 15, " of the want of frigates on the western seas to keep in the Jersey pirates;" March 17, " of the Jersey pirates taking several merchant-ships, and none of the Parliament frigates to help them;" March 19, "letters of the piracies committed by those of Jersey."[1]

Even after the appearance of Blake and Ascue off the Scilly Islands, Carteret, still confident in his own resources and secure in a fortress which since the days of Rollo had never been assailed with success, continued his destructive warfare on commerce. He had, indeed, no choice. Upwards of four thousand men, the remains of veteran armies and sea-roving adventurers, thronged the two little islands. He was bound to feed them, and it was desirable to keep the more daring spirits employed at sea. Of Jersey itself he had no fears. Its position was strong by nature, and had been rendered yet stronger by art. Storms rarely cease in that part of the English

---

[1] Whitelocke, under dates as above.

Channel. Sunken rocks, lying near the surface, not
only render the navigation extremely dangerous for
large vessels, even with good pilots, but cause violent
currents, cross currents, and cataracts at every ebb and
flow of tide. The coast of Jersey, rocky, steep and
broken, nature seemed to have fashioned as the ramparts of a vast and impregnable fortress. Skilful en-
gineers had added Elizabeth Castle, Mount Orgueil and
Cornet Castle to the natural defences. Elizabeth Castle,
built on a bold and isolated rock in St. Aubin's bay,
facing St. Hiliers, the chief town in Jersey, and about
a mile from the mainland, was at that time considered
one of the strongest military positions in the world.
This fortress, the key of his defensive operations, Sir
George Carteret commanded in person. Mount Orgueil
he entrusted to Sir Philip Carteret; and Cornet Castle,
in Guernsey, to Colonel Burgess. While the sea was
yet open to the marauders, they sent pressing entreaties
to Lord Jermyn and to the royal exiles for immediate
succour:—and in this position the Cavaliers awaited
the Roundhead squadron.[1]

While the expedition against these islands was fitting
out at Plymouth under his personal directions, Blake employed his leisure in visiting the various naval stations
on the coast, strengthening weak points, re-distributing
the naval force, stimulating the energy of his colleagues
and rectifying legions of abuses. His flag-ship, the
Victory, fairly flew about the Channel. One day its
bright pennon was streaming in the Downs, the next it
was found at Spithead or in Plymouth Sound. Where

---

[1] Falle's Jersey (1694), c. ii.; Heath, 306; Clarendon, v. 286-7.

work was to be done, apathy aroused, energy increased, there was the *Victory* and its indomitable Admiral. The tardy routine of the Navy Commission was the high rock against which his resistless will rolled with least effect. Week after week he urged this body to proceed with greater rapidity and resolution. The Scilly Isles reduced, these officials saw no reason for maintaining a force at the Land's End; but Blake told them it was necessary to keep several powerful vessels at that point; to send a frigate to watch the Isle of Man and check the Irish marauders who continued to infest St. George's Channel; and to station a regular garrison on St. Mary's Island.[1] When he quitted the Scilly Islands for Plymouth, he left a favourite officer, Colonel Bennett, in command of the Commonwealth forces there; and while the Scotch army remained in England he kept up a regular correspondence with him, considering that station as one of very great importance. Much of this correspondence is now lost; but the following brief note, relating to land as well as to sea events, has escaped the common doom.

" Plymouth, August 26, 1651.

" Yesterday I wrote unto the Com^r of the Militia, which I believe you have partaken of, — How that according to the intelligence I have received the enemy was possessed of Worcester. By the pacquet this morning, I am informed that the enemy bended his course towards that place, but to prevent him coming there was a considerable force put into it. He is at a stand,

---

[1] Blake to Navy Com., August 15, 1651; Dept. Mss.

knowing not where to go, and his forces mutinous in respect of their tedious marches. It hath pleased God to take out of this life my partner, Col. Popham, who died of a fever in the Downs, by reason whereof I believe my stay will not be long here. I have no more at present but to renew my desire that an eye may be had upon the disaffected."[1]

In the depôts and dockyards the abuses against which he had to struggle were of the most formidable kind. Many of his ships were not sea-worthy. The stores, provisions and warlike materials were very deficient; and the seamen's wages were often in arrear. He compelled the authorities in London to listen to complaints; and from the extracts of letters written by various captains of vessels which he submitted to their consideration, it is still possible to gather some idea of the extreme poverty of means with which he had to perform his wondrous exploits. An example or two will suffice for this purpose: Captain Pearce, he says, writing from Londonderry on the 27th of August of this year, "complains that the fleets on that coast generally stand in great need of victuals, desires speedy supplies thereof, otherwise must greatly suffer; goes to half allowance, drinks water; hath but seven days' provisions, most of it stinks; butter and cheese not edible." Captain Vessey, of the *Truelove*, writing from Liverpool in the same month, complains, he says, that "the frigate wants all manner of stores; stands in great need of trimming; is very leaky; when she bears up hath a foot of water above the ceiling; hath been out nineteen months;

---

[1] Add. Mss. 12098-10.

her men in great need of pay to provide clothes for winter." This was very much the state of the fleet throughout.[1] A letter written by Blake to the Commissioners at their office on Tower Hill, from Plymouth on the 28th of August, proves his minute attention to every thing connected with the welfare of his men, and exhibits one of the abuses—the plan of paying all the seamen's wages in London—which for a long time resisted all the influence brought to bear on it by the reformer.—"Gentlemen," this letter runs, "there hath been this summer divers mariners prest in this and other western ports into the States' ships; and, in respect their habitations are so far distant from London, many of them have, upon the going in of the ships they served in, been discharged here; and one Mr. Edward Pattison of this town, out of charity hath paid them their tickets, they being poor people and not able to look after it alone. This man acquaints me that for some tickets, notwithstanding he hath been without his money a good while, he is in danger to lose it through delay. I know not what the reason is, but I believe what he did was merely to relieve and ease the poor men. I therefore make it my desire to you that you will give orders for the payment of such tickets as he hath or shall present unto you, they agreeing both in entries and discharges with the muster-books, and thereby Mr. Pattison not put to unnecessary attendance. Therein you will not only oblige him but also your affectionate friend, Robert Blake."[2]

---

[1] Blake to Navy Com., Sept. 4, with enclosures; Dept. Mss.

[2] Ibid. August 28.

The rectification of abuses, and the political uncertainties which arose for a moment through the Scotch invasion of England, detained the fleet at Plymouth several months. Meanwhile Carteret maintained his reputation as a daring and successful cruiser. Undaunted by the fall of Sir John Grenville at Scilly, he swept the sea from Land's End to Portland Reach, and the Council had still the mortification to receive the letters which Whitelocke has thus briefly reported:—April 17, 1651, "letters of the Jersey pirates taking two barques laden in sight of Portland;" April 21, " of more prizes taken by the Jersey pirates, and of Captain Bennett's fighting two of them four hours;" July 14, "that five English vessels were taken by boats from Jersey, carrying four or five guns a piece;" July 18, "letters of two prizes taken by a Jersey frigate of eight guns, twenty-four oars and eighty men, and that there were twelve of those frigates belonging to Jersey;" August 7, " letters of much damage done by the Jersey pirates;" September 27, "letters of the Jersey pirates doing much mischief on the western coast."[1]

By the middle of October the English fleet was almost ready for sea. The battle of Worcester had put an end to all present embarrassments on land, and left the powers that ruled in Westminster time to think of such matters as national honour and the security of trade. Taking Colonel Haynes and his regiment on board, together with two other regiments of foot, and four troops of horse, Blake sailed from Plymouth sound; and on the 20th of October, after suffering from

---

[1] Whitelocke, under above dates.

a terrible storm which scattered and slightly damaged many of his ships, he obtained a precarious anchorage in St. Ouen's Bay on the west side of the island. The sea broke furiously on the rocky shore, and a heavy rain added to the difficulty of making observations. Still the officers of the *Victory* could see that the coast was alive with defenders, horse and foot, men active, courageous and well-disciplined.[1]

After a brief rest, the Admiral ordered his boats to be lowered at three in the morning, but the waves broke too grandly in their front to allow a hope of their being able to land. As soon as day dawned, a second attempt was made, but without success. Carteret had only to look on and see his enemy baffled by the elements. The boats put off, filled with armed marines, dismounted troopers and their horses, bodies of infantry with their pikes and matchlocks; but the huge sea rose before them like a vast rampart, and one or two boats which ventured into the raging surf, were overset in an instant. Blake then resolved to try the effect of a cannonade. The ships being got into position, the cannoneers began to play, and their fire was quickly answered from several little forts and redoubts in the bay, as well as from twenty-four brass field-pieces attached to the militia service. In the fury of the moment some of the frigates ran in close enough for the men on board t use their muskets, and many Cavaliers rushed into the water in the eagerness of their zeal; but as a cannonade of four

---

[1] Relation Ms. de la prise de l'Isle et des châteaux de Jersey par les rebelles d'Angleterre, trouvé parmi les papiers de Sire George de Carteret, —printed in Falle's Jersey (1694), 36.

N

hours' duration, in which the Roundhead gunners spared
neither powder nor shot, produced no apparent effect on
the garrison, the fleet drew off to a more sheltered position in St. Brelard's Bay, about a league distant, where
the commander made a new disposition of his power.[1]

One squadron was sent back to St. Ouen's Bay;
another was ordered to take up a strong position in St.
Aubin's Bay, over against St. Heliers, and ready to act
against Elizabeth Castle.   Other ships were commanded
to cruise off the coast of St. Clements, threatening every
hour to make a descent; and a further division was sent
to Grouville Bay, on the extreme east of the island, to
operate against Mount Orgueil Castle.   These movements perplexed the defenders, and Carteret was obliged
to detach a part of his forces to wait on and watch each
squadron of ships.   Blake himself remained at anchor
in St. Brelard's Bay, and the chief force of the Royalists
encamped on the rising grounds, ready to resist the
Roundheads should they attempt to land.[2]

A little after midnight, though a thin rain was still
falling, the moon broke out for a few minutes, and by her
pale and uncertain light Carteret saw that a large body of
foot was being lowered from the ships into flat-bottomed
boats brought from Plymouth for that service,—in all
ten battalions of four thousand men.   A brisk fire was
instantly opened on them from two small batteries which
had been erected in favourable positions on the shore, and
mounted with excellent ordnance.   The *Victory* replied
with its broadsides, and other of the Roundhead ships

---

[1] Relation Ms., &c., 37 ; History and Life, 42.
[2] Relation Ms. in Falle, 37.

joined in the cannonade. But either in consequence of the discovery of their intention, or because the tremendous swell of the sea prevented the necessary measures from being taken, the attempt to land that night was at last abandoned. When the battalions returned to their ships, new orders were given out. A squadron of nineteen sail was left in St. Brelard's Bay to occupy the attention of the camp, while Blake, with the remaining body, returned to his former position in St. Ouen's Bay, where he had found more sea-room, and had now resolved to effect his purpose of throwing Colonel Haynes and his troops on shore. Sir George Carteret left all the dragoons and his own company of fusiliers, supported by four companies of militia, to watch the nineteen ships and frigates, and started with the infantry on a harassing night-march along the beach; keeping the fleets in view as well as he could in the uncertain light of early morning. Blake's policy was to wear the men out by constant marches, alarms and cannonades. Every moment some of the fleet-guns thundered at the shore, or at the exposed column; and many times during the long march Carteret had to halt and bring his artillery into a position to return the fire. Nor could he gain a single moment's repose for his harassed comrades during the whole day. Instead of pulling up his fleet in the centre of the bay, as was expected, Blake held on his course, making for Letac, the extreme northern point of land, and thither Carteret was compelled to follow him. But as soon as the ships were all come up in front of that headland, the captains were signalled to tack about and return to the southern point, La Frouque, five or six miles distant.[1]

Sir George, active and vigilant as ever himself, could no longer keep his men together. They had been under arms three days and two nights, during which time rain had fallen without intermission; they had made several hasty marches and counter-marches over bad roads and broken ground; and they had stood the fierce though intermittent fire from the enemy's ships. At sunset he allowed them to depart for the neighbouring villages in search of refreshment and repose; he himself, with a few dragoons, alone remaining on the beach, along which, however, the camp-fires were lighted as usual. On the other side, the weather suddenly became more favourable for an attack. As night set in, the rain ceased, the roar of wind abated in violence, and the swell of sea lessened perceptibly; but not a star was visible, no moon arose to tell the tale of preparation; for years to come the pitchy darkness of the sky was recollected as an omen of disaster for the island. The fires along the shore appeared to warn the Admiral that his endeavour to throw Haynes' regiment on shore at that point would be attended with other difficulties than a threatening sea and a rocky coast on a dark night. Yet nothing could check his ardour. So long familiar with success, he despised every obstacle not evidently insurmountable; and towards the close of the civil war even the Roundhead soldiers had learned to feel that contempt for Cavalier prowess, which at an earlier period the Cavaliers

---

[1] Relation Ms. in Falle.

had affected to feel towards them. At eleven o'clock at night, the boats were again lowered, and by a desperate and gallant effort were run ashore. Holding their arms above their heads, the men leapt into the surf, many of them up to the neck in water, and pushed for land. While struggling to obtain firm footing, and free themselves from the returning surges, Carteret's horse rode down furiously with the design of forcing them back into the sea; but, forming his men as well as could be done in the confusion of such a scene and the darkness of a winter midnight, Haynes led them to the charge, and, after a sanguinary conflict of half-an-hour's duration, he drove the Cavalier horse from the field, and pursued them inland more than a mile.[1]

Early next morning, Haynes marched against a fort near his halting-place, but found it abandoned. Several pieces of cannon and some colours fell into his hands, but no enemy appeared to dispute his advance. During that and the next day other forts and positions of military importance were taken without a blow; and in three days the whole island, with the exception of Mount Orgueil and Elizabeth Castle, had surrendered. Finding it useless to contend in the open field with his dispirited troops against the victorious Roundheads, Sir George Carteret withdrew his entire force into Mount Orgueil and the Castle, which last place he had a reasonable prospect of maintaining against every assault. Money, guns, ammunition, stores, and provisions for eight months had been carefully piled up there in anticipation of the siege which now threatened it. Cut

---

[1] History and Life, 42; Whitelocke, Nov. 30; Falle, 39.

off from the mainland and surrounded by rocks and seas, commanding the island though not commanded by it, Elizabeth Castle was universally considered an impregnable fortress. The nearest point of land on which a fort could be raised against it was more than three-fourths of a mile distant, and the sunken rocks lay so near the surface all round, that a frigate or man-of-war could not approach it within several furlongs. With plenty of men and an occasional supply of provisions from France, Carteret hoped to hold this rock until a change of fortune came to his royal master; and into this fortress the chief Cavalier gentry, the clergy of the island and a picked garrison retired at the approach of the Roundheads on St. Heliers, which town they at once entered and secured.

Having already battered down a strong fort at St. Mary's, Blake believed he could also damage Elizabeth Castle from his fleet; and therefore while Colonel Haynes invested Mount Orgueil by land, he himself carried his frigates into St. Aubin's Bay, and planting them as near the fortifications as the pilot could find sea-room for them, he opened a tremendous fire on its old walls. The garrison answered with a loud cannonade. But at the very outset of this furious attack, an accidental shot from the *Victory* produced a most disastrous moral effect on the defenders. A cannon-ball struck the little church on the rock, splintered the stones and killed several persons; at which Lady Carteret was so alarmed that she earnestly entreated her husband to make terms with the Admiral before the island was blown to pieces. The commander was himself firm; but so many persons, male and female, came to him with their fears, that he was forced to send away his best boats with them that very night to France. Neither Lady Carteret nor the ladies and gentlemen who accompanied her in her hasty flight could have been of much use in the defence. But seeing these persons going on board under cover of the dark night, a part of the regular garrison, equally desirous of saving their own lives, made an attempt to get off at the same time; and all who were taken in the act of trying to escape were hanged as deserters. Still further to dispirit the defenders, Mount Orgueil surrendered after a fortnight's siege:—Sir Philip Carteret obtaining from Blake the promise of an amnesty and act of oblivion for himself and his comrades in arms, a promise which was in due time confirmed to them by Parliament. Twenty brass and iron guns, as many barrels of powder, a thousand stand of arms, and two months' provisions for seventy men, were the spoils of the victors. The land forces were then moved to a hill near St. Hilary's and opposite the Castle, but the ordinary field-artillery was of no use in that peculiar service, and Blake had to send to Plymouth for mortars of greater calibre. From these mortars a succession of missiles were thrown into the castle; many of the houses were knocked down and multitudes were killed by the exploding grenades; but, without one word of encouragement from his master, one message of hope from Lord Jermyn, Carteret gallantly held his little rock two months longer, though at a terrific sacrifice of human life,—when a large magazine of stores was blown up and eighty officers and men were buried in the ruins. This crowning calamity induced him to hoist a white flag, and after a parley, to surrender on condition of being taken, with such officers as chose to go, and landed safely at St. Maloes, on the coast of Normandy. The garrison had been reduced to three hundred and eighty men. A great park of artillery, and stores of powder, shot, bread, beer, beef, salt, wine and brandy, were found in the remaining magazines. After these signal successes, Cornet Castle, in Guernsey, surrendered without a blow,—and the English seas were at last cleared of every enemy to the Commonwealth of England.[1]

For this important service Blake received the special thanks of Parliament, as did also Colonel Haynes. A public thanksgiving was ordered for these victories and for the conquest of Limerick, which city had been taken about the same time. The election of members for the Council of State being about to take place, Blake was nominated by Parliament, in a full House, one of that supreme body. His hands were already pretty full. He was a Commissioner for sequestrating the Estates of Somerset Delinquents—a Commissioner for purging the Ministry of improper persons—a Commissioner of the Navy and Admiralty—a member of the House of Commons—and a member of the Council of State. And now, as if these offices implied no cares and duties, he was appointed, in the probable event of a fierce and sanguinary war with Holland, sole General-at-Sea for the ensuing year.[2]

---

[1] Relation Ms. in Falle, 41, 42; Parl. History, xx. 79; History and Life, 42-44; Clarendon, v. 286-7.

[2] Blake to Navy Com., Dec. 27, Dept. Mss.

But this accumulation of offices and honours did not prevent the great seaman from looking with care and courtesy to the interest of his humblest companions in glory. His letters at this as at every other time exhibit his characteristic kindness of heart, shewing the utmost readiness to hear complaints and to rectify grievances. One of his earliest suggestions to the Navy-Commissioners, after the reduction of the Channel Islands left them at leisure to think of abuses at home, was a strong recommendation for them to adopt the plan of paying the seamen's wages in the port in which they were discharged, and as soon as they came on shore; so as neither to give them the trouble of walking to London nor to keep them waiting several days at Portsmouth or Plymouth, in idleness, at great expense, and at a distance from all the salutary influences of family and home. His regard for minor and individual cases of distress was illustrated by numerous special applications to the Commissioners. Every sufferer found a zealous advocate in his beloved Admiral. And although abuses of many kinds continued to prevail at the Admiralty Office and in the dock-yards, defying every effort of the courageous naval reformer, there is good reason to suppose that when Blake pleaded the cause of his own seamen, he generally obtained justice for the applicants.[1]

---

[1] Blake to Navy Com., January 21, Dept. Mss.

CHAPTER VI.

1652.

The Dutch War.

A CHERISHED dream of the English Republicans had
been the idea of forming the United Provinces of Holland and the new insular Commonwealth into one
mighty Protestant state. The Dutch were then the
greatest naval power in the world. The sea seemed
to be their native element,—and their fleets of war and
commerce were known in every port, from the farthest
east to the remotest west. Their colonial empire was
only inferior in extent to that of Spain; while their
wealth, energy and valour, gave promise of its indefinite
expansion. England possessed a larger home territory,
better harbours, and a finer geographical position. Its
population was more numerous; its maritime resources
were scarcely, if at all, inferior; and its land forces,
after putting down the proudest chivalry of Europe,
were no longer to be compared with the mere mercenary troops of Italy and the Empire. The amalgama-
tion of the two Commonwealths would, therefore, have
produced a vast and powerful Republic, capable, should
the need arise, of combatting all the crowns of the Continent. Such a union would have been able to dictate
peace even to powers like France and Spain. It would
have secured the ascendency of Protestant ideas and a

liberal policy in the north and west of Europe; and would have furnished a vantage-ground from which knowledge and free institutions might have contended with greater effect against the ignorance, bigotry and despotism which in modern times have found their strongholds in the east and south. But this splendid conception was opposed by commercial jealousies and dynastic interests. William, second Prince of Orange of that name, had married in the palmy days of Stuart rule, a daughter of Charles I.; so that in addition to his princely antipathy to commonwealths, he was urged to thwart the idea of such an alliance by the powerful motive of a possible succession for his wife and children to the English throne. He was extremely popular with the lower classes of his countrymen; and so long as he lived, the two Protestant states remained on bad terms. He refused to extend to the Parliament's agents the ordinary protection of Dutch laws. Dorislaus, its first envoy, was murdered at the Hague by followers of Montrose. Strickland, who succeeded to the perilous office, suffered daily insults in the public streets. Yet no redress could be obtained. Recent prosperity, a career of victory unrelieved by chance or check, had raised the pride of Holland to the highest. Within a few years the renowned Admirals of the Republic had humbled the power of Spain, punished the insolence of Dunkirk, compelled the Prince of Salee and the Deys of Tunis and Algiers to sue for peace, and made the Sultan of Fez and Morocco tremble on his distant throne. After such successes, nothing seemed to them beyond the reach of their ambition; and many of their people, led by the Orange party, were anxious for a rupture with England at the moment of its supposed exhaustion, in the confident belief that in a few weeks they would be able to wrest from it that vain but fiercely disputed right to be considered mistress of the narrow seas.[1]

But the Prince of Orange died somewhat suddenly, leaving the heir to his honours and passions yet unborn; and the democratic party, comprising nearly all that was liberal and enlightened in Holland, seized the opportunity to abolish the office of Stadtholder and restore the pure form of republican government. Their success encouraged the English leaders to believe that, even if their favourite idea of a complete fusion could not be realised, a close alliance, offensive and defensive, might be formed between the two states. Oliver St. John was sent over as ambassador to the States-General to propose a treaty of trade and friendship. His reception was at first cordial and flattering; but the negociations went on slowly and uncertainly. After a long consideration of the English proposals, their High Mightinesses offered a counter project. Debates, interviews, and written explanations multiplied; time wore on; and at length St. John found that his leave of absence had expired. His pride was hurt at these delays. The exile court was still at the Hague,—and in addition to his ill success with the States-General, he was subject to frequent outrages from the Cavaliers. The Dutch, on their side, were angry with Parliament for having fixed a day for its agent's return, fancying it intended as a sarcasm or

---

[1] Thurloe, i. 112-124, 174; Colliber's Columna Rostrata, 93; Cornelius Van Tromp (1697), 6-11.

a menace. Probably the true cause of the delay was a desire on the part of Holland not to commit herself to the new Commonwealth until the result of the Scotch invasion should be seen :—St. John answered their complaints in haughty language, and took his leave, war between the two countries already raging in his heart.[1]

As soon as the battle of Worcester had put an end to every doubt as to the stability of the Commonwealth, Dutch statesmen saw their mistake ; and in turn the States-General sent envoys to assuage the wrath of Parliament, and endeavour to resume the negociation at the point where it had been interrupted. But new causes of offence were now in the way, and the terms once rejected could no longer be obtained. Some English merchants, in consequence of complaints made to the Council of State of their losses by Dutch privateers, had received letters of marque against the ships of that nation; and in a short time more than eighty prizes had been secured in the ports of our east coast. But a still more serious obstacle to negociation had arisen in passing the famous Navigation Act. The Dutch were a nation of traders. Their whale, cod and herring fisheries occupied a great number of vessels; but the largest and best part of their commercial navy was employed in the carrying trade. Amsterdam and Rotterdam were the exchanges of Europe ; and the shipowners of these rich ports made their largest fortunes by transporting the produce of art and nature from one country to another. Under the Stuarts, England had neglected this import-

---

[1] Parl. Hist. xix. 454-474; Whitelocke, 463; Mercurius Politicus, 44-46; Carte's Coll. i. 427; Heath, 285-287.

ant branch of naval industry; but the Navigation Act
in declaring that no goods, the produce of Asia, Africa
or America, should be imported into England except
in vessels either belonging to subjects of the Commonwealth, or to the countries from which the goods were
imported, put a period, so far as these islands, with all
their colonies, connexions and dependencies, were concerned, to that lucrative and fruitful branch of Dutch enterprise. The first prayer of the new Ambassador, therefore, was that this severe law of exclusion should be repealed, or if not repealed at once, that its action should
be suspended during the progress of negociation. But
while urging this point in the name of peace, they were
careful to hint before the Council of State that they
were then fitting out a powerful fleet for the protection
of their trade. Parliament took the hint as a menace,
and replied by ordering its captains to exact all those
honours to the red cross which had been claimed by
England in the narrow seas from the Saxon times. This
order soon raised new troubles. Commodore Young,
falling in with a Dutch fleet returning from Genoa, sent
to request the Admiral of the convoy to lower his flag;
the latter refused to comply with a demand so unexpected without first consulting his superiors; and Young
poured a broadside into the ships. A sharp action
ensued, but the Dutchman was obliged to strike. To
revenge what they professed to think an insult to their
colours, the States-General fitted out a fleet of forty-two
sail and placed it under the command of their renowned
Admiral, Tromp, with instructions to use his experienced
discretion as to when and how far he would insist on

the point of supremacy; but he was positively required
to repel on all occasions, and at all hazards, attacks on
the traders of the Republic, and to support the dignity
of its flag. Tromp's wily genius was well suited to the
execution of these vague and plastic orders.[1]

War had not yet been declared, and the ambassadors
were still in London talking of peace, when the Dutch
Admiral suddenly appeared in the Downs. Bourne,
stationed with a squadron of the fleet near Dover, despatched a messenger with intelligence of this visit to
Blake, then cruising in the *James* off Rye Bay, in the
usual manner of the summer guard. Suspecting that
some evil design was in contemplation, Blake instantly
gave his orders, and in a few hours his whole force was
under sail for the Straits. Next morning he saw for the
first time his celebrated enemy lying in and about Dover
roadstead; when he came within ten or twelve miles of
the nearest ships, Tromp weighed anchor and stood out to
sea, but without either lowering his flag or offering any
explanation of this act of defiance. Blake fired a signal-
gun to call attention to the omission. No answer was
returned. To a second and a third shot Tromp replied
derisively by a single gun, still keeping his course, with
the flag flying proudly at mast-head. Over against Calais
road, it was observed by the English that he fell in with
a ketch coming full speed from Holland, the captain of
which evidently brought important orders, for he soon
after veered round and made towards Blake, his own
ship, the *Brederode*, being in the van. The English offi-

---

[1] Scobell, ii. 176; Clarendon, v. 278; Columna Rostrata, 93; Cornelius Tromp, 12, 13; Granville Penn, i. 419-421.

cers were rather mystified by these movements; but in
spite of the presence of the Dutch ambassador in London, the Admiral felt a strong impression that Tromp had
received instructions to offer battle, and he lay-to and
got his squadron into as good a fighting posture as he
could on so short a notice. The Dutch had a vastly superior force. Tromp counted forty-two men-of-war and
frigates. Blake only fifteen. He had sent orders for
Bourne to join him with his squadron of eight ships,
but these were not yet in sight, and possibly would not
arrive in time for the engagement which seemed to
threaten. The disproportion of vessels did not, however,
indicate the true disproportion of force. As a rule the
English ships were larger than those of Holland, carrying more guns and a greater body of men; but, on the
other hand, the Dutch ships were manned by veteran
seamen, while the great body of men on board the English fleet were raw soldiers sent from the camp and entirely unaccustomed to the new service.[1]

When the two fleets came within musket-range, Blake,
affecting not to notice the enemy's menacing attitude,
shot out from his main body and advanced towards the
Brederode to speak with its commander about the refusal of honours formerly paid to the royal colours; but
the Dutch ship sent a broadside into the *James* and
stopt her short. Blake and several of his officers were
in the cabin when this salute burst on them, smashing
all the glass, and severely damaging the stern. He lifted
his eyes from his papers, and coolly observed—"Well,
it is not very civil in Van Tromp to take my flag-ship

---

[1] Blake to Navy Com., March 7, 1653, Dept. Mss.

for a brothel, and break my windows!" As he spoke, another broadside rolled from the decks of the *Brede-rode*. Curling his black whiskers round his fingers, as he always did in anger, he called his gunners to return the fire, and in a short time the battle became general.[1]

The English admirals then in service had not hither-to seen maritime war conducted on a grand scale, like Tromp and the officers who had served under his orders in the great contest with Spain; and only one of them, Vice-admiral Penn, had received a regular naval educa-tion. When the Council of State appointed Blake to the sole command against Holland, they gave him two blank commissions, that he might select his own vice and rear-admirals for the ensuing year; and in conjunc-tion with Cromwell, he had named Penn and Bourne to these important stations. Penn went on board the *Triumph*, sixty-eight guns, taking young Robert Blake, son of the Admiral's late brother Samuel, as his lieute-nant; Bourne raised his flag on board the *St. Andrew*, of sixty guns. But not supposing it possible that their navy would be assailed while the Dutch envoys were still in London soliciting peace, Penn had got leave of absence from his ship, and was then on a visit to his family; so that Blake had to contend with inferior power against the greatest nautical genius of the age, without having at his side a single person of practical knowledge as a seaman.

At four o'clock the contest began with a rapid suc-cession of broadsides. On the part of Blake at least,

---

[1] History and Life, 48-50; Granville Penn, i. 421-443; Clarendon, v. 279; Cornelius Tromp, 18-21.

no line appears to have been formed; fleet met fleet and ship grappled ship as they chanced to fall in each other's way. From the first onset, the *James*, a 50-gun ship, carrying 260 men, bore the brunt of the action.[1] The recollection of Lyme and Taunton, of Scilly and Carthagena, fierce as it was, faded before this terrific work. More than seventy cannon-balls were lodged in his hull; his masts were completely blown away; and his rigging was torn into ribands by the tremendous gunnery of the Dutch. His master, one of his mates, and several of his other officers fell, dead or wounded, at his side. For four hours the shot of the enemy flew about and around him without intermission. Six men were killed, thirty-five were desperately wounded, and many more were hurt; but his crew maintained the unequal contest with a bravery and resolution after his own heart. As night came down, their energies were roused to new life by the thunder of Bourne's cannon bursting suddenly in the enemy's rear. The sound of artillery, booming along the waters, had reached the rear-guard, consisting of the *St. Andrew* and seven other ships, and Bourne immediately crowded sail and stood out to sea in hope of sharing in the battle. He arrived in the crisis of the engagement, and his 300 additional guns sufficed to turn the scale of victory. Unable or unwilling to engage this new enemy, Tromp retired from the scene about nine o'clock with the fast-fading light, leaving his intended surprise and destruction of the English fleet at best a drawn battle. Blake was

---

[1] Add. Mss. 17, 503.

too much disabled to follow in his wake, his mizen-mast being shot away, his sails and cordage all torn and broken. He came to an anchor about four miles off the Ness, and spent the night in repairs and preparations for the morrow. But when day dawned the Dutch were not in sight. Far as the eye could reach, the Channel shewed no trace of an enemy:—and the Commonwealth was once more lord of the narrow seas. During the fight two Dutch ships had been boarded and taken; but one of them was so much damaged in the action that it was feared she would go down in the night, so that after rifling her holds and cabins the crew turned her adrift; the other capture, a ship of thirty guns, was brought in safely and manned for immediate service. Young Robert Blake greatly distinguished himself this day. In the absence of Vice-admiral Penn, he commanded the *Triumph,* and evinced such eminent skill and courage, that on Penn's removal to the *James,* he was appointed captain of that important vessel. With the one exception of the flag-ship, the fleet had not suffered materially. Only nine men were reported as slain in all the other ships. Of the Dutch, two hundred and fifty were taken prisoners, and nearly as many more were said to be killed.[1]

The sudden encounter of two powerful fleets in the midst of peace, without declaration of war or other previous formality to prepare men's minds for such a shock, produced an extraordinary sensation in the two coun-

---

[1] Elegiac Enumeration, 16; Somers Tracts, vii. 20-36; Cornelius Tromp, 17, 18; Clarendon, v. 279; Granville Penn, i. 422-427.

tries. In London, the mob rose at the cry of treachery, and would perhaps have burnt the house of the Dutch ambassadors at Chelsea, had not the government sent down a troop of horse for their protection. These ambassadors made strenuous efforts to explain the causes of the rencounter. They declared that Tromp was not the first to begin. They accounted for his appearance in the Downs by alleging stress of weather. They said he was about to lower his flag when Blake began to fire; they expressed deep regret at what had occurred, and urged, with great apparent earnestness, that violent counsels should give place to renewed attempts at negociation. Their Admiral also pretended that he had not violated the peace; that from first to last he had merely stood on his defence. He declared that had he chosen to make use of his immense superiority of force, he could have destroyed the English fleet. The people received this declaration with laughter and contempt. At last the ambassadors offered to disavow and disgrace their great Admiral; but the more they pressed their point, the sterner and more exacting Parliament became. England, it replied, had suffered insult and wrong; its duty was therefore to seek reparation for the past, security for the future. Every day war seemed nearer; every day the States-General seemed more resolved to adhere to their pacific policy. As a final effort they sent over their grand pensionary, Pauw, a man whose character and office were thought likely to give unusual weight to his overtures; but the demands of Parliament rose at every turn, and after a fruitless attempt to negociate, this eminent ambassador gave up the vain effort to reconcile the two powers, and took his leave.[1]

Blake continued master of the Channel. All pretence of reserve being thrown away in consequence of the late engagement, he exerted all his power to harass the enemy's trade, and to fit out such vessels as had fallen into his hands for immediate service against them. His cruisers brought prizes into port almost daily during the latter part of May and June. He captured ten merchant-men at one swoop. One day he received intelligence that a Dutch fleet of twenty-six traders, convoyed by three men-of-war, was coming up Channel:—they were all captured, traders and convoy, and the latter immediately manned and fitted for service.[2] In less than a month, to the surprise and ecstacy of the Londoners, he had sent into the river more than forty rich prizes captured in open sea from their powerful and vigilant enemy. The Dutch merchants were compelled to abandon the Straits. Their argosies from the South of Europe and from the Eastern and Western Indies had either to run for safety into French ports and send their cargoes overland at an immense loss, or make the long and dangerous voyage round by the North. This brilliant success inspired the Council of State with new life. Orders were given to strengthen Dover pier. Forty sail were added by a vote to the fleet. At Blake's suggestion six additional fire-ships were prepared. The seamen's wages were raised; and the Vice-admirals of all the maritime stations from Norfolk to Hampshire were

---

[1] Thurloe, i. 207-211; Heath, 314-321; Cornelius Tromp, 27-59.

[2] Council to Navy Com., June 17, Dept. Mss.

requested to summon together all mariners between the ages of fifteen and twenty, young, ardent, docile, and engage them in the State's service. Knowing the vast resources and inflexible spirit of the people with whom they were about to enter into serious conflict, the Council of State, Blake being a member, and in all matters connected with the navy its chief authority, resolved that the entire fleet should be raised to 250 sail and 14 fire-ships; and that the divisions should be commanded and located as follows :—30 sail were to go forthwith to the west channel, ply between Brest and Scilly, and keep the sea open towards the south; 20 sail were to go northward, disturb the Dutch fisheries and capture their Baltic traders; 30 sail were to ride in the Straits; and the remaining 170 sail and the fire-ships were to keep together under Blake's immediate orders to oppose and fight the enemy. These magnificent ideas were never realised in full :—but at the end of one month from the fight off Dover the energetic Admiral could count with patriotic pride no less than 105 vessels, carrying 3961 guns, under his flag. He was not, however, equally strong in men. His constant cry was—seamen, soldiers! And the Commissioners of the Navy were engaged day and night in devising means to supply him with this essential element of maritime power. Two regiments of foot were taken on board bodily, and from that time marines became a necessary part of the equipment of our men-of-war.[1]

Meanwhile the Dutch preparations for the campaign were made on the grandest scale. The dockyards of the

---

[1] Granville Penn, i. 428-430; History and Life, 56.

Texel, the Maas, and the Zuyder Zee resounded with
the note of coming strife. Sixty men-of-war, larger in
size and more perfect in equipment than had ever yet
been seen in those northern seas, were commenced.
Convoys not too far away were called back; merchant-
men of heavy tonnage were pressed into the service; the
ablest seamen found in their ports, irrespective of age or
nationality, were lured into the service by offers of high
wages and the hope of rich prizes; and in a few weeks
their renowned Admiral, ripe in age, honours and experience, saw himself at the head of 120 sail of ships—a
power more than sufficient in the opinion of every patriotic Dutchman to sweep the English navy from the
face of the earth.[1]

The swift and unexpected opening of the war had
placed the mercantile marine of both nations, especially
in the North Sea, at the mercy of privateers and cruising
squadrons. At that period but few English vessels ventured to the south of Europe; the distance checked the
enterprises of the timid, and the more substantial peril of
Algerine pirates and Salee rovers operated to prevent
the brave from seeking their fortunes in waters where
the might of England was as yet little known and still
less feared. In the opinion of these fierce marauders,
Holland was the only great naval power of Europe. More
than once she had chastised their insolence; and, as her
traders ploughed the southern waters in comparative
safety, the spices of the Levant, the silks of Italy and the
wines of Portugal, were chiefly brought to England in
Dutch bottoms. Baltic commerce, on the contrary, was

---

[1] Columna Rostrata, 94; Heath, 322; Granville Penn, i. 434.

chiefly carried in our own bottoms; and at that very
moment an unusual number of vessels were in the
North and Baltic Seas, Parliament, in anticipation of
war, having sent out several traders to purchase hemp,
tar, and other ship-stores for them in Sweden, Denmark, and Pomerania. These stores were now become
of essential importance. The dockyards were all bare;
not a frigate in the fleet was decently supplied; and in
the face of a contest which must occupy months and
might extend to years, it was necessary to send a strong
squadron to the north to collect these ships and convoy
them safely home with their precious cargoes. There
were other reasons which contributed their influence
towards compelling Blake's particular attention to the
squadron of the north. Ever since the atrocious action
at Amboyna, which wrested the Spice Islands from our
hands, the fleets of Holland had returned from either
east or west by the long route of the Orkneys, so as to
avoid bringing their precious freights within view of
Dover Castle; one of these rich argosies was now known
to be on the home voyage, and the Council of State was
anxious that it should be harassed, and if possible cut off.
Again, unable or unwilling to make use of the noble fisheries that nature has lavished on our coasts, the English
of the sixteenth and seventeenth centuries had allowed
their more enterprising neighbours to reap the harvest
almost unquestioned. The fisherman's life suited the
Dutchman's coarse and laborious habits. The hulks or
busses engaged in this trade, averaging from three hundred to five hundred tons burden, were each manned by
about a dozen persons; usually the master with his wife

and children, and about six or eight others, men and women. On board these herring-boats, children were able to
earn their own bread from the age of four or five. The
life was rude at best—the wages were always scanty. But
the people had learned to live on stormy and sterile seas,
to flourish on mud-banks and sandy plains. More than
once our ancestors had tried to establish rival fisheries,
but never with a chance of profit under such competition.
With that fine old Saxon chivalry, still found in some
portion of the lower classes, they refused to allow the
women to divide their coarse toils or share their daily
perils; nor had they yet learned to look without a sort
of horror on infant labour. Free from these scruples,
the Frisian had in his lower nature a commercial advantage against which it was ruinous to compete. The Dutch
family, huddled in a corner of the buss, found a part of its
coarse food in the waters on which it exercised its craft.
The English fisherman, who left his wife and children
at home, had to support them out of the nett profits of
his spoil. Thus the whole trade fell into the former
hands; and at the opening of the war between the two
countries the boats engaged in it were counted by thousands. Could the Dutch make good their claim to fish
among the Northern Islands? This was an open question. They did fish in those waters. But while the
fact was allowed, the right was denied; and on taking
the supreme direction of the war, Blake was anxious to
give practical effect to the denials of his government.
While the squadron was preparing for sea, information
came to hand that the spring fleet of these herring-busses,
consisting of more than six hundred sail, convoyed by

twelve men-of-war, was on its way home laden with fish. His first idea had been to send Sir George Ascue to the North, and stay in person to oppose Admiral Tromp; but as that great genius of strategy lay still in the Texel, making no sign of an immediate intention to put to sea, he changed this part of his plan, and resolved to go in person to the North. Sending swift messengers to the Baltic, to desire all the merchant-vessels, private and public, ready to return home, then in and about the Sound, to rendezvous at Elsinore, and there await his arrival,—he went down to Dover, installed Ascue as his lieutenant in the Channel, with orders to keep a sharp eye on Tromp's movements, and set sail in the *Resolution* for the North, attended by a magnificent array of sixty ships.[1]

On the 21st of June, Blake fired his parting salute in Dover road: so awful a burst of cannon had not been heard by the inhabitants of Kent since the days of the Armada. On the 9th of July letters reached the Council of State announcing that a gallant fleet, supposed to be General Blake's, had passed in sight of Dunbar. Two days later, despatches left Westminster in hot haste, by mounted couriers, to inform him that a sudden change had occurred in the enemy's dispositions,—that as soon as he was known to have passed the Frith of Forth the Dutch Admiral had quitted his lair,—that he was then riding with 102 men-of-war and ten fire-ships in the Downs, —that the whole coast was alarmed for its safety, none knowing where a blow would first be struck,—and that so far from Ascue being able to afford them any protection,

---

[1] History and Life, 58; Heath, 322; Granville Penn, i. 431.

he had himself been compelled to run under the guns of Dover Castle. The couriers rode day and night with urgent letters of recal; but before these came into the Admiral's hands, one of the three great objects of his expedition had been accomplished. Meeting the great herring-fleet off Bockness, his advanced guard of twenty sail fell furiously on the men-of-war, and after a gallant contest, prolonged by the obstinate valour of the Dutch against superior numbers for three hours, sunk three of the twelve and took the other nine. All the herring-busses, six hundred in number, fell into his power with their freights of herrings. But as these boats belonged to poor families, whose entire capital and means of life they constituted, he took from them, on a rough computation, every tenth herring as a royalty, and then warning the men never to fish again in the creeks and islands belonging to the Commonwealth of England without first obtaining from the Council of State a formal permission, he sent them home with all their boats and the remainder of their cargo untouched. This characteristic act of clemency called down severe censures on the Admiral in certain quarters. Many condemned such generosity to an enemy as Quixotic. " If the fish," said the politicians, " were of no use to the fleet, he should have thrown them into the sea." The answer was, " That they were human food, and that thousands would suffer, none would gain, by their destruction." Even men like Ludlow blamed him for not keeping possession of the poor fellows' boats. But Blake took no trouble to justify his noble instincts against such critics. His was indeed a happy fate :—

the only fault ever advanced by friend or foe against his public life was an excess of generosity towards his vanquished enemies![1]

Kent was up in arms to repel the menacing invader. Seamen living in the ports crowded on board Ascue's squadron with offers of service. The regular militia turned out. Between Deal and Sandown Castle a long double platform was erected, with cannon at intervals to sweep the shore should the Dutch attempt to land. But these warlike preparations, though they evinced the national spirit, did less to preserve the coast from outrage than those elements which have so often proved our best allies in the hour of danger. A calm kept the enemy spell-bound in mid-channel until the country had recovered from its first alarm. When the wind returned, it blew from the land, and with such steady violence, that with all his skill Tromp was unable to get near enough for even a passing broadside. To the south of his position, Ascue rode in perfect safety with his small squadron ; and some fresh ships, preparing to join him just before the Dutchman's appearance in the Straits, were retained in the Thames by a counter order. Tromp, it is believed, had expected to intercept this reinforcement as it left the river, and then by a sudden onset to crush Ascue under overwhelming cannonades. Success on these two points would have left Blake with about fifty sail — for he had despatched eight of his best frigates to strengthen the Downs squadron — against a fleet flushed with victory and thrice his power. But

---

[1] Elegiac Enumeration, 17 ; Balfour, iv. 257 ; Clarendon, v. 281; Cornelius Tromp, 61; Granville Penn, i. 434, 435.

the weather having foiled him in these hopes, the wily Dutchman returned with the strong gale then blowing to the Texel, where a vast fleet of merchants were impatiently waiting to set forth on their voyage under his protection. Convoying these vessels northward, he saw the Baltic traders through the Sound, the busses disperse to their fishing stations, and the Indiamen separate to pursue their several voyages out of all danger from English cruisers, — and then went in search of Blake's squadron, confident in his immense superiority of force, and not unwilling to put the fortunes of his country to the arbitration of a regular battle. Since his recent victory, Blake had suffered severely from storms, and his ships were scattered among the roadsteads of the Orkney Islands for repair; but on hearing that his great enemy had followed him into the North, he hastily prepared for an encounter of the two navies.

Towards evening, on the 5th of August, the fleets came in sight of each other between Fair Isle and Fould, almost half-way from the Orkneys to the Shetland group. Smarting under a recollection of former wrongs, both confident of success, Tromp trusting to his naval genius and superior force, Blake in the Lord of Hosts and the valour of his men, they eagerly prepared to engage. But the empire of the seas was to be then and there decided in favour of a new claimant. Whilst preparations were being made in the *Resolution* to attack the Dutch fleet, the sky gradually assumed a dark and threatening aspect. The wind, which had been extremely variable for some days, suddenly settled itself north-north-west. In the human excitement of the moment, these signs were not at first observed; but as the gale rose, and the sky continued to grow black and lurid, Blake signalled his ships to look out for the coming storm; and leave the enemy to shift for themselves, certain that there could be no engagement that day. At length it burst:—and the fiercest of mortal passions were stilled in a moment before the awful demonstrations of nature. The fitful gleams of light, now and then caught through the storm and darkness, told the commanders that another power had undertaken to disperse and separate their fleets. Many of the ships were soon unmanageable. Rudders were wrested violently off; sails were torn and twisted into knots, and the waves went through and through them every swell, throwing their white and seething foam into the very sky. The darkness, danger, and distance from aid and shelter, filled the imagination of the sailors with horror. "The fleet," says the Dutch writer of Cornelius Tromp, "being as it were buried by the sea in the most horrible abysses, rose out of them only to be tossed up to the clouds; here the masts were beaten down into the sea, there the deck was overflowed with the prevailing waves; the tempest was so much mistress of the ships, they could be governed no longer, and on every side appeared all the dreadful forerunners of a dismal wreck." The storm raged through the long night without abatement; and when day came down on the rolling waters, instead of the imperial fleets which rode so proudly among the rocks and islands a few hours previous, anxious in their fancied strength and majesty to put the freedom of the sea to an hour's arbitration,— a remnant of scattered, helpless and damaged ships were all that could be seen from the *Brederode* between land and sky. The Dutch had suffered terribly. More than one of their frigates had been dashed on the rocks, splintered into a myriad fragments, and every soul on board sent down into the foaming surge. Tromp picked up broken relics of three of his fire-ships:— their fate could not be doubted. They had all gone down. Most of his men-of-war and frigates were considerably damaged, and the greater part of his fleet was scattered beyond the possibility of recal. Some of the ships found refuge in the harbours of the Shetland group, others fled towards the Norwegian coast; and after spending several days in the vain attempt to collect the damaged elements of his power, Tromp was obliged to run into Scheveling with a remnant of only forty-two sail, to his own infinite chagrin and the extreme astonishment of his countrymen at the failure of an enterprise so vast and costly. Blake had been fortunate enough to keep his fleet together under shelter of the mainland of the Shetland Islands, and although he had not escaped without serious injury to many ships, he was able to keep the sea, and hang with his whole body of sixty-two sail, fleet and prizes, on the rear of the disabled Dutch. Finding the enemy disinclined to put out again from their harbours, he ravaged and insulted their coasts from Wadden to Zealand, and then ran across to Yarmouth with his prizes and nine hundred prisoners.[1]

In a few days his standard was again waving in the Downs from the masts of the *Resolution*. Ascue and

---

[1] Heath, 322 ; Cornelius Tromp, 62, 63.

De Ruiter had met and drawn a battle, but the spirit of the States-General seemed to rise with their unexpected want of success, and they prepared another large and gallant fleet for service in the Channel under command of the renowned admiral and statesman De Witt. Tromp retired into private life. Clamorous at a reverse in one so long accustomed to victory, a Dutch mob insulted his age and misfortune; and in a fit of disgust the veteran laid down his commission. De Ruiter, too, was anxious to retire from the responsibilities of command. He pleaded his long services, his old age, his failing health, but his countrymen would not listen: he must lead them once more as of old to glory and victory. When the new squadron was ready for sea, De Witt joined De Ruiter, and took the supreme command. To oppose this new danger, Blake called in the force under Ascue from Plymouth; and the two fleets—that of England composed of sixty-eight ships of various gunnage—that of Holland nearly but not quite equal to it in number of ships and guns—were once more in the same seas and ready to try their strength against each other.

But while cruising about the Channel in search of his more immediate enemy, Blake fell in with a French fleet under the Duke of Vendome, who had just engaged with and defeated the Spanish Admiral Count d'Oignon. This fleet was intended to relieve Dunkirk, then hotly pressed by the besieging Spaniards. The piratical town was in extremity; but the disaster of Count d'Oignon left the sea open to France, and Vendome ordered a relief squadron to rendezvous in Calais road, and take on board men, arms, stores and fresh provisions. As yet

there had been no formal declaration of war between
France and England. Though the privateers of Brest
and Dunkirk continued the old depredations, and English cruisers often retaliated on French vessels, such disorders were not considered as seriously compromising
the political relations of the two governments. But as
soon as Blake learned that Vendome was collecting ships
and stores for Dunkirk in the port of Calais, without
waiting for instructions from London, or even reporting
his intentions to his colleagues of the Council of State,
he stood over for that harbour, where he found seven
men-of-war, a small frigate, six fire-ships and a number
of transports with men and provisions on board already
collected and under sail. What was to be done? With
that accession of strength Dunkirk would have been able
to defy the Archduke Leopold for an indefinite period.
English interests, commercial and political, required the
downfall of that nest of privateers; the Council of State
were anxious to see the town change hands; and they
had already conceived a hope—afterwards realised—that
the Spaniards might be induced on certain terms to cede
their conquest. Blake knew the opinion of his countrymen on this subject too well to doubt how far he could
go without incurring serious personal responsibility, if,
in striking a blow which would involve the government
in trouble with the great Cardinal, he could achieve a
sudden and complete success. He therefore rode into
Calais road; and in spite of the threats, protests and
explanations of Vendome, he attacked the men-of-war,
while part of his fleet chased the transports and fire-
ships along the coast. As the resistance was not se-

P

rious, the whole body of the French squadron, war-ships, fire-ships and transports, admirals, officers and men, were in a few hours safely harboured under the guns of Dover Castle. Dunkirk immediately surren-dered to the Archduke Leopold:—and the seizure of Vendome's squadron remained, not only as an illus-tration of the extraordinary powers exercised by Blake at sea, but a striking instance of bold conception and equally rapid and effective execution.[1]

These prizes safely harboured, the cruise in search of De Witt and De Ruiter was resumed. On the 28th of September, Penn, still on board the *James*, came in sight of the Dutchmen off the North Foreland ; on see-ing the signal, Blake, at that moment more than a league in advance of his main body, rode up to the vanguard and gave his brief but emphatic orders—" As soon as some more of our fleet comes up, bear in among them !" Blake was ever ready for action : he trusted in God and kept his powder dry. But De Witt was taken unawares; his ships were in disorder ; a bad spirit prevailed among the men ; and De Ruiter urged him to avoid a battle. His pride rendered him deaf to this sage councillor, and he resolved to fight even at a disadvantage rather than exhibit to the world the spectacle of a Dutch admiral in retreat before the presumptuous islanders. His dis-positions were made hastily and in confusion. De Ruiter was to lead the van, he himself the main body, De Wilde the rear. Evertz was stationed with a reserve to watch the action from a short distance, and send out succours where they should be most needed. At the last mo-

---

[1] Elegiac Enumeration, 14, 15; Columna Rostrata, 105 ; Heath, 325.

ment De Witt sent an advice-boat round to each of his ships to beg the captains to do their duty in their respective posts on that great day. But this prayer was not heard. Apathy, intrigue and discontent were on every deck. The *Brederode*, Tromp's old flag-ship, was in the fleet, but the officers and men refused to allow the new Admiral to come on board her; and just before the action began his standard was removed to a huge Indiaman. Resenting the disgrace of their favourite leader, several other ships either disputed the new Admiral's orders, or obeyed them without the zeal which is essential to victory. But unwarned by these signs of disaffection—perhaps hoping that success would restore confidence and loyalty to his crews—De Witt hauled his foresails to the masts and formed his fleet into line.

About four o'clock in the afternoon, the English being then well up together, a single order was given out from the *Resolution*—to hold back their fire till close in with the enemy,—and the flag-ship, followed by the *James*, the *Sovereign* and the whole body of the vanguard, bore down on De Witt's line, which kept up an intermittent and harmless fire as it advanced. At this moment the Dutch tacked, and the two fleets came into almost instant collision. The crash of the first broadsides was terrific, for the ships were so near together, that an unusual quantity of shot went home. For more than an hour the roar of artillery was incessant. After that its action was less furious; there were occasional pauses in the storm; and the Dutch ships clearing off to a greater distance, the sulphurous atmosphere broke in many places, and the winds drifted it away in huge

masses. But although the Dutch fell back, they fell
back fighting and with their faces to the enemy. With
obstinate valour they continued the battle until night
fell like a funeral pall on the scene of slaughter. The
Dutch had suffered most severely in men, the English
in masts and rigging. The most experienced admirals
in both fleets were of opinion that De Witt could not
have held out an hour longer without being entirely
broken and annihilated. De Ruiter had commanded
his division with consummate skill and bravery. A
great part of his own crew was swept away; his main-
yard was turned over to the left side; his main-sails,
mizen-sails and rigging were all torn to shreds; his hull
was seriously shattered; and he had received no less
than four shots between wind and water. De Witt had
atoned in a great measure for his rashness in fighting
such an enemy under the circumstances of his fleet, by
his courage and conduct during the action. Nevertheless, Holland was unmistakably worsted. Under the
first shock of the onset, two of its ships went down.
Two others had been boarded and taken, one of them
the Rear-admiral by Captain Mildmay in the *Nonsuch*,
together with the two captains, and all the crews on
deck. Throughout the Dutch fleet, the loss of life had
been great.[1] And to the infinite vexation of De Witt,
about twenty of his captains, either disaffected to his
person or unwilling to renew on the morrow so destructive an engagement, took advantage of the dark night
to quit the main body with the ships under their com-

---

[1] Blake to Council of State, Oct. 2, 1652; Cornelius Tromp, 77, 78 ;
Penn's Account (Granville Penn, i. 446-450); History and Life, 63.

mand and make for Zealand, whither they carried the
first news of the disaster.

All that night Blake observed lights burning in the
enemy's ships, and assuming that they would fight again
at daybreak, every hand on board the English fleet was
employed in repairing sails, masts and cordage — in securing the prisoners already taken — in waiting on and
soothing the wounded sailors—and in the sad and pious
duties connected with the burial of the dead. The grey
light dawned on the sleepless crews still at their necessary labours, and before sunrise the whole fleet was in
motion bearing up towards the enemy, who at first
seemed disposed to renew the bloody work of the previous day ; but before the English van had got within
range of cannon-shot a change of opinion took place,
they hoisted full sail and stood up the Channel. De Witt
had wished to fight. But Evertz and De Ruiter overruled his voice in the council of war, where it was resolved that an attempt should be made to collect the
shattered and scattered remnants of their fleet ; to gain
one of their own ports and communicate with their masters; to repair, refit, and re-man their ships; and then
await the commands of the States-General. Blake kept
as close on their rear as the disabled state of his ships
would allow ; and having chased them into the Göree,
where the shallows afforded them ample protection, he
was obliged to rest content with returning the insults
offered to our own coasts by Admiral Tromp earlier in
the summer.[1]

---

[1] Blake to Council of State, Oct. 2 ; Clarendon, v. 281; Corneliu
Tromp, 78-81.

Nothing could exceed the avidity with which reports of the battle of the North Foreland were read in London. It was the first great naval action which the nation had fought since the reign of Elizabeth; and indeed there was room for a little honest exultation. The prowess of England had now been arrayed against the best seamen and most experienced admirals in the world, and the English had come off victorious. At the very first trial of strength, they had established themselves as equal to the acknowledged masters of maritime war. Hitherto Tromp, Evertz, and De Ruiter had been regarded by Europe as peerless, if not invincible, commanders. Yet an English land-officer, with only three years' experience of the sea, had learned to contend with these renowned admirals on equal terms; rough soldiers, drafted from the camp, had, in the same period, ceased altogether to feel awe in the presence of the veteran sailors who had swept the imperial navies of Spain from the face of the ocean. Blake was fast rising into the first name in our naval history. His southern campaign, made while his genius was still unaided by experience, had placed him in general estimation by the side of Drake and Frobisher. His drawn battle with Tromp, his victory over De Ruiter and De Witt, raised him into the highest rank of living admirals.

Parliament shared the liberal enthusiasm of the people. With a somewhat premature contempt of their powerful enemy, they had desired Blake to dismiss a part of his fleet back to the merchant service from which it had been taken;[1] they allowed the fortifi-

---

[1] Blake to Navy Com., Sept. 20, Dept. Mss.

cations erected between Deal and Sandown to be destroyed; and they ordered the guns planted on the line of breastworks to be removed into the two castles. At Blake's urgent request they gave orders for thirty new frigates to be built; but for the moment all was confidence and security as to the future. The Council of State began a diligent study of the *Mare Clausum*, Selden's learned book on the right of England to assert the dominion of the narrow seas and to exclude the Dutch from any participation in the advantages of the northern fisheries. They had the book translated into English; and questions which had tested the learning and intellect of men like Grotius and Selden were debated in taverns, and practically settled in Council Chambers. Vendome's complaints were treated by the Council of State with haughty indifference. They already fancied their power supreme in the Channel; but they had not yet learned to understand the magnitude of their enemy's genius and resources.[1]

---

[1] Ludlow, i. 367; Whitelock, 545; Le Clerc, i. 324; Granville Penn, i. 454, 455.

CHAPTER VII.

Tromp.

DE WITT's return to Holland with the discomfited fleet was the signal for disorders in that country. His enemies of the Orange party charged him with rashness, cowardice and treason. The common sailors, turbulent and disobedient before the engagement, pushed their dislike to the verge of mutiny after their defeat. Even on the flag-ship his position was most disagreeable, if his life were not in danger. Before going on board in the Texel he had been compelled by a decent regard for naval discipline to hang two of his seamen in Amsterdam, and at the execution he had been under the still more unfortunate necessity of shooting several citizens in order to prevent a rescue in the streets. In his day of power and of untried fortunes these acts of severity were borne in silent rage; but when he returned from sea with broken power and faded laurels, the popular passions rose against him like the surges of their own stormy coast. In Flushing he was mobbed as soon as he landed — and his proud heart was almost broken by the insult. In anger and disgust, he took to a sick chamber. De Ruiter shared in some measure the unpopularity of his chief, and he also offered to resign his commission. The moment of general alarm and indignation—for they had so often triumphed over every enemy at sea, they could not yet understand that their reverses were other than the result of gross misconduct,—sent the inconsiderate people to the feet of their old commander. They now remembered, that if Tromp's success in the early part of the war had not been such as they had expected, he at least had not suffered a signal defeat; if he had lost a powerful squadron, they had the consolation to feel that nature and not man had been the cause of its sudden overthrow. When the failure of his rivals allowed them time to estimate his claims with less haste and less passion, they could not but see that his reputation still towered above that of every other seaman in Holland; while, on the other hand, personal feeling and the incidents of his career had fitted him in a peculiar manner for the chief command in a war against England.

At ten years old, Tromp was present in his father's ship at the famous battle fought against Spain under the walls of Gibraltar in 1607. Shortly after that memorable event, he was captured by an English cruiser after a brisk engagement in which his father lost his life. Two years and a half he was compelled to serve in the menial capacity of cabin-boy on board the captor:—and thus were the seeds of hatred to England and the English sown in his proud and passionate heart. Once planted, this hatred grew with his growth and strengthened with his strength. For a long time his life was passed on board fishing-boats and merchant-men; but his nautical genius was irresistible, and he fought his way through legions of obstacles to high command. At thirty years old he was confessedly the ablest navigator in Holland. More than twenty years he had now commanded his country's fleets with success against Spain,—and had done more than any other individual to humble the pride and reduce the power of that extensive empire. The disastrous opening of the English war was no impeachment of his naval genius; and the insult offered to his former successes in stripping him of his great employments because nature had raised a destructive storm in the northern latitudes, appeared to the States-General gratuitous and unworthy as soon as they discovered that his future services were necessary to the Republic. The old Admiral's passion was also soothed by royal good offices. The King of Denmark, alarmed at the sudden growth of England's maritime power, made interest with the leading Dutch statesmen with a view to promote a vigorous renewal of hostilities, and at his special intercession Tromp was restored to his former offices and honours, the most eminent of his rivals in naval ability and domestic influence, De Witt, De Ruiter, Evertz and Floritz, being appointed to serve under him as his Vice and Rear-admirals. De Witt, too much mortified at his recent failure to have any wish to re-appear on the same scene in an inferior place, excused himself from serving on the ground of ill-health, De Ruiter therefore again went on board as second in command.[1]

Other nations became interested in the quarrels of the two Republics. The war had barely commenced before the States-General sent ambassadors to Denmark, Poland and other powers in the north of Europe to

---

[1] Heath, 326; Cornelius Tromp, 83; History and Life, 64.

engage them in a common league against England. Frederick III., King of Denmark and Norway, listened to these proposals; and though he did not as yet choose to commit himself by an open acknowledgment of his leanings, he sought by an indirect and unexplained course of action to forward the views of his powerful continental friends. Under pretence of securing them against Dutch cruisers, Frederick refused to allow the ships which Blake had ordered to rendezvous at Elsinore to pass the Sound:—an idle pretence, since the English were at that time masters at sea. As the hemp, tar and other stores from the Baltic on board these ships were urgently needed in the dockyards, Parliament wrote to King Frederick desiring him as a friend and ally of the Commonwealth, to deliver up to their Admiral all the goods and ships then lying in his ports, and at their request Blake detached Captain Ball with twenty men-of-war and frigates to add force to this reasonable desire, and in the event of its receiving favourable attention to convoy the ships home in safety. After an absence of some weeks, Ball returned as he went out. Pressed to declare itself, the Court of Denmark vamped up a story about some old debts contracted by the late King of England on account of the German war, and claimed a right to detain the government vessels until these debts were liquidated. The expected supply of stores was therefore not obtained,—and the Commonwealth had a new enemy to deal with in the north of Europe.[1]

The term for which Blake had been commissioned to act as sole General and Admiral of the Fleet being on

---

[1] Heath, 327, 328.

the point of expiration, he requested that two colleagues should be joined with him in the command as in the first years of his naval service had been the case. A rare instance of self-denial! During his absence in the north he had seen the disadvantage of leaving the Downs to an inferior officer, however able; and in the belief that such a division of the supreme command would be serviceable to the country he set aside every personal consideration and proposed to have two officers, enjoying the full confidence of the Council of State, associated with him in the new commission. Popham being dead the choice of admirals fell on Colonel Deane, his former colleague, and General Monk; but both these officers were then employed in suppressing the last remnants of the war in Scotland, and they could not for some time to come take any active part in the naval war.[1]

Severe weather being now set in and the Dutchmen busy in their dockyards with the preparation of another vast armament, Blake made the usual winter distribution of the fleet. Besides the twenty ships sent to Elsinore under Ball, Penn sailed with a similar squadron towards the North to convoy a fleet of colliers from Newcastle to London; a division of twelve ships was stationed in Plymouth Sound; fifteen of the most damaged vessels were ordered into the river for repair; and with the remainder of his force, consisting of thirty-seven men-of-war and frigates, the fire-ships and a few hoys,— Blake rode in the Channel, cruising from port to port between Essex and Hampshire, and expecting no enemy to appear until the return of fine weather. In this he was

---

[1] Skinner's Monk, 49; Heath, 331.

mistaken. Tromp's energy and influence had infused
an extraordinary degree of activity into the marine department, the harbours and dockyards of Holland. In
an incredibly short time they had fitted out and manned
a vast fleet; and as soon as the English squadrons were
dispersed for the winter stations, he secretly and unexpectedly drew out his ships and appeared off the
Goodwin Sands with more than a hundred sail of the
line, frigates and fire-ships. His plan was bold and well
conceived. Throwing himself suddenly into the Downs
with this overwhelming force, he intended to close up
the Thames and cut off re-inforcements from Chatham
or the Lea, to fall on Blake's little squadron like an
avalanche, and either crush or drive it down Channel
towards the Land's End, and then, with the entire coast
at his mercy, to dictate peace to the Commonwealth on
his own terms. At that time the thought of a winter campaign filled men's minds with terror; but Tromp relied
on the effect of a swift and daring blow to conclude the
war in a few days. Blake was scarcely aware that the
Dutch were stirring before their ships were seen from
the out-look of the *Triumph*, to which vessel he had
removed his pennon. On the 9th of December the
two fleets were in presence between Dover and Calais;
and the knowledge that Tromp was on board assured
the English Admiral that serious mischief was meant.
A council of war was called on board the *Triumph*.
Blake described the situation of the two countries at that
moment, glanced at the superior force of the enemy, at
the distance of his own squadrons, and ended by declaring his resolution to fight, if it were necessary, but

on no account to fall down the Channel, leaving the coast-towns to be insulted, and perhaps destroyed by that mighty and uncrippled armament. The captains accepted his decision with alacrity, and returned to their several ships to report the result of their conference. All that day the two admirals watched each other's motions, the object being to gain the weather-gage. The night proved cold and tempestuous, even for mid winter, and the ships were unable to keep well together. With the appearance of light the manœuvres of the previous day were renewed, the *Triumph* and the *Brederode* dodging each other for several hours in a slight and variable wind, their somewhat oblique course inclining slowly towards the Nase. At three in the afternoon the fleets were near to each other off that Essex head-land. Tromp's patience was worn out, and anxious to engage, he made a sudden effort to get alongside the English Admiral at an advantage; but a rapid and decisive movement carried the *Triumph* clean under his bow to the weather-gage. In passing, the two ships exchanged broadsides. Blake was closely followed in his dexterous movement by the *Garland*, and missing the *Triumph* Tromp ran against her with such violence as in an instant to break her bowspit and ship's-head with the weight of the crash. The *Garland* and the *Brederode* quickly engaged, the English ship of only forty-eight guns fighting with consummate bravery against its powerful enemy, until the *Bonadventure*, a trader of thirty guns, came to the rescue, and placed the Dutch Admiral himself in peril. Tromp encouraged his men by shouts and gestures to renewed efforts; he appealed to their love of country, their pride of race, their affection for himself. But all his exertions would have availed but little, had not Evertz seen his exposed position, and brought his own ship to bear on the *Bonadventure*, thus placing the gallant little merchantman between the fire of two powerful admirals. The four ships were all grappled together; but the English held out manfully against tremendous odds for more than an hour, when the contest was decided in favour of number of men and weight of metal. Out of two hundred men on board the *Garland* at the beginning of the action, the captain and sixty officers and men were killed, and a still greater number were severely wounded; the *Bonadventure* had suffered to an equal extent; and the survivors being no longer able to defend their respective decks, the Dutchmen boarded and captured both the vessels. The *Triumph*, the *Vanguard* and the *Victory* bore the chief brunt of the action. At one time these three vessels were engaged with twenty of the enemy; and although they also suffered most severely in men, and were greatly damaged in their hulls, masts and rigging, they all came off safely from the desperate encounter. Night, which at that season of the year came down early, was already separating the fleets, when Blake heard for the first time of the unequal battle waged between the two Dutch Admirals and the *Garland* and *Bonadventure;* and notwithstanding the fatigue of his men, he gave orders to bear up to the *Brederode*, and endeavour to recover the captures. Other of the enemy's ships, how-ever, crossed his line, and a more destructive conflict than had yet taken place ensued. Blake was surrounded

by the Dutch ships.   Three several times the *Triumph*
was boarded in gallant style ; but each time the boarders
were driven back to their boats with fearful slaughter.
The flag-ship was reduced to a wreck.   The foretop-
mast was shot away.   The mainstay was gone.   The
sails and tackling were all in ribands.   The hull was
shattered and pierced with hundreds of shots.   The
wonder was how she could keep her head above water,
and had it not been for the *Sapphire*, a trader of thirty
guns, and the *Vanguard*, which stood by him with unwavering steadiness and devotion, the English Admiral
must have fallen before such overwhelming numbers in
spite of his iron will and dauntless courage.   Thick fog
and December darkness at length put an end to the
struggle.   Under cover of night Blake drew off his
ships, the *Triumph* being the last to retire from the
scene of action, towards Dover roads.   Tromp could
not, or would not, follow on his rear.   Next day the
weather was thick with fog ; the enemy was not in
sight.   The disabled vessels were ill prepared to brave
the fury of the south-west winds ; and, master of his
own movements, the Admiral proposed to run into the
Thames, and anchor in Lea-road to repair damages,
ascertain the enemy's intentions, make some necessary
alterations in the fleet, and wait the recal and concentration of his distant squadrons.   The Dutch had not
gained an easy victory.   Their loss in men was extremely
great.   One of their vessels had been blown into the
air, every man on board perishing.   Tromp's ship and
De Ruiter's ship were both put out of service, and
many others were seriously crippled.   But their victory

was unquestionable: for the moment they were once again masters of the Channel.[1]

There seem to have been three principal causes of this disaster—the first and last that England experienced under Blake's command—any one of them sufficient to account for it:—(1.) an overwhelming superiority of force on the part of Tromp; (2.) the extreme weakness to which some of the vessels were reduced for want of men; and (3.) cowardice or disaffection to the service, manifested at a critical moment of the battle by several captains in his little fleet. To the first of these causes Blake himself professed to attach only a secondary importance. Had all the thirty-seven ships behaved like the *Garland, Sapphire, Vanguard, Bonadventure, Victory,* and *Triumph,* the result would probably have been other than it was; and even his defeat, if the retirement of a squadron before a fleet three times its strength can be so called, was less galling to his proud nature than the idea of having officers under his command who at such a time could fail in duty to their country. In the letter which conveyed to the Council of State the first news of the reverse of fortune, he says:—" I am bound to let your honours know that there was much baseness of spirit, not among the merchant-men only, but in many of the State's ships. And therefore I make it my earnest request that your honours would be pleased to send down some gentlemen to take an impartial and strict examination of the deportment of several commanders, that

---

[1] Blake to Council of State, December 1, 1652 ; Granville Penn, i. 456-459; Cornelius Tromp, 83-86 ; Heath, 330.

Q

you may know who are to be confided in and who are not. It will then be time to take into consideration the grounds of some other errors and defects, especially the discouragement and want of seamen. I shall be bold at present to name one—not the least,—which is, the great number of private men-of-war, especially out of the Thames. And I hope it will not be unseasonable for me, in behalf of myself, to desire your honours that you would think of giving me, your unworthy servant, a discharge from this employment as far too great for me, especially since your honours have added two such able gentlemen [Monk and Deane] for the undertaking of that charge; so that I may spend the remainder of my days in private retirement, and in prayers to the Lord for blessings on you and on this nation."[1]

But instead of receiving the acceptance of his offer to resign, Blake soon found that the misfortune which might have ruined another man had given him strength and influence in the country. The Council of State wrote by return of courier to express their unanimous thanks for his gallant conduct in the late action, and to assure him that all his proposals,—except the one which referred to his own retirement,—should be adopted. Never had he been so necessary to them as at that moment, and his hints and requests were immediately carried into effect, so far as lay with the Council. Three of their own body, Colonel Walton, Mr. Chaloner, and Colonel Morley were sent down to inquire into the alleged misconduct of certain officers, to report on the ineffective condition of

---

[1] Blake to Council of State, Dec. 1.

the fleet, and, in case of need, to assist in a Council of
War to be called by the Admiral after their arrival.
Messengers were sent to recal the convoys to the Downs.
Orders were sent to Deane and Monk to hold themselves
in readiness to go on board at twenty-four hours' notice,
and assume the responsibilities of their new rank. Cruisers and other vessels lying at Harwich and elsewhere on
the near coasts were instructed to repair to the general
rendezvous. A resolution was carried to raise the effective marine force to 30,000 men. More care was taken
with the store magazines. The Navy Commissioners,
long crippled by the perfidious policy of the Danish
King, were empowered in this emergency to seize on
hemp, tar and pitch, wherever these important articles
could be found. But not a whisper was heard against
the Admiral either in the Council or in the city. There
was no attempt on the part of the Navy Commissioners
to meddle with his schemes or to abridge his authority.
The Council of State reposed an almost unbounded confidence in his genius and fidelity. Five days after the
engagement off the Nase, they ordered—" that a letter
be written to General Blake, to acquaint him with what
the Council hath done for the giving him an addition of
strength, — to let him know that (in regard the state of
affairs is before him, and he hath a perfect understanding of them) *the Council do leave to him upon the place
to do what he may for his own defence and the service of
the Commonwealth.*" The next day they wrote again
in the same spirit :—" The Council suggest objections
to General Blake going with his fleet into Lea road, and
recommend Harwich as a better position: *but still leave*

*it to him to act according as his Council of War shall
advise upon the place."*[1]

Curiously enough, the first disaster experienced by
Blake at sea gave him power to effect reforms in the
service and to root out abuses which had defied all his
efforts in the day of his success.   One great abuse was
abolished that in his opinion lay at the source of the
late defeat.   To encourage merchants and others having
vessels capable of armament to place them during the
war at the disposal of Government, an Order of Council had hitherto allowed the masters of such vessels to
command them after the change of service; by which
means many persons came to occupy, as a private right,
important offices in the navy who had no real attachment to the new order of things, and there was good
reason to suspect that some of the secret partisans of
the Stuarts had crept into places of trust in this way
for the express purpose of betraying the Commonwealth
at the first favourable opportunity.   These Royalists
kept the exiled court well informed as to the state of
the navy, and the exiles in turn communicated the latest
information to the States-General.   Thus the Admiral
had not only to fight his great and astute adversary, but
to struggle against intrigues abroad and treason at home.
Before Tromp sailed from the Texel, Charles Stuart
had caused a secret memoir to be drawn up by Lord
Clarendon and the Marquis of Ormonde—to be presented
to M. Borrel, Dutch Ambassador in Paris—in which he
proposed to the States-General a plan for creating divisions in the English fleet and consequent excitement

---

[1] Orders of Council of State, Dec. 2 to Dec. 5.

and weakness in the country. He declared that he was aware that many captains in the Commonwealth navy were his own friends; and he offered to go in person on board the Dutch fleet as a private officer, seeking no command, except of such vessels as should desert to him from their enemy. De Witt, however, as a sincere Republican, refused to accept this doubtful aid; but a certain knowledge of the fact on which the proposal was based, that many of Blake's officers served under false colours and were ripe for an act of treason, was of vast importance to Tromp in the arrangement of his bold and masterly campaign. Certain incidents in the late battle left no moral doubt that several captains had acted with direct or indirect reference to the enemy's design; and without being able to bring the crime of treason home to them, the Admiral took the occasion to insist on having a regulation adopted by the supreme Council, that in future all the captains and other officers should receive their appointments from the State.[1]

As the inquiries of the three members, Walton, Morley and Chaloner proceeded, several officers were suspended, either for neglect of duty, lack of courage or other faults, against whom no suspicion of treachery or disaffection could arise. It was necessary to purge the fleet of its weak, as well as of its faithless, captains. No naval scrutiny was ever conducted with greater justice, openness and severity. The three members reported to the Admiral the results of their investigation in each case, and he delivered sentence of arrest or dis-

[1] Clarendon, v. 282, 283; Clarendon to Secretary Nicholas, January 18, 1652-3; Granville Penn, i. 427.

missal with a stern rigour, even when the law fell in its full weight on his own household and his own family. Francis Harvey, his secretary, was cashiered. Captains Young, Taylor, Saltonstill and others were put under arrest until the pleasure of the Council of State should be known. His brother Benjamin, to whom he was strongly attached as a brother and an officer, fell under suspicion of some neglect of duty ; and however painful the exercise of power under such circumstances, he was instantly broken and sent on shore. This rigid measure of justice against his own flesh and blood silenced every complaint ; and the service gained immeasurably in spirit, discipline and confidence.[1]

While these reforms, recruitments and renovations were proceeding under Blake's immediate eye, Tromp rode up and down the Channel with a broom at his mast-head, a somewhat prosaic emblem of his right to sweep the narrow seas ; and the States-General, still more elated with their victory than the Admiral himself, put out a proclamation against our manufactures—sent intelligence of their great successes to foreign powers— and interdicted all correspondence and communication with the British Islands, pretending, as if they were already assured victors, to place them in a state of naval blockade. Ballads, by-words and scurrilous caricatures delighted the ears and eyes of the excited populace. The names of the vessels captured in the fight afforded Dutch wits a theme for abuse : they had carried off the " garland," they said, from the islanders; and there were squibs and jokes about the " bon-adventure " having

_____

[1] Orders of Council of State, January 28, 1652-3.

realised the prophecy of its name in falling into their hands. But what concerned the Council of State much more than these usual incidents of success, was a report that Tromp contemplated making a descent on the Isles of Jersey and Guernsey, and a very natural fear that the trading part of the community would suffer from the cruisers of their watchful and active enemy. These alarms hastened their preparations for the second winter campaign; and on the 8th of February Blake, still in the *Triumph,* sailed from Queensborough, at the head of sixty men-of-war and frigates, having Monk and Deane with twelve hundred soldiers from the camp on board. Penn was the Vice-admiral, Lawson the Rear-admiral. In the Straits the Portsmouth squadron of twenty sail came in, and with this addition to his effective strength, Blake resolved to seek the Dutch fleet and give battle. Tromp had gone southward to meet a large fleet of traders, ordered by the States-General to rendezvous at the Isle of Rhe, opposite Rochelle, and convoy them home; but intelligence had there reached him that the English were about to quit the Thames in his absence with sixty sail, and he intended to arrive at the river mouth in time to block it up, prevent their departure, and keep the Portsmouth squadron from effecting a junction with the main body. Blake had stolen a march on the Dutch Admiral, and when the latter turned Cape de la Hogue, he was surprised to find the English with a force equal to his own prepared to dispute the passage of a sea so lately swept by his potential broom. Confident, however, of victory, he accepted with joy the offer of a battle which fortune had enabled him to decline without disadvantage had such been his pleasure.[1]

Day was just breaking on the morning of February 18, when the vanguard of the Dutch Admiral was descried from the mast-head of the *Triumph*. Blake dressed and went to the out-look. Nature could scarcely boast a grander spectacle than rose before him as the sun came forth, shewing that heaving wintry sea covered with ships, and lighting their sails and pennons with its pale radiance. The darkness of the weather had prevented mutual recognition until the foremost ships were within a league or so of each other. Fortunately the English Admirals were all together, the *Triumph* having Penn's ship, the *Speaker*, and Lawson's, the *Fairfax*, both within call; but Monk was some miles astern in the *Vanguard*, and the main body of the fleet lay about a league and a half apart at the moment when the Dutchmen came in sight. Tromp saw his advantage and pressed it home. With the wind in his favour he might have carried his convoy to the Scheldt in safety, and returned at his leisure to give battle; but he chose to play a bolder game, and fancying the enemy would be found unequal with a vanguard of some twenty ships to resist the weight of his attack, he sent his fleet of traders a little to windward, out of gun range, with orders for them to wait there and witness the engagement. Personal combined with public reasons to lend a thrilling interest to the coming battle. The two nations had now had time to collect their best forces. Their largest ships were in the array. The most renowned admirals

---

[1] Heath, 332; Granville Penn, i. 474, and ii. 614.

were on board the respective fleets: Blake, Deane, Penn and Lawson on the one side ; Tromp, Evertz, De Ruiter, Swers, Floritz and De Wilde, all great names in history, on the other. It was the first time Blake and Tromp had met on equal terms : even the common seamen felt that the day was come to test their relative prowess, and they burned with zeal to begin the struggle. At the outset, all the advantages of position were with the Dutch, their ships had the wind, and were close up together ; and when their extended line of fire opened on the English vanguard, it seemed almost impossible for about twenty ships to withstand the crash of such tremendous broadsides. As usual, the *Triumph* was the first to engage, and the *Brederode*, ever in the van, advanced to meet her, reserving fire till the two vessels were within musket-shot of each other, and her charge could be delivered with the most deadly effect. With a strong breeze in his favour Tromp shot by the *Triumph*, pouring a fearful broadside into her as he passed ; and then, suddenly tacking round, fired a second close under her sails, splintering masts and spars, tearing canvass and cordage, and strewing the decks with heaps of killed and wounded men. With this fiery salute the two Admirals parted company for the day, Penn dashing in with the *Speaker* and other vessels to cover Blake from some part of the circle of fire in which he lay exposed to destruction. The battle became general as the other divisions of the English fleet came up. On both sides the wreck was awful. In less than an hour after the first shot was launched from the guns of the *Triumph*, the sea was covered with spars, torn sails and

broken planks. Almost every ship engaged in the action
had already had its cables cut asunder and its masts shot
away. One moment an English crew were seen boarding
a Dutch man-of-war, the next moment the boarders were
driven back, and their own vessel was assailed in turn.
Here there was a ship wrapt in flames; there one was
going down with all her men on deck, their cries unheard
or their terrors unheeded by friend or foe; elsewhere a
fearful explosion sent decks and crews whirling into the
black and lurid atmosphere. It is said in contemporary
accounts, that the tremendous roar of the artillery could
be heard along the shores of the Channel, from Boulogne on the one side to Portland on the other. About
mid-day Monk came up with the white division, and
from time to time the other ships joined in the contest,
thenceforward fought on nearly equal terms. De Ruiter kept up the credit of his old renown. Early in the
battle he had singled out and engaged with the *Prosperous*, a hired merchantman of forty guns, commanded by
Captain Barker; but the fire of the English ship was
maintained with such resolute steadiness that he grew
impatient with the result of his distant fighting; and ordering a boarding-party to prepare for action, he ran his
ship alongside the enemy, when his Dutchmen gallantly
leaped on her deck pistol and sword in hand. The
close combat lasted a few seconds only. Driving the
assailants back to their ship, Barker threatened De
Ruiter in his turn; but the brave old seaman, shouting
in his fierce humour to the men, " *Come, my lads, that
was nothing—at them again!*" led them to a second and
more furious assault. With their numbers reduced and

their ship unmanageable, Barker and his officers were
unable to resist this murderous onset, and they were
all made prisoners. At that very instant Blake came
to their assistance with several vessels. The prize
was instantly recovered, and De Ruiter himself almost
surrounded by the English. Vice-admiral Evertz and
Captains Swers and Kriuk hastened to relieve their
countryman from his dangerous position, and the battle
soon raged round this new centre with extraordinary
violence. Penn's ship, the *Speaker*, was so shattered
by the guns, that she was considered no longer fit for
such service; and as soon as night put an end to the
engagement of that first day, he was despatched to the
Isle of Wight for the guard left at that station. Kriuk,
in the *Ostrich*, fought like a true sailor, till his rigging
and masts were shot away to the very hull, and his deck
was covered with the dead bodies of his comrades. At
last, he was boarded by the English; but as the unfortunate vessel appeared to be sinking, and her officers
and crew were nearly all killed or wounded, the boarders
made a hasty plunder of her contents and left her to her
fate. De Wilde offered his aid in an effort to bring her
off; but a sudden calm came on, and not having a yard
of sail still spread, the attempt to tow her away failed,
and she was again abandoned. Next morning, Blake
found her floating at her own will, the unburied corpses
lying where they had fallen the previous day, and not
a living soul on board! The fearless Captain Swers
—afterwards the distinguished admiral of that name—
was taken prisoner. Seeing his comrade, Captain De
Port, roughly used by two English frigates, he flew to

the rescue with his ship, and the four enemies were immediately locked together. De Port's ship was struck between wind and water and began to fill; he himself was severely wounded by the fall of a huge splinter; nevertheless, he continued to encourage his men by shouts, and to flourish his hanger as he lay on his back writhing in agony, until ship and crew all went down into the great deep together. Effective as the Dutch cannonade had hitherto been thought, it was no match for the destructive fire of the English frigates; and after a desperate struggle, in which the enemies proved themselves worthy of each other, Swers' ship also went down, himself and several of his officers and crew being taken on board the frigates and their lives preserved. Towards dusk, Blake felt himself strong enough to detach a number of his swiftest sailers with orders to gain the wind, and if possible prevent the escape of that vast fleet of rich traders; but Tromp saw the movements of this squadron, and guessing its motive fell back with a great part of his fleet, so as to cover the convoy. This retreat put an end to the first day's engagement; for seeing their Admiral turn his face from the enemy, some of the Dutch captains hoisted sail and fled away under cover of the gathering darkness. Blake remained master of the scene of action, but his ships were too far damaged and his men too much exhausted to permit of an active night-chase in mid-winter. Heroic valour had characterised the officers and men on both sides. The Dutch had had eight men-of-war either taken by the enemy or destroyed. The *Prosperous*, the *Oak*, the *Assistance*, the *Sampson*, and several other English ships had been boarded and captured during some period of the day, though every vessel was afterwards recovered. The *Sampson* was our only loss on that day. Its brave commander, Captain Button, and nearly all his crew being slain, Blake took out of her the remaining officers and men and allowed her to drift away. This excepted, no other ship in the English fleet had suffered so severely as the *Triumph*. Her able captain, Andrew Ball, fell that day covered with glory; Sparrow, the Admiral's new secretary, was shot down at his side; and nearly half of the entire crew had been swept into eternity. Blake himself was wounded in the thigh, and the same ball which lamed him for the remainder of his life, tore away part of Deane's buff coat. The enemy's loss in men could not be ascertained; it was known to be very great by the entire clearance of more than one vessel, and the decks and guns of the captured ships were so horribly spattered with blood and brains, as to sicken and appal the most callous of the victors.[1]

As soon as night came down, Blake's first care was to relieve the agonies of the wounded by sending them on shore to the well-prepared hospitals, where persons of all ranks and opinions vied with each other in the endeavour to promote their comfort and recovery; collections of money, clothes and linen being made for them throughout the West and the defects of the service made good by the spontaneous enthusiasm of the people. His own wound, though not really dangerous,

---

[1] Blake, Deane, and Monk to Speaker of the House, Feb. 27, in Parl. Hist. xx. 116-127; Cornelius Tromp, 88-94; Clarendon, v. 285; Heath, 335; History and Life, 69; Hoste's Art des Armées Navales, 90.

demanded repose and proper medical treatment; but he
would on no account listen to the friends who urged
him to go on shore and seek for himself the relief which
he had put in the way of his humblest comrade.   The
two fleets lay almost close together, with their lights
streaming all night across the wintry sea as beacons
for each other's guidance.   Until dawn the next day,
every effective hand on board the English fleet was employed in restoring sails, stopping leaks, cleaning guns,
and otherwise repairing the waste of war; every thing
was made ready to renew the contest on the morrow,
for a dead calm had succeeded to the fresh breeze blowing when the battle began, and if this calm should continue, it was thought impossible for the Dutch to avoid
another battle.   But as day broke a light wind sprang
up, and Tromp, anxious now to take home his convoy
in safety, disposed his fleet in the form of a crescent,
the two hundred traders in his centre, and crowding
every inch of sail that he could spread out stood directly
up the Channel.   Blake followed with his whole power;
the breeze which favoured the flight also aiding the
pursuit; yet it was twelve o'clock before the *Triumph*
came within gunshot of the rearmost enemy, and nearly
two before the main body came up with them off Dun-
geness.   Again compelled to fight, Tromp ordered the
merchants to make sail for the nearest Dutch port, keeping close under the French shore between Calais and
Dunkirk for protection, and then turned like a pan-
ther on his pursuer.   The battle was renewed on both
sides with fury.   De Ruiter gave fresh proofs of his
courage; but the fortune of war was still against him.

After some hours of this second engagement his vessel became unmanageable, and would have fallen into the enemy's hands had not Tromp seen his danger and sent Captain Duin to bring him out from the fight. With great difficulty he was extricated from his position and carried away. An hour or so later Tromp also began to fall back towards Boulogne, still, however, contesting every wave, and the mingled rout and battle lasted until night again separated the hostile hosts.

Fortunately for the English fleet, though the air was bitterly cold, the sky was unusually clear for winter, so that the enemy's lights served them as polar stars and enabled their ships to keep pretty close together and well up for the new battle of the morrow. On the second day Blake had captured or destroyed five Dutch men-of-war. The advantages gained by the recent reforms came out clearly in face of the enemy : — the Admirals had not a single complaint to make as to the courage, steadiness and unity of purpose displayed by the inferior officers. In the Dutch fleet, on the contrary, want of concert, party-bitterness and personal envy, combined to clog the genius of the great commander. At the close of the second day's engagement several captains of ships sent word to the *Brederode* that they could resist no longer, pleading want of powder as an excuse, and Tromp was compelled to send these men away from the main body in the night so as to prevent the treason and cowardice from spreading to the other ships. To conceal the true nature and cause of this defection, he made a pretence of giving them instructions to take up a new position to windward of the convoy, and make such a show of resistance as would keep the English frigates from coming too near. But this device failed of its own weakness. When daylight dawned, Blake saw at a glance that the fleet had been considerably reduced, and inferring that a squadron had been despatched in the night to cover the flight of the merchants, he sent off a division of fleet sailers, drawing little water, in pursuit of them, while he himself bore down once more with the main body on his reduced but still unconquered enemy. Tromp fought, as usual, with the most desperate courage: but he had now little hope, with his broken and divided power, of doing more than occupy Blake until his richly laden convoy could run into the nearest port. Even this was doubtful. After the first shock of the third day's battle, he sent Captain Van Ness to the merchants, with orders for them to crowd sail and make for Calais road, as he found himself unable to afford them more than a few hours' protection from the enemy. As the fight grew fiercer, he sent his Fiscal or Treasurer to urge them to press on faster, or the English frigates would soon be amongst them. But the wind was then blowing from the French coast, and notwithstanding his energetic attempts, Van Ness was unable to carry such a number of disorganised ships sufficiently near land to be out of danger. More than half the Dutch frigates and men-of-war had now been taken, sunk or scattered; and considering that it was a species of insanity in Tromp to continue the engagement until they were all destroyed, the other captains, contrary to their express orders, retreated on the flying convoy. Confusion then reached its height. Some of the English frigates came up; and the merchants, in their alarm and disorder, ran foul of each other, knocked themselves to pieces or fell blindly into the enemy's power. Still fighting with the retreating men-of-war, Blake arrived in the midst of this strange scene late in the afternoon, and finding several ships run against him, as if desirous of being captured, the thought occurred to him that this was a device of his wily adversary to stay the victorious pursuit, and give time to rally some part of the discomfited fleet,— and he issued strict and instant commands that every war-ship still in a condition to follow and fight the enemy should press on with all its force against the main body, leaving the traders in their rear to be watched and seized by the frigates already assigned to that service, or driven into ports whence it would be easy to recover them should the Dutch fleet be swept utterly from the Channel. Darkness alone put an end to the exciting chase. Tromp ran in under the French shore, some four miles from Calais, where he anchored the remnant of his once mighty fleet—now reduced to less than half the former number of masts, besides being damaged in every part. Blake consulted pilots and others well acquainted with the coast, as to what Tromp could do in his new position; and the general opinion of these men was, that the Dutch could not weather the coast of Artois, as the wind and tide then were, and would be compelled to come out again to sea in order to get home. He therefore cast his anchors and sat down to repair his damages. The night was unusually dark, with a high gale blowing, so that the enemy's

lights could not be seen; and when day again dawned
the sea was clear in that direction, Tromp having slipped
away and tided towards Dunkirk, whence he got off
into the harbours of Zealand. By twelve o'clock in the
morning, Blake was ready to give chase; but no enemy
being then visible, and feeling that it would be useless to
follow the runaways into the flats and shallows of their
own coast, he stood over towards England, and the gale
still rising, carried his fleet and prizes into Stoake's
Bay, whence he and his colleagues in command wrote
to inform the House of their success.[1]

Extremely false and exaggerated accounts of the
great Battle of Portland were published in the two
countries. Excepting the loss of their traders, the
States-General tried to make the world believe that
their fleet had done as much mischief as it had suffered:
—but when Tromp was asked to sail against the enemy
unencumbered by a convoy, he frankly confessed that
his best war-ships had already lost or destroyed.
In their report to Parliament, the English commanders
stated that their loss was confined to the *Sampson*, the
vessel turned adrift the first night of the engagement,—
and that their gain from the enemy was seventeen or
eighteen men-of-war and a large fleet of merchant-ships,
the precise number not being ascertainable at once, as
the prizes had been carried into different ports. Sixteen
sail were brought into Dover. Altogether it is probable
that more than fifty of these vessels fell into English
hands. On both sides the loss of life was great. The

---

[1] Elegiac Enumeration, 17, 18; Blake, Deane and Monk to Speaker,
Feb. 27; Cornelius Tromp, 94-105; Hoste, 90.

Dutch captains, Balk, Van Zaanen, De Port, Spanhem, Regemorter, Fokkes and Allart were all slain: Swers, Schey and Van Zeelst were taken prisoners. England had to mourn the deaths of three of her bravest captains —Ball, Mildmay and Barker. Blake himself was severely wounded, as were also his gallant Rear-admiral, Lawson, and many other of the most distinguished persons on board.[1]

In London the first news of this terrible battle was received with boundless enthusiasm. At last the two nations had met on a fair field; the genius, strength and courage of the officers and men had been fairly tried; and the Commonwealth had gained a splendid victory. Special letters of thanks and congratulation were written to the three commanders. A day of general thanksgiving was appointed. Parliament began an immediate subscription in behalf of the wives and children of such as had fallen in the action: and a short time afterwards a public provision was made by the State itself for their support. Troops of horse escorted the prisoners from the various ports where they had been landed to London, and in every town through which these cavalcades passed on the journey the people rang the joy-bells in celebration of the battle. As to Blake himself, less mindful of his own wound than he was of the hurts of his humblest companion, he remained in St. Helen's road and about the Solent for some weeks after he had received it, refitting his ships, taking in fresh stores, and preparing to chastise the Brest privateers, who still infested the seas and made spoil of English and other traders engaged in

---

[1] Heath, 335, 336; Hist. Parl. xx. 120.

the commerce with Ireland.[1]   But in April he received
information on which he could rely that Tromp was
making great efforts to equip another fleet.   With a
hundred sail he appeared before the Texel, where he
found about seventy Dutch men-of-war and frigates;
his vanguard fired into them as soon as he came within
gunshot, when they hastily retreated, leaving fifty of their
doggers behind as prizes for the enemy.   Tromp had
already gone out on convoy service; but no longer able
or willing to try the Channel passage, he was obliged to
go round the north of Scotland to meet the fleet of Spanish and Levant merchants.   He contrived by consummate seamanship to bring his ships safe home, though
the wits of London and Westminster had their laugh at
the expense of that top-gallant humour which had so
lately threatened to brush the English navy from the
seas in which he no longer dared to shew his pennons.
Leaving him for the present secure in his fortified and
inaccessible ports, Blake sailed towards the North with
a small squadron, while Monk and Deane returned with
eighty sail into the Downs where they witnessed and ac-
quiesced in Cromwell's dispersion of the Long Parliament and in his assumption of supreme power.[2]

The precise objects of this northern cruise have not
been clearly stated.   But as it had the effect of removing from the Downs and from the great majority of his
naval comrades a popular commander, known for his
sincere attachment to the Commonwealth, at the very
moment when Cromwell had resolved to venture on the

---

[1] Blake and Penn to Navy Com., March 7-18, Dept. Mss.

[2] Hist. Parl. xx. 121; Cornelius Tromp, 165.

rash, indecent and unlawful act of dispersing by brute
force the representatives of the nation, it is not difficult
to surmise by whose intrigues the Council of State had
been induced to urge it. His separation from the fleet
—his removal to a distance from the scene of action—
were necessary precautions; from the other generals
and admirals Cromwell had little to fear. Monk was
the obsequious creature of his will. Deane was a mere
soldier without opinions. Penn was never likely to be
found on the weaker side. But Blake, like other sincere and moderate Republicans, had accepted the death
of Charles as the term of monarchy in this country.
A Council of State, freely elected out of the whole
body of representatives, and responsible to Parliament
for their public conduct, seems to have been the form of
government which he desired to see prevail. Soldier as
he was, he strongly repudiated the rule of the sword.
Between Blake and Cromwell there were strong points
of contrast as well as of resemblance. Both were sincerely
religious, undauntedly brave, fertile in expedients, irresistible in action. Born in the same year, they began
and almost closed their lives at the same time. Both
were country gentlemen of moderate fortune. Both
were of middle age when the revolution came. Without
previous knowledge or professional training, both attained to the highest honours of the respective services.
But there the parallel ends. Blake's patriotism was as
pure as Cromwell's was selfish. Anxious only for the
glory and interest of his country, the great seaman took
little or no care of his personal aggrandisement. His
contempt of money, his impatience with the mere vani-

ties of power, were supreme. With his most creditable aspirations the Lord-General mingled views of personal profit; he coveted power, place and patronage for himself —wealthy and aristocratic connexions for his children. Open to the lowest order of corrupt influences in his own person, Cromwell never scrupled to appeal to the sense of private interest in others. Blake abhorred bribery in all its shapes; he even carried his objection so far as to declare against the custom of giving parliamentary rewards for any but the most extraordinary and meritorious services. By nature Cromwell was dark and suspicious; Blake was frank and open to a fault; his heart was in his hand, and his mind ever on his lips. In military genius, in command over men, in faculty for organising crude materials into actual power—they were perhaps at once equal and unequalled. In the highest moral attributes of manhood—in honesty, modesty, generosity, sincerity and magnanimity, Blake was far superior to Cromwell; and if he ultimately became in the world's eye the second man in England, it was chiefly, if not solely, because his nature and his principles forbad him to contend with the weapons of his rival.

On the famous 20th of April 1653, Blake was quietly cruising with twenty ships between the Friths of Forth and Moray, when the troopers marched down to Westminster and cleared the House. Vane, Sidney, Lenthall, Marten and others opposed the illegal violence of the Lord-General. He abused them in coarse and characteristic language, added insult to injury, and turned them out of doors. Next day he dissolved the Council of State. On the 25th a council of officers in London declared for

Cromwell, and the same afternoon brought despatches from Deane and Monk, with their adhesion and that of certain captains of their fleet to the number of thirty-three. Penn and the officers with him all signed to the same effect. But neither the Admiral himself, his brother Benjamin, nor his nephew Robert, set their hands to these documents, so that the name of Blake does not occur in the papers which carried to the usurper an assurance that his violence would not be opposed by the navy.[1]

That Blake was dissatisfied with a change that soon condemned Algernon Sidney to the privacy of Penshurst, consigned Sir Harry Vane to a prison, and drove many of the liberal and moderate men whose opinions he shared, into private life, there is no reason to doubt. To his friends and associates he made no secret of his resentment. Had he been in his place in the Council of State when Cromwell entered, there would probably have been a louder and more important protest against the act of usurpation than that made by the Lord-President Bradshawe. But he was far away, and deeply engrossed with the duties of the service, when the deed of violence was done in Westminster; and before the intelligence reached him on his distant station, the change was an historical fact, formally accepted by the army and the fleet. From that moment he gave up politics. The gentry of Somersetshire returned him as their representative in the new Parliament; but he never sat again, or appeared in the House, except on the business of his department. The fears and intrigues of the

[1] Perfect Diurnal, April 25, May 2; Whitelock, 529; Ludlow, ii. 455; Hist. Parl. xx. 137; Clarendon, v. 316.

usurper caused him to be excluded from the new Council of State. In a Parliament without real power, even his fearless truth and uncompromising honesty could do little harm to the Lord-General's interests; while his very name on the rolls of the New Representative, lent a dignity to that assembly which Cromwell understood, and his admirers still claim as a sort of triumph for their hero. The case was different as regards the Council of State. Within that smaller and more powerful body, he might have proved a dangerous adviser and opponent so long as the great question of a settlement of the nation was still under discussion: it was, therefore, a necessary precaution, that, for a time at least, he should be excluded. Blake's opinions were known to be unfavourable to military rule, not only in England, but on the continent generally; and when the Dutch heard of a sudden revolution having been accomplished by the army in London, they at once leapt to the conclusion that their most redoubtable naval enemy would no longer carry on the war with the same vigour.[1]

In these hopes they were deceived. Calling his captains together as soon as the messengers arrived at the fleet before Aberdeen with the news of the day, he told them, that whatever might be their private opinions, he considered it to be his duty and their duty to act in their several posts, while out at sea, with good faith, and in such a way as would best conduce to the public peace and welfare. He spoke of the irregularities which had occurred in London; but he would not admit that in

---

[1] Thurloe, i. 293; Carlyle's Cromwell, iii. 260; Hist. Parl. xx. 178-183.

such a crisis, threatened as the country was on every side with foreign enemies, the fleet had any right to plunge the country into the horrors of civil war. When pressed by some of his captains to declare against the clique of army officers and their leader, he at once took up a position which he never afterwards abandoned. " No," he said, " it is not for us to mind affairs of State, but to keep foreigners from fooling us." Though he suspected Cromwell and abhorred military rule, he had manliness and patriotism enough not to deprive his country of such services as he could render, because it had allowed itself to submit in an irregular way to a power not of his choosing. And fortunately this resolution was taken with his usual rapidity; for Tromp, Evertz, De Ruiter, and De Witt, under the impression that the fleets of England were divided from each other and torn by discords, sailed from the Göree with 120 ships, brought together and manned in haste, for Dover road, into which they drove a few stragglers, took two or three prizes, and began to fire on the town. The fleet then in and about the narrow seas was divided into three squadrons. Deane and Monk, with the red flag, in the *Resolution*, had under their immediate orders 38 sail, carrying 1440 guns and 6169 men; the white division, under Penn, consisted of 33 sail, with 1189 guns and 5085 men; Lawson commanded the blue, composed of 34 ships, having on board 1189 guns, and 5015 men; making a grand total of 105 ships, 3840 guns, and 16,269 men. The Dutch were about equal in guns and men, though they had a greater number of vessels. Blake, meanwhile, having learned by mounted couriers riding

day and night that Tromp was in the Channel, and had
already fired into Dover, spread his sails and poured
impetuously down the north coast before a full breeze,
burning with desire to revenge that insult and re-establish
his invaded supremacy in the narrow seas.　Early in the
morning of June 2d, the two great fleets sighted each other
about three leagues from the Gable.　Lawson pressed
on in advance of his comrades, and charged through the
enemy between eleven and twelve o'clock in the fore-
noon, separating De Ruiter's squadron from the rest and
engaging it in a severe contest before the main body on
either side could be brought to bear.　In about an hour
Tromp was at the elbow of his gallant comrade, and at
three o'clock the firing was quite general.　One of the
first cannon-shots that swept the *Resolution* killed General Deane: Monk threw his cloak over the mangled
corpse of his colleague, and shouted to the men to avenge
his death.　Tromp had given out an extra quantity of
liquor, and for some hours the Dutchmen fought with
reckless and extraordinary courage; but when darkness
put an end to a long day's engagement, he found himself not less damaged than the enemy.　All that night,
while the hostile fleets, at barely gunshot distance from
each other, were trying in haste and disorder to repair
somewhat the waste of the past few hours, Blake was
riding with his division, full sail and with streaming
lights, for the scene of action, unaware of the day's
events, the loss of his old friend Deane, and the doubtful position of the great fleet.　All night the officers
and men, not a little dispirited at the death of one of
their old generals, watched and waited anxiously for the

signals of the Sea King. The summer morning dawned
early, but no trace of his coming could be descried on
the horizon. Fortunately, Tromp was unaware that
Blake was expected in the course of the day, believing
him to be too far north to be recalled so soon, and he
spent the whole morning in a series of skilful movements
intended to recover the weather-gage; but, owing to a
sudden calm which came on, he was unsuccessful in this
attempt, and about noon the fleets were again within
range of the great guns. The battle was renewed, as if
by mutual consent, at the point where it had ceased the
night before: it was maintained with energy; but neither
party could claim an advantage over the other until the
expected squadron hove in sight. Early in the afternoon, high above the din of battle, and breaking through
it as the thunder-clap bursts through the roar of wind
and rain in a southern storm, the explosions of his terrible artillery was heard by the anxious and excited seamen on the Hollanders' rear and flank; and the sound,
telling the tale of carnage and destruction in every crash,
roused them into new and more formidable life. The
young Captain Robert Blake was the first man to engage
the enemy; he broke through the Dutch line, vomiting
death from every gun, and was received with a tremendous cheer from the sailors of the fleet, to whom he
brought ocular proofs of their great commander's arrival on the scene. At four o'clock the battle ended and
the rout began. Tromp fought with the energy of despair; but nothing could stand that impetuous onset.
The men of the *Brederode*, roused to fury by the cries
and reproaches of their Admiral, boarded the Vice-ad-

miral—the *James*—but were repulsed by Penn's crew
who entered the *Brederode* with them, gained possession
of the quarter-deck, and would probably have captured
the ship, had not Tromp, resolved not to fall alive into the
enemy's hands, thrown a light into the powder-magazine,
and caused an explosion which sent the upper-deck and
the gallant boarders who occupied it into mid air—the
planks shivered into a thousand splinters—the men
horribly scorched and mutilated.   By a miracle Tromp
himself was scarcely hurt; but a report of his death was
spread about, and many of his captains, feeling that all
was lost, turned and fled.   De Ruiter and De Witt exerted themselves in vain.   After his marvellous escape,
Tromp quitted the disabled *Brederode* for a fast-sailing
frigate, in which he flew through the fleet to assure them
of his safety, encouraging the brave, threatening the
waverers, and firing on the timid as they fled.   But it
was now too late: the day was irretrievably lost, and the
brave old sailor at last and with great reluctance gave his
sanction to the orders for retreat.   As the flight became
general, a fresh gale sprung up.   Allowing them no
pause, the English admirals pressed hotly on their rear,
sunk many of their ships, captured several others, and
would have destroyed the entire armament had they been
favoured with two hours more daylight.   But favoured
by the dark night, Tromp sought shelter in the road before Ostend, and the next day escaped with the remnant
of his fleet into Weilingen.   Blake and Monk had to
report that among their captures they counted 1350
Dutch prisoners, including six captains, Verburg, Schel-
linger, Laurence, Duin, Fietersz, and Westergo: eleven

men-of-war, including a vice-admiral and two rear-admirals ; two water-hoys and one fly-boat. The other
ascertainable losses of the enemy included six men-of-
war sunk, two blown up and one burnt. In their own
fleet they counted 126 men slain and 236 wounded.
Several of their ships had had their bows shot away, and
the masts and rigging of many others were much shattered and destroyed.[1]

Intelligence of this great defeat threw the United
Provinces into a most dangerous ferment. The mob
rose in various towns, deposed the magistrates, and accused the government of incapacity and treason. The
Admirals offered to resign their commissions. Tromp
told the Deputies of the States that it was impossible to
fight the islanders any longer, unless their fleet could be
reinforced by a great number of large ships; and De
Ruiter boldly declared that he would go to sea no more
with such a fleet as they then possessed. In the Assembly of the States, De Witt spoke the truth still more
clearly out :—" Why," he said, " should I keep silence
any longer? I am here before my sovereigns ; I am free
to speak :—and I must say that the English are at present masters both of us and of the seas." This was the
opinion of the well-informed in both countries. The
naval power of Holland was for the time completely
broken, and the final battle of the war, hazarded and
lost two months later, was but an expiring effort made

---

[1] Monk to Navy Com., June 3; Blake and Monk to Cromwell,
June 4; Several Proceedings in State Affairs, June 2-9; History and
Life, 72-75; Tromp to the States-General, June 13 and 14 ; Skinner,
50-51.

with crippled means and under circumstances of the greatest discouragement. The condition of the Dutch flag-ship was but a little worse than that of their navy throughout:— "The *Brederode*," says Tromp, in his report to the States-General, " has received several shots between wind and water; and though we have had her caulked as well as possible, she still leaks so fast, that last night, in spite of all our pumps, the water gained on us above five feet in height: till the present time we have contrived to keep her above water; but if after all we find our labour lost, we shall be obliged to run her ashore." Under these circumstances the States began to think of peace, and a vessel carrying a white flag was sent with an agent on board, who was instructed to go to London to prepare the way for two fresh ambassadors fully empowered to arrange the preliminaries of a treaty.[1]

Though it kept the sea, the English fleet was in scarcely better condition than the enemy. After sending the wounded men on shore at Ipswich, where hospitals had been prepared for their reception, with strict orders that every care should be taken of their wounds, and every comfort afforded them during the progress of their recovery,[2]— Blake pursued the flying enemy, keeping his great ships out at sea to avoid the shoals and sandbanks, but running his frigates close in land and scouring every bay and inlet. His objects were, to place the coast of Holland from the Zwin to the Texel in a state of blockade—to intercept and destroy the Dutch trade—

---

[1] Cornelius Tromp, 131; Heath, 344, 345.

[2] Blake to Captain Salte, June 7, 1653, Dept. Mss.

to hinder the herring-busses and whaling-boats from going out on the usual summer voyage—and to keep the fleet closed up in the Texel and prevent its junction with that refitting in the Weilingen; and having determined on his plan, he collected such of his ships as appeared to be unable to remain at sea for some weeks to come, and sent them back to England with the prizes, himself remaining with the other portion of his fleet in the Dutch waters, capturing stray ships and holding the long chain of towns and ports between Ostend and the Ems in a state of perpetual alarm and irritation. His letters written at this time from before the Texel and the Vlie shew with how wide a range of obstacles he had to contend, and add new elements to the admiration excited by his victorious career. Five days after the battle he writes to the Board of Admiralty :—

"GENTLEMEN,—Since ours of the 6th present, we are got between the Texell and the Vlie, where we shall endeavour to hinder any men-of-war coming out from thence to make a conjunction with the Dutch fleet now at the Weilingen, as well as hinder their fishing and merchandising trade so near as we can.

" The ships sent for England with the Dutch prizes, of which you had an account in our last, we do desire they may be refitted and sent unto us so soon as possibly you can, and that the Commissioners of the Navy may be sent unto, to give order for as much victuals and water to be put on board them as they can well stow, also that so many other ships with victuals and water as can be got ready in that time, may come along with them, and for those victualling and water-ships now with

us, we shall use our best endeavours to get it out as fast
as we can, and dispose of it to each ship according to
their necessity so far as it will go, and then send them
back for recruits, whereby the charge of hiring more
ships for that service may be saved; but as yet we have
not had time.

"We do desire that two or three of the best-sailing
frigates may be hastened to us with powder and shot,
which is our great want.

"We have sent orders to all those ships and vessels
in Yarmouth road to repair unto us with all expedition,
and do desire that for the future no more ships-of-war
or others may be sent thither, but that they repair into
the Zwin, where we shall send to them and for them as
the service requires.

"We would gladly know certainly what quantity of
victuals there lies now ready at Hull, Yarmouth, and
Harwich upon any occasion.

"It is supposed as soon as the enemy is in a capacity
to shew his head, he will endeavour to attempt somewhat upon our own coast; but we hope you will take
care that he may be prevented, and if he shall come
again and shoot into Dover pier, that you will not be
much startled at it, though we assure you there shall
be nothing wanting in us to hinder him in that or any
thing else that may disturb the peace of this Commonwealth, so far as the Lord shall enable us.

"We do desire all diligence may be used to supply
us with seamen, and that the first ships that come may
bring as many with them as they can. We are," &c.[1]

---

[1] Blake and Monk to Navy Com., June 9, Dept. Mss.

Next day he wrote again, complaining that the ships were in very bad condition and much in want of powder and shot. But supplies came in slowly. Want and sickness increased day by day. On the 12th he wrote again:

"The 11th present came many letters of yours to our hands, several of them, bearing date in May last, are duplicates of some we formerly received, and have already answered as to the material things therein. The same day also came Colonel Goffe, Major Bourne and Captain Hatsell, and seven ships-of-war, with eleven victuallers and water-ships in their company. What their lading particularly is we cannot as yet give you an account; but so soon as it comes to our hands, we shall communicate it unto you, which we hope will be by the next; only this we have in general, that there are 140 barrels of powder in the *Samuel* merchant, and 172 in the *John and Katherine* (besides a quantity of shot) over and above their proportion; also 700 soldiers, which might have been serviceable unto us had care been taken to have sent bedding and cloths along with them, according to your resolutions at Chatham in that particular, which we hoped would have been adhered to; for want whereof they are likely to occasion much sickness amongst us, instead of answering your expectations.

"As soon as we have disposed of the victuals now come to us, we shall send the ships that brought it back again with what speed we can, that they may be recruited and returned to us; and we hope you will use all diligence for the hastening back the ships we sent into the river as a convoy to the Dutch prizes; we having many ships here will be unfit for service before they get to us,

s

let them make what haste they can. We sent the other day eleven ships and frigates to Harwich to wash and tallow, and then to complete three months victuals, as also to take in the ammunition remaining at Yarmouth for the fleet, and so to return with all speed.

" For those ships and frigates of Captain Badily's squadron, which we understand are in a capacity for service, wanting some men, we desire they may be supplied and hastened to us, the rather because we are informed there are eleven or twelve great frigates newly launched at Amsterdam, Enchuysen, and thereabouts, which carry fifty guns a piece, besides the ten men-of-war which came home with the French fleet. We understand some hammocks are come in a hoy to Harwich, for which we have sent, but hear not of the other necessaries of wood and candles, so often mentioned unto you, of which the fleet wants a proportion of six weeks to even with our present victualling. The 1000lbs. is now come in the *John and Katherine,* and John Poortmans intends to get it aboard to-day, which we hope will yet be serviceable; for the *Cock* and *Brier* which you mention are on their way towards us; the latter of them we conceive may be very useful in her station on the western coast, and therefore do not desire her here. We have desired Major Bourne to remain about Harwich and Yarmouth, the better to despatch to us the ships and frigates that are or shall be sent thither, and such other vessels with provisions as are necessary for the fleet; and also to maintain a constant and mutual correspondence between the Council of State and yourselves with us. The supply of ammunition you have made unto us, especially of shot, will not answer our present wants in that behalf, wherefore we desire the continuance of your care therein, that what further quantities can be suddenly provided may be sent unto us accordingly."[1]

About a fortnight later he complained that his stores and provisions were all run short; the beer, he said, was sour, the bread bad, the butter rancid, the cheese rotten. The amount of sickness on board was very great; and in spite of the enemy's present weakness, and the immense advantage of holding them in close blockade, he expressed a fear that, unless relieved, he would be compelled by want and sickness to return to England. His own health was bad, the consequence of his neglected wound, but of that he said little. The close of his letter, in which he had described one of his captures, gave excellent reasons for maintaining the blockade:

"It hath pleased God this last week," it ran, " to deliver several merchant-ships of the enemy into our hands, which was thus: Upon the 19th present some of our frigates, appointed to ply to and again before the Vlie, met with eleven sail, which proved to be Dutch ships, some of them come from the West Indies; and being ships of force, they fought for some time, but at length committed themselves to sailing as their securest way; whereby five of them escaped, but four are taken, one sunk, and another burnt. In this encounter Captain Vessey, Commander of the *Martin,* was slain, whom we understand hath left a poor widow with a great charge of children, whose condition we leave to your consideration. Upon the 22d some other of our frigates met

---

[1] Blake and Monk to Navy Com., June 12, Dept. Mss.

about thirty sail more to the northward of the Vlie, which being ships of no force endeavoured wholly an escape; but yet eleven of them were taken and some of the remainder scattered, and the rest got into port; two of these came from Swethland laden with guns, all new, whereof two are brass, and most of them carrying a bullet from 24lbs. weight to twelve, as we are informed, which we hope will be as seasonable for us as for them, had they escaped; there were no more amongst them had any guns but these two, the rest are richly laden for the most part; they are not all come into the fleet as yet; when they are, we shall send them in under the convoy of such ships as are least useful, also such sick and wounded men as are not fit to be kept on board; upon whose arrival in Lea road, whither we shall order them, we do desire speedy directions may be given concerning them as may stand with the good of the service. We intend also (if the Lord will) to make a trip over with the whole fleet upon the English shore, to see them out of danger, and then to return with what speed we can, leaving in the meantime so many of the best frigates we have to lie between the Dogger Bank and the Riff, to intercept the enemy's ships of trade expected home. We earnestly desire you will hasten unto us as many clean ships as you can, apprehending more service might be done than now is, had we a considerable number of them; also that you would send to Major Bourne that those ships now tallowing at Harwich may be expedited to us.

" We still continue before this place, sometimes at an anchor, at other times under sail."[1]

---

[1] Blake and Monk to Navy Com., June 28, Dept. Mss.

One more extract from this correspondence will complete the dreary picture of this victorious fleet, and will bring down the story of the war to the point where Blake was compelled by illness to go on shore :

"Since our last, wherein we acquainted you with our resolutions to sail with the main body of the fleet for Sowle Bay, we have had blowing weather for the most part, whereby we were driven to leeward as far as Flamborough Head; but are now, through the goodness of God, come thus far on our way, and hope to get into the place of rendezvous this night, or to-morrow morning at furthest, where all diligence shall be used to accomplish the end of our coming thither; and therefore desire that what victualling ships and others can be sent from London within the time limited for our staying upon this coast, may be expedited to us, and we have written to Major Bourne in the like manner for such provisions as can be sent unto us from Yarmouth and Harwich. Our men fall sick very fast every day, having at present on board this ship upwards of eighty sick men, and some of them very dangerously, which we hear is generally through the whole fleet alike, proportionable to the number of men on board; so that we shall be constrained to send a considerable number unto Ipswich for their recovery; where there is room enough for them and good accommodation, as we understand by a letter from Dr. Whistler lately come to our hands, to whom we have written that special care might be taken of them, and suitable provision made for them, according to their conditions; and do desire a considerable number of seamen may be sent unto us with what expedition you can, or else it is apprehended we shall be very weakly manned, to do service answerable to what is expected from us.

" We have this morning sent away the *Worcester* frigate for Chatham, being very foul, and wanting a new foremast, which could not be supplied here. We should have ordered him to stay in Lea road to receive your directions, but that we apprehended much time would be lost that way, being appointed to make his repair unto the fleet with all expedition. The captain of her is a godly and valiant man, whom, with Captain Newbery, commander of the *Entrance*, we do especially recommend for two of the best frigates now a building, which if you shall approve of and appoint unto, we shall deliver them commissions upon notice given. We hope you do not forget to send us paper and canvass for cartridges, with a considerable quantity of old junk for wads, our necessity in this particular having been several times made known unto you. There are two honest captains more whom we desire to recommend unto you for removes into some of the new frigates now a building, with good strength, viz. Captain Bragg in the *Marmaduke* and Captain Hermon in the *Welcome;* they are already in ships of good force but slow sailers, and do apprehend they would do more and better service if better provided. We earnestly desire you will send down to us as much victuals as will complete us to the last of September, if you can, or else the quantity of butter, cheese and bread that was lost in the *Golliott* hoy, of which we gave you an account already, being much in want thereof. We also desire you will hasten unto us what clean ships and frigates you can from London, for want whereof so much service cannot be done as otherwise might be."[1]

Next morning the fleet put in, and Blake was carried on shore more dead than alive, leaving Monk, Penn and Lawson on board to carry out and complete his plan for the final reduction of Holland.[2]

One more blow, and all was over. Taking advantage of the temporary absence of the blockading fleet, the Dutch squadrons of the Texel and Weilingen put to sea and effected a junction with each other on the south coast; but their shattered power was no longer capable of bearding their powerful enemy, and when the English admirals hove in sight at the close of the month, they endeavoured by flight to avoid another battle. Penn and Lawson won their brightest laurels in this final conflict with Tromp, Evertz and De Ruiter. The fighting began at dusk; but night soon parted the combatants. Next day a heavy gale and thick dirty weather prevented a renewal of the action. On the third day the last shot was fired. The aged and able Admiral of Holland received a musket-ball in his heart; and after his death the captains of his fleet fled away, the English for the first and only time in that war pursuing the fugitives without mercy, as the ruthless Monk had commanded them to give no quarter. They made no prisoners; they killed all who fell in their way; and after a few hours the contest became a massacre rather than a battle. The States-General, now thoroughly humbled, sent

---

[1] Blake and Monk to Navy Com., July 4, Dept. Mss.
[2] Monk to Navy Com., July 5.

ambassadors to sue for peace; the negociations were carried on without further interruption; and early in the following spring a treaty was made in which they formally conceded to England the honours of the flag—agreed to banish the royalist exiles from Holland—gave the East India Company compensation for its losses—settled a sum of money on the heirs of their Amboyna victims—and made amends to the English traders who had suffered in the Baltic. In modern times there had been no maritime war to compare with this, either as to the interests concerned or the magnitude of the operations conducted. In less than two years the English Sea-General and his officers had, according to our own computations, captured or destroyed seventeen hundred ships; the Hollanders themselves admitted that they had lost more than eleven hundred vessels. These twenty months war with England cost the States-General more money than they had expended during the twenty years war against Spain.[1]

Honours and decorations awaited the successful admirals in England. The Council of State proposed that Parliament should order two gold chains, each of 300l. value, to be made and presented to the two surviving generals, Blake and Monk. Two other chains, valued at 100l. each, were given to Penn and Lawson. Four chains of 40l. each were presented to the four flag-officers. Rewards and promotions fell to the lot of many of the inferior officers. Penn was raised to the rank of Sea-General in the place of Deane. Lawson

---

[1] Thurloe, i. 392-448; Paul Hoste, 78; Columna Rostrata, 132, 3; Sagredo Ms. in Lingard, xi. 225; Skinner, 51-53; Clarendon, v. 317-320.

was made Vice-admiral. Captain Badily—who had
recently fought and lost the battle of Porto Longone,
the only event of any importance which had occurred in
the Mediterranean during the Dutch war—was made
Rear-admiral at the same time. A sum of 1040*l.* was
voted for medals for the inferior officers and men.
Bonfires were lighted in all public places, and most conspicuously on Tower Hill. A day of general thanksgiving, as usual with the Roundheads after a great victory, was appointed. But all this time Blake lay at
home in a dangerous fever, and only heard the public
exultation at his marvellous successes through the occasional echoes which, in spite of medical precautions,
came to disturb the repose of a sick room.[1]

[1] Elegiac Enumeration, 18 ; Hist. Parl. xx. 206; Order in Council,
August 6, 1653.

CHAPTER VIII.

The Mediterranean.

DURING the remainder of the summer months of 1653, it is at least probable that Blake lay sick at Knoll, a country-house attached to an estate which he had purchased about two miles from Bridgwater. Fever, of a slow but obstinate character, arising in the first instance from his neglected wound, combined with other ailments, including dropsy and scurvy, then common to all men leading a seafaring life — to lay him for a while completely prostrate. But a land-diet, gentle exercise and his native air gradually produced a change for the better in his condition. Knoll was at all times a favourite retreat. When absent from his political and professional duties, it was his delight to run down to Bridgwater for a few days or weeks, and with his chosen books and one or two devout and abstemious friends, to indulge in all the luxuries of seclusion. He was by nature self-absorbed and taciturn. A long walk, during which he appeared to his simple neighbours to be lost in profound thought, as if working out in his own mind the details of one of his great battles, or busy with some abstruse point of Puritan theology, usually occupied his morning. If accompanied by one of his brothers or by some other intimate friend, he was still for the most part silent. Good-humoured always, and enjoying sarcasm when of a grave, high class, he yet never talked from the loquacious instinct, or encouraged others so to employ their time and talents in his presence. Even his lively and rattling brother Humphrey, his almost constant companion when on shore, caught, from long habit, the great man's contemplative and self-communing gait and manner; and when his friends rallied him on the subject in after-years, he used to say that he had caught the trick of silence while walking by the Admiral's side in his long morning musings on Knoll hill. A plain dinner satisfied his wants. Religious conversation, reading and the details of business, generally filled up the evening until supper-time; after family prayers, always pronounced by the General himself, and a frugal supper, he would invariably call for his cup of sack and a dry crust of bread, and while he drank two or three horns of Canary, would smile and chat in his own dry manner with his friends and domestics, asking minute questions about their neighbours and acquaintance; or when scholars or clergymen shared his simple repast, affecting a droll anxiety, rich and pleasant in the conqueror of Tromp, to prove by the aptness and abundance of his quotations that, in becoming an admiral, he had not forfeited his claim to be considered a good classic.[1]

During the whole period of this recovery he was in constant communication with his colleagues the Sea-Generals and with the Navy Commissioners. When his commission expired, it was again renewed; and not

---

[1] History and Life, 116.

an order of any consequence was given in that branch
of the public service on which his opinion was not first
taken. His brother Humphrey was named, with John
Sparrow, Richard Hill, Robert Turpin and Richard
Blackwall, a Commissioner for the condemnation and
sale of prizes,—an extremely responsible and lucrative
office.[1] In December an Act of Parliament named a
new list of Lords Commissioners of the Admiralty, at
the head of which his name appeared. A few weeks
later, though still suffering from ill-health, and lamed
for life by his late wound, he returned to active service,
going on board the *Swiftsure* at Spithead, with the new
Sea-General Penn, whose plain good sense and wide
range of nautical information were of great use to him
in his high station. The Dutch negociation was not
proceeding so rapidly as could have been wished; the
ambassadors, with the proverbial slowness of their nation, dallying with the English claims, he determined to
bring them to the point at once by an active renewal of
hostilities, no truce having been entered into by the two
powers. He had also some accounts to settle with the
Brest privateers, that port having lately grown into
another Dunkirk.[2] Spreading out his winter guard, he
closed up the south entrance of the Channel, and spent
most of his time in daily chase of such adventurous
craft as dared to try the narrow seas in preference to
the long voyage round the Orkney Islands, until the
treaty with Holland was actually signed and ratified by
the two governments. With this result he was ex-

---

[1] Admiralty Mss. 70, State-Paper Office.

[2] Blake and Penn's despatch, January 25, 1654-5, Dept. Mss.

tremely well pleased. Though his highest renown had
been gained in the Dutch war, that war had never
met with his private approval. Holland, like England,
was a Protestant State, and it galled him to think that
the two guardians of free thought and reformed religion should be wasting each other's power, while Popish
Spain looked haughtily on. A war against that empire
was his passion by day, his dream by night; like a true
Puritan, he suspected and hated the Spaniards as the real
children of Anti-Christ; and could he have chosen, he
would have waged none but anti-Popish and anti-pira-
tical wars. When he went on board the *Swiftsure*, he
carried in his pocket instructions from the Council of
State to lie at the entrance of Brest harbour and prevent
ingress or egress, until satisfaction was obtained for the
injuries done to English commerce; but on consulting
pilots and captains well acquainted with the coasts of
Bretagne, he found that the strong westerly winds generally blowing there would render it extremely hazardous for vessels to attempt to ride near the shore.
He therefore stationed a part of his squadron at convenient points, to watch and overawe the depredators,
while the main body kept out at sea in search of the
Hollanders.[1]

The progress of the Dutch treaty put an end to
the necessity for a winter campaign. The colleagues
returned to London; and Blake went down to Bridgwater in a new character, the formidable Sea-General
being suddenly transformed into a commissioner for

---

[1] Blake and Penn to Lords of Admiralty on Feb. 4, 14, 17, and 25,
all in Deptford Mss.; Elegiac Enumeration, 18, 19.

purging the churches of England, Puritan, Independent, Presbyterian, and all other, of ignorant, scandalous and inefficient pastors. From the cockpit of a man-of-war he passed into the chapter-houses of Somersetshire, carrying that stern and resolute spirit of reform into his new sphere of action which had already made him so conspicuous at the Navy Board. For the moment, the active part of his professional career seemed about to close; and a new world of public duties was opening before him, when government, having its own reasons, public and private, for wishing to keep him and his comrades at a distance from London, commenced the preparations for a new expedition. Cromwell kept the objects of this naval armament a profound mystery. Of course, it was soon noised abroad that the islanders were fitting out a new fleet; but the service on which it was to be employed—the commanders to whose skill and fidelity it would be entrusted—could only be surmised by friend or foe. France and Spain, constrained by the late issue of events to think with less scorn of the new Commonwealth, both waited with anxiety the fall of the thunderbolt. The war which had long raged between these two great European powers, exhausting both countries without producing a decided preponderance in either, rendered the friendship of England, now mistress at sea, of the utmost importance to both parties. That the armament then preparing was intended to take a part in the contest was assumed on all sides:—but into which scale would the swords of the Sea-Generals be thrown? Causes of dissatisfaction, both general and special, were not wanting with either country. Spain was the great Catholic power, and therefore the natural enemy of Puritan England. Its commercial system was prohibitive, and therefore opposed to the interests of our merchants and manufacturers. Its arrogance offended the national pride. The favour which it had shewn to Prince Rupert and the revolted fleet during the doubtful fortunes of the Commonwealth, was neither forgotten nor forgiven. But France, on its part, had afforded an asylum to the royal exiles, had allowed its subjects to attack the merchants of the Channel, had interdicted the importation of English silks and woollens into that country, and without an open declaration of war, both private and national cruisers of the two states had long carried letters of marque against each other, which they had executed at every opportunity. Up to the close of the Dutch war, England had favoured the cause of Spain as against France. Agents of that state had been allowed to recruit their armies in Ireland, and the succours so raised had enabled them to reduce Gravelines and invest Dunkirk. At a critical moment Blake himself had captured the relief-guard under the Duke of Vendôme, and caused the loss of this stronghold. But the urgent inquiries made by the representatives of the two crowns as to the object of the new armament were evasively answered by Cromwell, and no one could tell in what quarter the menacing storm would burst.[1]

Meanwhile the work of equipment was carried on throughout the summer and autumn months. As the ships became ready for sea, and the plans of the government came to maturity, the fleet was divided into two

[1] Thurloe, ii. 588, 638, 731; Clarendon, vi. 6; Scobell, ii. 335-347.

grand divisions : the first, entrusted to Blake, consisted of the flag-ship *St. George*, carrying 60 guns and
350 men, and twenty-four other sail, carrying altogether 4100 men and 874 guns ; the second, placed under
Penn, consisted of the flag-ship *Swiftsure*, and thirty-
seven other ships, besides two ketches, one hoy, and one
dogger-boat, the whole carrying 4410 seamen and 1114
guns.   On board the latter squadron about 3000 soldiers
were also placed, with General Venables at their head.
The gallant Captain Robert Blake went out with his
uncle ; Benjamin Blake, restored to his former rank, commanded the *Gloucester*, of 54 guns, in the Penn division.

Towards the close of the year 1653 these mysterious
armaments sailed from the Solent with sealed orders, the
smaller squadron passing by Brest towards the south of
Europe, the stronger bearing right away into the Atlantic, as if bound for the Isle of Barbadoes ; leaving the
minds of men, not only in England but on the Continent,
in a state of profound uncertainty as to their ultimate
aims.   At first popular opinion inclined to believe that a
great blow was to be struck at France ; and this belief
was fostered by the arts of the wily cardinal then ruling
the destinies of that country.   Every day rumours were
spread of an approaching rupture between the two
powers, and a body of troops was sent down to Dieppe,
as if to repel an expected invasion in that quarter.   Pub·
lic belief was so far mystified by Cromwell and Maza·
rine that it was commonly reported that Blake, with his
entire division, was about to enter the service of Spain,
and the price at which this powerful aid had been pur·
chased was actually named.   Many weeks elapsed before

the people learned the real nature of this armed demon-stration.[1]

The secret aim of the new government was to deal a great and sudden blow at the pride and power of Spain. Though the expedition had other objects, this was its paramount purpose. Envy of her colonial wealth, hatred of her religion, and impatience of her narrow views of commerce, combined with the recollection of ancient and unredressed wrongs of a more political character to give point and popularity to a war against Spain. Blake, with his flying squadron, was desired to watch the ports and rivers of that country, to intercept any ships enter-ing or leaving them, and, if possible, to cut off all commu-nication between Madrid and the West Indian Islands; while Penn and Venables, after raising a large additional force at Barbadoes and other English settlements in those seas, were to make an attempt on Hispaniola and San Juan, or, failing these, on the mainland of South America, between Oronooco and Porto Bello. The con-ception of this double campaign was masterly; Blake holding the mother country in a state of profound iso-lation, while Penn and Venables invaded and captured her distant colonies; and had it been executed with equal vigour and precision, it is more than probable that England would have founded an empire in South Ame-rica as well as in the North. But during the few weeks which must necessarily elapse before Blake's co-operation would be required in this service—no war being as yet declared against Spain, nor any intimation afforded her that the West India squadron was directed against her

---

[1] Heath, 366; Thurloe, iii. 103, iv. 452; Granville Penn, ii. 17, 18.

possessions—he undertook to seek redress for certain minor and more miscellaneous wrongs. Our traders still suffered from the privateers of Brest and Toulon. The Duke of Guise threatened an invasion of Naples, which it was thought due to English interests to impede, and, if possible, prevent. Rovers from Salee, Tunis, Tripoli, and Algiers, then and long afterwards the pests of European commerce, had recently captured and sold into slavery several crews of our merchantmen. The Commonwealth had also cause of offence against the grand Duke of Tuscany, who had formerly supported the revolted fleet, and allowed Rupert to sell his prizes in the port of Leghorn. The Knights of Malta too, equally zealous against heretics and infidels, had piratically seized some English ships. All these wrongs, suffered during the troubles on land, he received a roving commission to inquire into, rectify and redress; his powers being to that end as vague and extensive as the work to be done was novel and undefinable.[1]

Early in December, his squadron anchored in Cadiz road. He was received, not only by the Spanish authorities, but by the captains and officers of all nations then at that great emporium of trade, with extraordinary demonstrations of respect. The English residents crowded the beach, eager to catch a glimpse of their renowned countryman. A Dutch admiral, lying there with his fleet, lowered his flag in honour of the red cross. One of our tenders, parting from the fleet, fell in with a Brest admiral, on his way with seven ships-of-war to join the Toulon fleet, fitting out to cover the

---

[1] Burchett, 385; Thurloe, iii. 547.

operations of the Duke of Guise and check the movements of the English in the waters of Italy and France;
but on learning that it belonged to the English squadron
then at Cadiz, the Frenchman sent for the captain into
his cabin, when he told him he was at liberty to return,
invited him to drink Blake's health in a cup of Bur-
gundy, and ordered a salute of five guns. The renown
of his exploits had gone before him to the warlike ports
and towns of Barbary; and some Algerine cruisers,
having a number of English captives on board, brought
them as presents to appease his wrath. Every prince
and people in the south who had insulted or outraged
the Commonwealth learned to tremble at his approach.
In his imagination the Grand Duke of Tuscany already
heard the thunder of his cannon booming across the
waters of Leghorn. The terrified Pope gave orders for
a solemn procession, and the sacred Host was exposed
for forty hours, to avert the threatening calamity from
the dominions of the Church.[1]

As peace had not yet been ratified between France
and England, the Brest admiral, finding Blake's ships
spread cross the entrance of the Straits, feared to attempt
a passage in presence of so uncertain a friend, and fell
back with his re-inforcement to Lisbon. Meanwhile
news reached Cadiz that the fleet of the Duke of Guise
was still at Naples; and the English immediately drew
in their anchors and passed the rock of Gibraltar under
full sail, making their course directly for the southern
limb of Italy. When they arrived at Naples, the Duke
was gone; but whether into the Gulf of Venice, or that

---

[1] History and Life, 80; Thurloe, iii. 1.

of Genoa, they could not learn from any trustworthy
source. What appeared to be the best accounts described him as having sailed for Leghorn; and as soon
as the fleet had taken in bread and water, they quitted
the Bay of Naples—where they had received every kindness from the people, — and followed in pursuit of the
enemy along the Papal coast, well pleased with the
idea of making Anti-Christ tremble in the midst of his
altars and palaces. The alarm of the Holy City was extreme. Many of the rich citizens fled away from Rome.
Some buried their wealth in secret places — others
carried their effects, for greater safety, into the Um-
brian Appenines. Trains of monks paraded the streets
in penitential garb, and new works were hastily raised
about the chapel of Loretto to preserve it from pillage.
When the cause of all this ferment arrived with fourteen
sail in sight of the towers of Leghorn, he sent his
secretary on shore to desire instant redress from the
Grand Duke for the owners of all vessels which had been
seized and sold in his territories by Rupert and Maurice,
fixing the money value of these various injuries at the
sum of 60,000*l.* sterling. The Duke hesitated and protested; but on finding the Sea-General urgent and inflexible in his demand, he offered to pay down a part
of the money, and to confer with his friend and ally, the
sovereign Pontiff, about the residue. Blake replied,
that the Pope had nothing to do with the matter, and
that he expected the Grand Duke would at once pay
down the entire sum. This peremptory message brought
down thirty-five thousand Spanish pistoles and twenty-
five thousand Italian, together with information that some

of Rupert's piratical seizures had been disposed of in Roman ports. This information was peculiarly acceptable; and on its receipt Blake sent an officer to Rome with a demand for reparation. Doubts, equivocations, and even refusals followed on the part of the newly-elected Pontiff, Alexander VII. But remonstrances and supplications were of no avail; the right was clear; the power to enforce it was at hand; and ultimately the Pope's fiscal was obliged to pay down to the heretics twenty thousand pistoles : — probably the only money ever brought from Roman coffers to enrich the public treasury of England.[1]

Ever mindful of the religious interests of his countrymen, the Sea-General wrote a letter to the Grand Duke of Tuscany, urging him to permit the Protestants of England and other countries, whom pleasure or business might induce to settle in his dominions, full liberty to follow their own form of worship — a privilege not then formally conceded by any Catholic power in the South, though Jews, Greeks and Armenians, were all permitted the open exercise of their religion at that very time in Florence! No threat accompanied this request; but the imposing power of the Puritan Commonwealth and the marvellous successes of Gustavus Adolphus in Poland, roused the fears of even the least tolerant of the Italian princes, and the Duke rather deferred than denied the request of the bold heretic, alleging as his excuse for delay, the want of precedent for such a concession in any Catholic country. Blake contented the English

---

[1] Thurloe, iii. 1, 41, 103, iv. 464; Heath, 366; History and Life, 81, 82.

residents in Florence and Leghorn by a promise that, on his return to England, he would urge the government to adopt measures for effecting their object. Other business now demanded his attention. French pirate cruisers, reported to be growing more and more formidable to our peaceful traders in and about the Balearic Islands, required a check; he therefore sent the *Langport* and three other frigates to ply between Capo Palos and Majorca. Intelligence also reached him to the effect that a general rendezvous of all the Moslem fleets had been ordered by the Grand Seigneur at Tunis on an affair of great moment, probably with a view to an attack on Venice or some other Christian state. New orders likewise came to hand from London touching the Spanish Silver Fleets, then slowly wending their way from the New World towards Cadiz, which made it absolutely necessary for him to despatch his affairs in the Mediterranean and sail with convenient haste for the western coast of Spain.[1]

But sickness, foul weather and contrary winds detained the fleet near Leghorn. Two French vessels from the Levant, brought in as prizes, unfortunately communicated the plague to their captors. Blake himself was struck down by this new and terrible disease, and for several weeks he was unable to hold a pen or even indite a letter.[2] The winter storms also put the fleet in daily peril. On the 19th of January, Blake wrote from Leghorn to the Commissioners in London :—" My last unto you was only a postscript of the 5th January—sent by

---

[1] Carlyle's Cromwell, iv. 16; Thurloe, iii. 232, iv. 92.
[2] Blake Despatches, in Add. Mss. 9304-130.

the way of Antwerp—added to a duplicate of my former
of the same, being then under sail bound for Trapani.
Since which time it hath pleased God to exercise us with
variety of wind and weather, and with divers mixed pro-
vidences and strange dispensations never to be forgotten
by us, especially in regard that He hath been pleased in
them all to rouse His compassion to prevail against His
threatenings, and His mercy to triumph over His judgment. The day we set sail we had a fair wind at N.E.,
with clear weather and great hopes of the continuance
thereof, forasmuch as it had been a long time foul and
stormy before, almost ever since we came into the road.
The next day we had the wind at E. and E.S.E., sometimes at S.E. and S.S.E., but not much wind. We were
then engaged among many islands; a place of no small
danger, especially for a fleet. At night we, hauling up
our sails and it growing calm, we drove upon a sudden
so near Capua, that if it had not pleased God to spring
up a fresh gale in the very nick, the ship would have
been in hazard, almost inevitable, of perishing there.
The *Worcester* and *Langport* were in the same danger
with us, being nearer the shore than we, especially the
Langport, which was in much less than the ship's length
of it, being a steep and upright rocky place. The (*St.*)
Andrew and some others were also in no small danger.
But it pleased God wonderfully and in great mercy to
bring us all off in safety without any loss but of an
anchor and cable of the *Langport*. The next day, re-
taining still some hope of a favourable wind and weather
to carry us on our intended voyage, we kept plying and
turning to windward, and so continued till yesterday

morning, at what (which) time, there being no likelihood of obtaining our first intention, the wind S.S.E.
blowing very hard and murky weather, we were forced
to bear up for this place; where, although not without
much danger in our way, by reason of a shoal and rock
lying under water upon which divers ships have been
wrecked, we arrived yesterday by a most merciful and
good hand of providence, leading us, as it were, by the
brink of destruction into safety: for which we, in our
gratitude, have great cause everlastingly to praise the
Lord and His wonderful goodness, and to rejoice in these
His salvations with fear and trembling. So we doubt
not, when the papers shall come to your hands, your
hearts will likewise be filled with the thoughts of the
same and of His unspeakable love."[1]

The first day of good weather the fleet left Leghorn
road for Tunis, intending to pay a flying visit to Tripoli
and Algiers, after arranging some open questions with
the Dey, to impress those formidable corsairs with a
salutary dread of English power. On the 8th of February they anchored in Goletta road, having on the way
sent out a vessel to recal some frigates formerly left at
Trapani in Sicily; but even before his arrival on the
coast of Africa, Blake had learned that no gathering of
the Barbary powers was likely to take place at that time.
Nevertheless, there were accounts to settle with these
pirates; for years they had been in the habit of plundering English vessels, and carrying English crews into
the interior as slaves. Some of their depredations were
quite recent; and it was suspected that many Christian

---

[1] Blake's Despatches, in Add. Mss. 9304-98.

captives lived in their city in all the suffering and degra-
dation of slavery. War was their charter, its spoils their
source of revenue. The Dutch had tried more than
once to make peace with them, but they would not hear
the word : pirates by birth, education and policy, they
knew no power but that of the sword, admitted no law
but that of necessity. The Dey of this warlike and
lawless race hearing that the strange people, whose flag
had not waved in those seas within memory of the oldest
Mussulman, intended to visit his port and demand reparation for the past, guarantees for the future, formed a
temporary camp of several thousand horse and foot, light-
ened his heavy ships, and drew them in shore under the
guns of his great castles of Goletta and Porto Ferino,
raised a new platform, strengthened by batteries along
the inner line of the bay, brought out from the arsenal
his largest guns, and then, with all the pride and confidence of a barbarian, he waited the enemy's approach.[1]

Wisely considering that wherever the pirate powers
appeared in unusual force it would be for the honour
and interest of England to be near at hand, Blake, acting on the false report of an intended gathering, had
made a somewhat hasty and unprepared appearance before the walls of Tunis ; he had come to fight or to make
a passing observation, as the case might seem to require, rather than to higgle about terms and conditions,
to measure words and concoct articles with the usual
tediousness of diplomacy. For such slow work his fleet
was in no condition. The very sea in which he rode at
large was strange and hostile to him and to his country.

---

[1] Blake's Despatches, in Add. Mss. 9304-106; Thurloe, iii. 232.

England had then no Malta, Corfu and Gibraltar as the
bases of naval operations in the Mediterranean; on the
contrary, Blake found that in almost every gulf and on
almost every island of that sea, in Malta, Venice, Genoa,
Leghorn, Algiers, Tunis and Marseilles, there existed a
rival and an enemy. Hardly could he rely on the shelter
of one friendly port. Most of his supplies had to be
obtained from England; and there were not more than
three or four harbours, Naples, Cagliari, and Trapani,
for instance, in which he could obtain a common com-
modity such as bread, for either love or money. Foul
weather had seriously injured his ships, and the stock of
provisions already ran short; but being now within sight
from the graceful minarets of the town, it was thought
best before retiring, to try the effect of a summons, such
as had carried consternation through the palaces of Rome
and Florence. An officer was therefore sent on shore with
a letter from the Admiral to the Dey, giving an account
of the recent seizure, by Tunis pirates, of the *Princess*
and some other English ships, the names and cargoes of
which were duly specified, and concluding with a demand in the name of the Commonwealth of England
for their restitution, together with the instant release of
all English captives. After several questions and explanations had passed between the two powers, Commissioners were mutually named to consider these demands,
and they met on board the flag-ship, the *St. George.*
The agents of the Dey, professing the utmost readiness
to make peace, would undertake to respect the flag of
England in all times to come, but they steadily refused
to give up the prizes which they had already acquired.

Finding them puffed up with a vain pride in their own strength, the English commander ceased to negociate, sent some of his frigates forward to block up the entrance of the harbour, whilst he carried the *St. George* as close as he could under the guns of Porto Ferino, in order to obtain a good view of the coast and its means of defence. A council of officers, after a long debate, advised an attempt to enter the port with their whole squadron, and attack the great ships of the enemy under the very embrasures of the castle; but on consulting the locker, and finding there a great scarcity both of bread and liquor,— only five days' drink and fourteen days' bread,—Blake felt that it would not be wise to attempt so perilous a service without better provision. Under these circumstances he left Captain Stayner, one of his most distinguished officers, with the *Plymouth* and five other ships, to keep guard over the harbour, and if possible prevent the pirate fleet from escaping to sea, while he sailed with the remainder of his force to Cagliari, a friendly station on the south-eastern limb of the Island of Sardinia, to refit and provision.[1]

At Cagliari Blake found the *Langport* and the other frigates which he had sent from Leghorn to the Balearic Islands, with a new French frigate in prize and 3000 dollars obtained for the wreck of another French cruiser disabled by them and run on shore at Majorca. But Cagliari could not supply bread enough for the wants of the English squadron, and the Sea-General was obliged to send out vessels in all directions in search of this essen-

---

[1] Blake's Despatch, in Add. Mss. 9304; Winstanley's England's Worthies, 563; Thurloe, iii. 232.

tial article of diet. The *Langport* and the *Diamond* were despatched to Majorca and the Spanish coast for bread; the *Maidstone* and the *Hampshire* went to Genoa and the ports of Northern Italy for bread; the *Hope* was permanently stationed on the Sardinian coast to procure bread; two frigates were despatched to Algiers for bread or biscuit.[1] The want of these necessaries delayed his operations some weeks; but on the 8th of March, the *St. George* was once more under the guns of Porto Ferino, and an English officer at the Dey's palace trying to induce him to make reparation and render up the English captives without bloodshed. Vain of his strength, and confident that Blake had sailed away on the former occasion from fear of his tremendous artillery, the barbarian replied in insolent terms to every proposal made by this agent. He refused them the commonest civilities: even permission to take on board a little fresh water.—" Tell the Dey," said Blake, curling his whiskers in scorn and anger, " that God has given the benefit of water to all his creatures; and for men to deny it to each other is equally insolent and wicked."— The barbarian replied with defiance. " Here," said he to Blake's officers, " here are our Castles of Goletta and Porto Ferino: do your worst; and do not think to brave us with the sight of your great fleet."—A short consultation of the English captains took place, and the commander laid before them his plan. " We judged it necessary," he afterwards wrote to Secretary Thurloe, " for the honour of the fleet, our nation and religion, seeing they would not deal with us as friends, to make

---

[1] Blake's Despatch, in Add. Mss. 9304.

them feel us as enemies, and it was therefore determined in a council of war to endeavour the firing of their ships in Porto Ferino."[1]

The artillerymen on shore were at their guns, the horse was drawn up and the infantry disposed along the line of the harbour to repel the anticipated attempt to land, when, to the extreme surprise of the Dey, the English fleet again drew off, and stood out to sea without firing a single gun. Gradually the white sails faded from his sight. Night came down, but no enemy appeared in the offing. Next day all was still silent: the English fleet had vanished from before their eyes like the mirage of their own deserts. A second day elapsed, a third, fourth and fifth, but nothing was seen of those haughty islanders, of whose courage they had heard so much in the ports of Italy and Spain. To the spirit of defiance succeeded a feeling of contempt. All Tunis believed they had looked their last on that famous red cross; by degrees a false sense of security crept over the excited corsairs; their watchfulness relaxed, their ardour melted away; and when Blake suddenly returned from Trapani—whither he had sailed for the very purpose of throwing the pirates off their guard —he found them in a less organised and enthusiastic attitude of defence, though their means were still such as an ordinary man would have thought it madness to encounter.[2]

Late in the afternoon of April 3d, 1655, the English flag was once more descried from the towers of Porto

---

[1] Thurloe, iii. 232, 326, 390; History and Life, 83; Heath, 374.

[2] Blake to Thurloe, April 4, 1655.

Ferino. Soon after break of day on the following morning, without firing a single gun, the whole squadron
rode into the harbour before a light gale, and to the
amazement of the Turkish janizaries and artillerymen
on shore coolly proceeded to drop anchors within half
musket-range of the great batteries. The English had
prepared themselves for a terrible day. Long before it
was yet light they came on deck, and at a signal from
the *St. George* divine service was performed throughout
the fleet in an extremely solemn and impressive manner.
This pious act completed, orders were given to advance.
Captain Cobham, in the *Newcastle* frigate, was the first
to gain the corsair harbour; but he was quickly followed by the *Taunton, Foresight, Amity, Mermaid,* and
Merlin. Close in their wake came the great ships, the
St. Andrew, Vice-admiral Badily, first; the *Plymouth,,*
Captain Stayner, second; and the *St. George,* third.
These and other war-ships stationed themselves directly
in front of the castles and as near to them as they could
float.[1] The boldness of this movement awed the stout
hearts of the corsairs for a few seconds, but they soon recovered presence of mind, and here and there a ready
gun sent its iron contents crashing in amongst the masts
and rigging. The Dey now gave his final instructions, and the first broadsides from the English ships
were answered from the immense park of artillery displayed along the shore—not less than a hundred and
twenty guns of large calibre vomiting out death from
their brazen throats at the first discharge. In a short
time the fire of Porto Ferino was made to bear on the

---

[1] Book of the Continuation of Foreign Passages (1657), 30.

line of great ships, these fiercely replying with their tremendous broadsides against its solid masonry; and for two hours the air was torn and the sky obscured by the incessant volleys of flame and smoke, dense, hot and sulphurous. At the onset all the issues of the day seemed to lie with the artillery. Fortunately, the gale which in the early morning had carried the English fleet into the harbour, continued to blow during the battle, throwing volumes of impenetrable smoke in the faces of the corsairs and helping to prevent their cannoneers from taking accurate aim. On the other side, almost every shot from the ships told with effect on the castles, batteries and platform. Some of the guns were silenced and many parts of the breastwork were cleared by the cannonade; but the conflict was still undecided when Blake made a new movement, which had been in his mind from the first, but was not deemed practicable until that moment. Drafting a certain number of picked men from each ship, he lowered the long boats and sent them, under cover of the black sky, with instructions to row alongside the great corsair vessels, and throw into them a quantity of lighted brands and torches. One of his favourite officers, John Stoaks—a man who had served with distinction in the Dutch war, commanding the *Dragon* in the battle of Portland, the *Laurel* in that of the Texel, and who was at this time captain of the *St. George* —was selected for the execution of this important trust; and he achieved his perilous task with such consummate address, that in spite of a galling fire from the musketeers on shore, he succeeded in effecting a lodgment under the ports of the huge pirates, and threw into them his

burning brands. The work of destruction was then swift
and awful. The whole of the nine great ships-of-war,
the naval strength of the Tunisians, were at once wrapt
in fire. Even the assailants felt cowed at an event so sudden and so terrible, and the battle almost ceased at the
instant, as if both parties were entranced by the gorge-
ous spectacle. The frantic corsairs made many efforts
to stop the progress of destruction; but wherever the
fire appeared to slacken for an instant, a broadside from
one of the English frigates raked its deck, stirred up
the burning embers, and scattered the daring fellows
who had ventured to go on board. At last the decks
were abandoned by the pirates, and the red glare of the
consuming squadron shot up freely and furiously against
the sky, tinging with a hot and lurid light a scene which
the April sun could scarcely reach through the artificial
pall of battle. In four hours from the crash of the first
broadside, the work was done. The pirate ships, so
long the terror of peaceful traders, were burnt to their
very keels. The batteries on shore were completely
silenced, and most of the guns planted on the raised platform were either damaged or dismounted. The walls
of Goletta and of Porto Ferino had been much shaken;
several breaches had been made in them; and both strongholds might have been carried by assault had there existed any reason for their capture. But Blake's ends
had been accomplished in the destruction of the fleet. His
losses in this celebrated action amounted to no more that
twenty-five killed and about forty wounded; the loss of
life on shore, though the men fought behind breast
works and other cover, must have been very considerable

though it was of course impossible for the English to obtain an exact account of the casualties.[1]

After reading the pirates this tremendous lesson— to which there was scarcely a parallel in history until Exmouth's splendid bombardment of Algiers in our own time,—the English squadron sailed for Tripoli on the same errand; but the Dey of that place, warned by the fate of Tunis, received them with every demonstration of honour and regard; he acceded with apparent zeal to their demands, and entered into a treaty to respect the Commonwealth flag at all times and in all places. This summary dealing with the dependent powers of Turkey brought the governments of London and Constantinople into connexion and correspondence. Blake himself seems to have had some doubts whether his instructions, vague and ample as they were, would be held to justify him in entering the ports of a power with which his country was not actually at war, and destroying its fleets and fortifications. Had not the Dey's haughty words chafed his spirit, it is not certain that he would have proceeded so far without waiting for fresh instructions; and as soon as the action at Tunis was over, he despatched a full account of the incident to Sir Thomas Bendish, Cromwell's ambassador at Constantinople, which that functionary was desired to lay before the Grand Vizier should any complaints be made on the subject. The Turks were then at war with the Venetian Republic, and the destruction of so large a portion of their

---

[1] Elegiac Enumeration, 20, 21; Blake to Thurloe, April 4, 1655; Heath, 374; Clarendon, vi. 11; Book of the Continuation of Foreign Passages, 31.

fleet by an enemy hitherto unknown in the affairs of the Mediterranean roused their anger to a high degree; but the Grand Vizier hesitated to involve himself with a new and powerful enemy by any hasty expression of his resentment. Tunisian agents went to Constantinople to complain of Blake to the Grand Seigneur. They attributed their inability to defend their fleet and castles to the want of heavier guns; and the government immediately ordered six pieces of brass ordnance of the largest calibre to be despatched to Porto Ferino. Bendish was led to consider the Grand Vizier satisfied with Blake's explanations; but the incident was nevertheless a sharp thorn in his master's side; and for several months the English traders at Smyrna lived in fear of retaliations. Fear or policy, however, prevailed in the divan, and so long as the formidable Sea-General lived, the English residents in the Levant continued to pursue their peaceful enterprises without molestation.[1]

After settling his affairs at Tripoli, Blake ran into the Adriatic, where the Venetians received him with such honours as are given to royal visitors. His late actions had spoken in the most convincing language to the able and astute rulers of Venice, and they lost no time in offering friendship to the western Republic. On his return towards the Straits of Gibraltar, he again called at Tunis to inquire if the Dey were prepared to treat of peace. In answer to his first summons, a white flag was raised at the castle of Porto Ferino; and after some negociation of a merely technical nature, a treaty was signed and ratified in terms equally

---

[1] History and Life, 84; Thurloe, iii. 390, 513.

honourable and advantageous to England. The humbled
corsair even consented to allow an English consular
agent to reside at his court! A flying visit to the island
of Malta served to teach the proud and unprincipled
Templars some respect for the rights and properties of
heretical Englishmen. These priestly marauders believed themselves a serious power in the Mediterranean;
in some degree they made a pretence of being the guardians and the arbiters of Catholic Europe. When the
expedition under the Duke of Guise appeared before
Valetta, they haughtily refused to allow it the shelter
of their port. But the unceremonious manner in which
the Puritan Sea-General had exacted reparation from
the princes of Italy, and even laid his hands on Pope
Alexander's own coffers, warned them that their clerical character would afford them no protection from the
strong arm of English justice, and they prudently submitted to restore to their lawful owners the spoils of
their warfare against the heretics.[1]

There only remained Algiers. But force was no
longer necessary in dealing with the great pirate cities;
the blow struck against the system at Tunis had effectually cowed the corsairs from Tripoli to the shores of Fez
and Morocco. When the English squadron rode into
the Bay of Algiers, boldly as if on a visit of courtesy to
a friendly power, and Blake sent his officer, as usual,
to demand restitution of property and the liberation of
Christian slaves, the Dey received the messenger with
great civility, paid a handsome compliment to the English
Admiral, and to shew his good will sent a present of

---

[1] Elegiac Enumeration, 21, 22; History and Life, 84, 85.

live cattle to the fleet — an extremely seasonable and politic gift, which at once made him popular with the ill-fed seamen. With regard to the specific demands of the Admiral, he answered with great adroitness, that the ships and men captured by his people in times past, whether from the English or from other nations, had become the property of private individuals, most of whom had bought them at full price in open market; that they had been seized during a period of recognised and inveterate war between Islam and Christendom, when no treaties existed, and when therefore none could be broken; that he could not restore the captives without using violence towards his subjects, and creating general discontent, if not rebellion, in his dominions. He urged, moreover, that, considering the general prevalence of piracy in Europe as well as in Africa, the English required too much when they demanded the unconditional surrender of his prizes. Finally, if these objections should seem to the Admiral as clear as they did to himself, he said he would procure the liberation of all English captives then in his country at a moderate ransom per head, and enter for himself and his people into a solemn engagement not to molest English traders for all time to come. The humble tone of the pirate prince recommended his line of argument; a contract was therefore made for the ransom of all the captives at a fixed price, and the poor wretches were liberated and sent on board the ships of their deliverers. Before the fleet sailed from the harbour a noble and touching incident occurred, adding one more to the long list of illustrations of the English seaman's character.

The ships were lying in-shore, not far from the mole-head, when a number of men were observed swimming towards them, pursued by several turbaned Moors in boats; and on coming under the bows of our vessels, the fugitives cried to the sailors in Dutch to save them from their Moslem pursuers.   Forgetting that only a few months before they had been at war with their country-men, regardless of every consideration beyond the humane instincts of the moment, the sailors helped the poor wretches to clamber up, when they discovered that they were runaway slaves, and the men in chase of them their masters. Here, then, was a new difficulty! The Dey claimed the fugitives in virtue of the new treaty, and appealed to the accepted principle of compensation for all restored captives.   But the idea of giving back Christian men, even enemies, from the freedom of an English man-of-war into the hands of pirates and infidels was not to be entertained by Puritan sailors.   Some one suggested to his fellows a subscription : how much the Admiral himself paid into this fund he has carefully concealed, but every seaman in the fleet generously agreed to give up a dollar of his wages to buy the poor Hollanders their freedom.   A bargain was soon made, the money was paid by the fleet-treasurer, and the liberated men went home to tell their countrymen this story of the magnanimous islanders.[1]

Before the end of April 1655, Blake had brought this extraordinary cruise to a triumphant issue.   In six months he had established himself as a power in that great midland sea from which his countrymen had been

---

[1] Blake Despatch, Oct. 9, 1655, Deptford Mss.; Thurloe, iii. 527.

politically excluded since the age of the Crusades.   He
had redressed with a high hand the grievances of many
years, and had taught nations to which the very name of
Englishman was a strange sound, to respect its honour
and its rights.   The pirates of Barbary had been chastised as they had never yet been in history.   The petty
princes of Italy had been made to feel the power of the
northern Protestants.   The Pope himself had learned to
tremble on his seven hills; and the distant echoes of our
guns had startled the Council-chambers of Venice and
Constantinople.   Blake sent home not less than sixteen
ships laden with treasure, received in satisfaction of
former injuries, or taken by force from hostile states.
Some of the Italian princes sent embassies to London to
cultivate the friendship of Cromwell.   The representatives of the Grand Duke of Tuscany and the Doge of
Venice distinguished themselves in these missions by the
splendour of their appointments.   The former had orders to solicit the honour of a present of the Protector's
portrait, which was painted for his master by Cooper,
and hung in the ducal palace among the choicest pro-
ducts of Italian art.[1]

---

[1] History and Life, 89, 90.

CHAPTER IX.

1654-1656.

𝔖𝔭𝔞𝔫𝔦𝔰𝔥 𝔚𝔞𝔯.

THE correspondence between Blake and Cromwell, so far as it related to the affairs of Spain and the course to be pursued by the southern fleet, had been carried on in cipher, and all the instructions sent from London were regarded as secret. But the time was now come to throw off the mask. During the six months occupied by the series of bold and successful exploits which had established on both shores of the Mediterranean so salutary an awe of English prowess, the object of the expedition under Penn and Venables remained a profound mystery. Penn himself, when he sailed from Portsmouth, was unaware of the precise service on which his squadron was to be employed, for his orders were not to open the letter of final instructions until far enough from Europe to prevent any risk of their nature transpiring:—a very necessary precaution as the event proved, for that worldly seaman, already foreseeing the downfall of the Commonwealth, and anxious to secure to himself the future gratitude of the royal family by unexpected and splendid services in their cause, no sooner found himself at the head of a large fleet than he put himself into communication with the exile court at Cologne, offering to desert with his entire power from the

Commonwealth, and sail into whatever port should be named for that purpose. Had he known on what errand he was about to proceed when this proposal was made, he would unquestionably have told the Stuarts, who, in their turn, would have eagerly seized the opportunity of strengthening their interests at Madrid by forwarding such a piece of state intelligence ; and on the receipt of it there is no reason to suppose that Philip IV. would have refused to grant the use of one of his harbours in the Low Countries for the reception of the revolters. But having nowhere to receive so large a fleet—nor any means of supporting it, except piracy,—from which he was perhaps warned by the mysterious fate of his cousin Maurice,—Charles for a time declined the traitorous offer, and desired the Admiral to reserve his loyalty for some happier season. The expedition therefore sailed on its unknown voyage ; and it was not until late in the spring of 1655 that news arrived in Europe from the west relating the particulars of an attack made by Penn and Venables on the great Spanish settlement of His-paniola.[1]

The idea of a secret expedition to invade the peace of an island in possession of a power against which war had not been formally declared, would be to the last de-gree offensive to modern notions of public honour. But in Cromwell's time the peace of Europe was not fixed on certain bases. Commerce and colonies lay almost beyond the pale of law and treaties. No French ad-miral would have thought it right to plunder Lyme or

---

[1] Granville Penn, ii. 14, 15; Clarendon, vi. 5, 6; Carte's Coll. ii. 53.

Sandown; but not one in ten would have considered it wrong to seize the merchants of either port on the high seas.   By a curious political distinction countries might be at war in one latitude, though not in all—at sea when not on land.   The seizure of Vendôme's fleet had not led to a war between France and England.   The destruction of Rupert's squadron in the harbours of Carthagena had not interrupted the relations, such as they were, between London and Madrid.   Europe, indeed, had never known such a thing as peace on the high seas; from the Northern jarl to the African corsair, the strong arm had ruled from the feudal times on the highway of nations.   Even when England and Spain had seemed to be on the best terms with each other in Europe, envy, jealousy and distrust reigned in the New World, and the elements of discord often broke out there into open violence and bloodshed.   Cromwell affected to satisfy his conscience with the pretence that war already existed between the two countries in that hemisphere, and that an armament was needed for the protection of English interests in America.[1]

Real causes for a war with Spain were neither few nor remote, though it is probable that the most active were such as would exercise little influence over the minds of statesmen in the nineteenth century.   The first and gravest was the religious situation. Spain was ultra-Catholic, England ultra-Protestant. The most powerful and most warlike sects which supported Cromwell sincerely believed that Spain was the devil's stronghold in Europe.   The Reformed faith — tolerated in the Holy

---

[1] Thurloe, i. 760.

Roman Empire, in France, still more recently in Portugal—had never found mercy at Madrid. Racks, wheels, boiling oil, and other yet more delicate means of torture, opposed the spread of new doctrines throughout Spain and the Indies; while frequent burnings and gibbetings were employed to keep the masses true to the creed of their fathers. The horror excited in Puritan England by the report of such atrocities was naturally heightened by the fact, that now and then a foreign resident—even an Englishman—fell under the frowns of the Holy Office, and whatever his country or his creed, suffered, without appeal, the sort of judgment bestowed by that terrible tribunal. In fact, the Inquisition was the great obstacle to a solid and durable peace between the two powers. When the Spanish Ambassador first proposed an alliance, Cromwell made this one of his two essential conditions:—that English merchants living in Spain should be allowed to exercise their own religion, have the use of Bibles and such other pious books as they might require, and be free from the control of the Holy Office. The Ambassador refused even to transmit this demand to his master, and the attempt at negociation failed. Other causes tended to excite the war-feeling. The murder of Ascham had not been forgotten or forgiven; nor the favours extended and the shelter afforded to Rupert and his revolted ships at Cadiz and Carthagena. Among political reasons, the obstinate refusal to allow foreign traders to visit any of the ports of America and the West India Islands, was the first and strongest. Liberty of trade—freedom from the Holy Office: these were the two conditions on which the Protector offered to treat. "What," exclaimed the Ambassador, "my master has but two eyes, and you ask him to pluck out both at once!" Not being able to make terms with the Catholic court, Cromwell resolved, as far as it lay in him, to cripple its resources, and thus force it to respect the commerce and religion of Englishmen.[1]

Though Mazarin, acting on his famous maxim of state, seemed willing to give way on every point before the energetic rulers of the new Commonwealth, the causes of quarrel with France were not yet fully removed. The cruisers of the two countries still carried letters of marque against each other's ships; and daily encounters took place at sea without either accelerating or retarding the long and tedious negociations of M. Bordeaux. For three years this agent had been in London asking for peace. Crafty diplomatists fancied that Cromwell employed his time in maturely weighing the relative advantages of a French or a Spanish alliance, and the ambassadors of the rival powers intrigued day and night to gain his adhesion. To the surprise of the old formalists, he at length took a decisive attitude against Spain, without first attempting to hurry on the settlement of his differences with France. Fearless of every consequence, while Penn and Venables went out to attack Hispaniola, Blake harassed the trade of Marseilles and kept the Toulon fleet locked up in the Mediterranean harbours. Whenever his cruisers found ships at sea sailing to or from French ports, they seized them as lawful prizes. One of his frigates took a Ham-

---

[1] Ayscough Mss. 6125; Burton, i. clviii. et seqq.; Thurloe, i. 761; History and Life, 85, 86.

burg vessel bound for Marseilles, which he condemned.[1]
Another captured two Hamburgers and a Hollander; but
as he found by their papers that two of these were not
bound for French ports, they were set free; the other,
carrying goods to Rouen, was confiscated. Such incidents occurred almost daily. Loud and bitter complaints were made by men in business at the delay of
peace; discontents spread to other classes; and Bordeaux was urged by his countrymen to conclude a treaty
with the Commonwealth at almost any sacrifice, rather
than continue a state of things so wounding to the pride
and disastrous to the commerce of France.[2]

Even the pride of Louis XIV. yielded to the interests of his country. He treated on Cromwell's own
terms. The point of honour and precedence was waived;
Louis consented to banish the Stuart Princes, together
with Hyde, Ormonde, and fifteen other of their adherents, from the soil of France; maritime hostilities were
at once to cease between the two nations; and the treaty
was on the very eve of signature, when news arrived in
London of the horrible massacre of the Vaudois by the
soldiers of the Duke of Savoy, an intimate friend and
ally of the King of France. No event in history had
ever fired the Protestant passions of the English people
like the atrocious invasion of those Piedmont valleys.
Fasts, prayers, denunciations, offered themselves as vents
for the national fervour; collections of money were made
for the sufferers in all the churches of London; and some
of the bolder spirits proposed to send an army to the

---

[1] Letter of Intelligence, Cadiz, June 13, 1655, Dept. Mss.

[2] Thurloe, iii. 487, 619-653.

Savoy Alps ; a project to which the Government was
not altogether averse. But for the moment Cromwell
trusted to his influence over Mazarin as the best means
of obtaining justice for those poor Protestant villagers.
He told Bordeaux that he would not make peace with
his master until he knew his sentiments on the subject of the massacre and banishment of the Vaudois;
and Blake received orders to uphold Protestant interests in the south with all the power at his command.
The presence of an English fleet in the Mediterranean
gave plenary force to Cromwell's suggestions. At first
the Ambassador of Louis contended that France had
nothing to do with the matter,—that the Duke of Savoy
was an independent prince, — that the Vaudois were
rebels as well as heretics, and had justly incurred chastisement at the hands of their sovereign. Cromwell remained inexorable ; and Bordeaux's master was at last
compelled to interfere. Under the double pressure of
English and French remonstrance, the Duke of Savoy
granted a full amnesty to the Vaudois, and confirmed
to them their ancient right to exercise their own forms
of divine worship by a new decree.[1]

Cromwell's letters informed Blake that, in consequence of the blow about to be struck in the Western
Archipelago, his presence with the fleet, if not his more
active services, would be required on the Atlantic coast
of Spain ; and in consequence of these orders he sailed
from Algiers towards the Straits of Gibraltar. But as the
two countries were still at peace, he called at Malaga for

---

[1] Dumont, vi. part ii. 121; Thurloe, iii. 469-745. Morland, in hi
History of the Churches in Piedmont, gives ample details of this affair.

fresh water, when an extremely characteristic incident
occurred. A party of English sailors from his fleet, in
rambling about the town, suddenly came upon a procession of priests carrying a Host through the streets,
and instead of falling on their knees before the sacred
symbol, like the pious Spaniards, the Puritan seamen
laughed at and derided those who did so, until their
want of reverence provoked one of the clergy to call on
the populace to avenge the insult aimed at their religion.
A street fight ensued ; and with advantages of numbers
and local knowledge on their side, the Malagayans beat
the scoffers back to their ships, whither they carried an
English version of the fray to their commander. Indignation and true policy concurred in inducing Blake to
treat the affair gravely. In Lisbon, Venice and other
Catholic ports, mob-law had been applied to the sailors
of English merchant-vessels on the ground of alleged
want of respect for the mummeries of foreign worship ;
and considering the new relations which the two countries were about to assume, he judged it due to the
honour of his flag and necessary to the safety of his
countrymen, to shew the Spaniards that he could and
would redress such wrongs with promptitude and severity. Half measures, he felt, would be useless in such
a case ; so sending a trumpeter into the town, he demanded, not retaliation on the offending mob, as was
expected, but that the priest who had set them on
should be given up to justice. The Spaniards were
astounded. Give up a Catholic priest to the judgment
of heretics ! The Governor of Malaga replied that he
had no power over the offender, as in Spain the servants

of the Church were not responsible to the civil power.
" I will not stay to inquire," said the stern Englishman,
" who has the power to send the offender to me ; but if
he be not on board the *St. George* within three hours,
I will burn your city to the ground." And so he dismissed the messenger. No excuse, no protest, was admitted; and before the three hours had expired the priest
made his appearance in the fleet. Blake now called
accusers and accused together; heard the story on both
sides ; and decided that the seamen had behaved with
rudeness and impropriety towards the natives, and thereby provoked the attack of which they complained. He
told the priest that if he had sent an account of what
had occurred to him, the men should have been severely
punished, as he would not suffer them to affront the
religion of any people at whose ports they touched ;
but he expressed his extreme displeasure at their having
taken the law into their own hands, as he would have
them and all the world know that an Englishman was
not to be judged and punished except by Englishmen.
With this warning for the future, Blake, satisfied that
the man had been given up and was then completely
at his mercy, treated him with civility and sent him
back unharmed to his friends, who, on hearing an account of the affair, were delighted and astonished at
the magnanimity displayed by the terrible commander.
Cromwell was mightily pleased with this little incident.
He took the letters referring to it in his own hand to
the Council, read them out with a smiling face, and when
he had finished reading, declared that by such means

they would make the name of Englishman as great as that of Roman was in Rome's most palmy days.[1]

Early in June the fleet passed the Straits and anchored once more in the Bay of Cadiz, where they received a more than usually hospitable reception. By the treaties then existing between the two states, not more than ten English ships-of-war could claim to enter any Spanish port at one time; yet as a mark of extraordinary confidence and respect, when the Governor of Cadiz sent down a present of bread, flesh and vegetables to the *St. George*, he desired it to be intimated to the Admiral, that although the capitulations declared that " there cannot come in hither above ten ships-of-war at once, nevertheless his lordship might come in with all his forces and welcome." But Blake, expecting every hour to receive intelligence from London which would compel him to exchange pacific greetings for acts of vigorous hostility, would have refused this invitation even had he not suspected that a snare might be concealed under this show of extreme courtesy. He excused himself on the plea that he had only touched at Cadiz on his way, and could stay no longer than was required to take fresh water and other necessaries on board. In the city every effort was made to learn what he intended to do next. Whether his fleet was bound for England, Lisbon or the Barbary coast, could not be ascertained even by the secret agents of the Council of State. But among the best-informed English residents in Cadiz, rumour fixed on Salee, the famous rovers of which still harassed our

---

[1] Burnett, Own Times, i. 147, 148.

southern trade, as the scene in which the next grand naval spectacle would be exhibited.[1]

This mystery was soon cleared up. Barely had Blake shipped his cables at Cadiz harbour when news arrived from the Archipelago. Penn, it turned out, had sailed from Barbadoes to Hispaniola. There the regiments were landed and given up to the sole direction of Venables; who, through cowardice, incapacity or treason—for he also, though unknown to Penn, was in correspondence with the Stuarts,—frittered away his most favourable opportunities, and finally led his men into a disastrous situation, from which they were only rescued by the intrepidity of Admiral Goodson and a body of seamen, sent from the fleet for that purpose. The English had retired from the island disgraced and discomfited : — so far the expedition, begun with secret treason, had ended in a signal failure. But after this first overthrow, as the sealed orders required Penn to establish an interest in any part of the Spanish Indies, he sailed for Jamaica, landed his troops, put down a feeble attempt at resistance, and added that fine island to the permanent colonial empire of his country.[2]

When this intelligence reached Madrid, Philip declared war against England—seized the persons of all English residents, merchants, factors and agents connected with the interests of their commerce, and laid an embargo on all their merchandise and properties, amongst others on those of Nicholas Blake, the Admiral's brother. The reported failure of the attempt on His-

---

[1] Letter of Intelligence, Cadiz, June 13, Dept. Mss.
[2] Harl. Misc. vi. 373-390 ; Granville Penn, ii. 21-132.

paniola raised the spirits of the court to an extravagant
height : the Governor of the island was made a grandee
and pensioned ; even the messenger who brought the
news to Spain had 1500 ducats a-year settled on him
for life.   Blake's rapid and effective cruise in the Mediterranean, following in the immediate rear of the brilliant actions of the Dutch war, had caused the maritime
powers of Europe, and particularly Spain, from its own
experience of the Dutch admirals, to regard with blended
interest and alarm what appeared to be the invincible
prowess and fortunes of the young Commonwealth.   The
first signal check to that ascending power was therefore
hailed with a delight out of all real proportion to its
importance.   In the safety of Hispaniola, Philip forgot
the loss of Jamaica ; in the escape of his Silver Fleets
from the English squadron in the West Indies, he overlooked the more resolute and watchful enemy who lay
in wait for them under the very guns of Cadiz.[1]

While staying in the Channel before Cadiz, Blake
had learned from his scouts that the Silver Fleet was
expected from America in four or five weeks, and war
being then inevitable, he stood across to Cape Santa
Maria, the most southern point of land in Portugal, intending to make the bay or bays lying between that
promontory and Cape St. Vincent the basis of his summer
operations ; with his frigates and fast sailers ranging the
sea in a vast circle as far as wind and weather would
permit, in search of the anticipated prize.   In the Spanish harbour ten large galleons were being prepared for
sea — six of them, it was reported, being intended for

---

[1] Thurloe, iv. 19, 20, 21, 44.

service at Hispaniola, the others for the Mediterranean;
but Blake suspecting that they were designed as a convoy
for the Silver Fleet, he endeavoured by absence from the
port, by insult and by other provocations to force them
to come out. But nothing would induce them to stir.
Nearly a month the *St. George* rode before the little
town of Lagos. The war-ships kept out at sea, the frigates menaced the coast; still the galleons did not move.
At last, in the full belief that Philip would not allow
his admirals to risk a battle—a belief founded on information reaching London through various and independent channels — Cromwell desired Blake to send home
part of his fleet, so as to reduce the heavy expenses of
the war; but before these instructions could be carried
into effect, news arrived at Lagos that the merchants of
Seville, Cadiz, and San Lucar, seeing the government neglect to provide the necessary protection for their trade,
had combined to equip at their private expense a squadron strong enough to put to sea for convoy service, and
even give battle in case of need ; and under these circumstances he abandoned the idea of sending back any
part of his fleet, and as speedily as he was able got such
of his vessels as were sea-worthy, and several that were
not, together. On the 4th of July he wrote to Cromwell
in reference to the state of his ships :—" Seeing it hath
pleased your Highness to command my longer stay in
and about these parts with the rest of the ships, I shall
make bold to offer one humble desire, which I conceive
to be my duty for the service of the Commonwealth
and the better effecting the ends proposed,—that your
Highness will be pleased to consider the condition of

our fleet, especially of the great ships, which are very foul and defective, particularly the ship in which I am being very leaky and the mainmast unsound." Yet it was in vessels of this character that he had ruined Prince Rupert, cleared the Channel Islands, fought the battle of Portland, and chastised the pirates of Porto Ferino! Early in August the Spanish squadron, consisting of 28 men-of-war, and six fire-ships, with 36 long-boats, and 6000 troops on board, sailed from Cadiz, with the apparent intention of fighting the English.[1]

Towards the middle of the month the two squadrons came in sight off the coast of Portugal, Blake having been southward in search of the Spaniards; but, after dodging each other for some days, they separated without exchanging a single shot, for reasons which are explained at length in the following letter from Blake to the Lord Protector:

MAY IT PLEASE YOUR HIGHNESS,—Your commands of the 30th July I received by the *Assurance* frigate the 13th instant, with the intelligence of a great fleet prepared to come out of Cadiz and their design from your secretary, which in part we have found to be true, as I shall give your Highness an account.

The 6th inst. I received a letter from Captain Smith (which comes herewith), whereupon we stood away for the coast of Barbary, as far as Mamora, within three leagues; but having no news of the fleet there, we made towards the Bay of Cadiz, sending two frigates before to gain intelligence, who returned to us the 12th instant

---

[1] Thurloe, iii. 541, 611, 620, 698.

with this, that the fleet sailed from thence seven days
before, and were plying off Cape St. Vincent, to which
place we hastened; and the 15th, in the morning, espied
them to the windward of us, we being then off the Bay
of Lagos, whither we desired to go for water; but they
bearing up upon us, with intent (as we thought) to fight
us, I called a council of war, which unanimously resolved
to engage the first opportunity, being moved thereunto
with an eager desire we had to see some end of our tedious
expectation, and to prevent that accession of strength
mentioned in the secretary's intelligence (whereof we
likewise had notice from other hands), and also out of a
despair of being able to keep the sea many days longer
for want of liquor. But the Spanish fleet forthwith
tacked and stood the other way, and we after them all
that night. In the morning we were fair by them; but
there being little wind (not enough to work our ships)
and a great sea, so that we could not make use of our
lower tier, and also a thick fog, we did nothing that day;
their fleet being then thirty-one in all. The next day we
continued in the same resolution, and sent some frigates
ahead to gain the wind, and to engage them; but the
evening approaching, and a great part of our fleet far
astern, we thought it best to desist for that time. These
checks of Providence did put us upon second thoughts,
and a strict review of the instructions which I had received; the which being all perused and compared together at a council of war, we could not find in them
any authority given unto us to attack this party, but
rather the contrary; and we had reason also to conceive
it was not the intention of your Highness that we should

be the first breakers of the peace, seeing your Highness
having notice of the coming forth of the Spanish fleet did
not give us any new direction at all touching the same in
your last order of the 30th of July. Upon these grounds
we receded from our first resolution, and took into consideration the state of our fleet, which we found in all
things to be extremely defective, but more particularly
in want of liquor; some of the ships having not beverage
for above four days, and the whole not able to make above
eight, and that at short allowance; and no small part
both of our beverage and water stinking. Hereupon it
was debated amongst us whether we should return to the
Bay of Lagos or go to Lisbon for supplies, there being
no other place but those two. To go to Lagos it was
not held good, both because all that country could not
afford us one pipe of beverage wine, and to get water
there very difficult, and upon the least wind from the
south or east almost impossible, and the place a dangerous road for such a fleet to anchor in, which we must
have done for getting a quantity of water, beside many
other inconveniences. It was therefore resolved that we
should go to Lisbon. Nevertheless, we kept in sight two
days after, and on the 22d inst. we lay a great part of
the day with our sails hauled up, until they were very
near us; but perceiving they had no intention to engage
us, nor any commission to that purpose, as we thought,
and also understood by a small frigate of theirs of twenty-four guns, the captain whereof coming accidentally
amongst us, I commanded aboard, who told us the same;
and withal that they knew nothing of the expected fleet
at all, but only that they were bound to attend the com-

ing of the same. Hereupon, our liquor growing less, we stood away for Lisbon, where we arrived on the 24th instant, and anchored in the road of Cascaes. . . . How these passages of Providence will be looked upon, or what construction our carriage in this business may receive, I know not (although it hath been with all integrity of heart), but this we know, that our condition is dark and sad, and, without especial mercy, like to be very miserable :—our ships extremely foul, winter drawing on, our victuals expiring, all stores failing, our men falling sick through the badness of drink, and eating their victuals boiled in salt water for two months' space; the coming of a supply uncertain (we received not one word from the Commissioners of the Admiralty and Navy by the last), and though it come timely, yet if beer come not with it, we shall be undone that way. We have no place or friend, our recruits here slow, and our mariners (which I most apprehend) apt to fall into discontents through their long keeping abroad. Our only comfort is that we have a God to lean upon, although we walk in darkness and see no light. I shall not trouble your Highness with any complaints of myself, of the indisposition of my body, or troubles of my mind; my many infirmities will one day, I doubt not, sufficiently plead for me or against me, so that I may be free of so great a burden, consoling myself in the mean time in the Lord, and in the firm purpose of my heart with all faithfulness and sincerity to discharge the trust while reposed in me. . . . . As soon as we have got a sufficient proportion of liquor, which I hope may be in five or six days, we intend (God willing) to sail to the southward cape, and to spend some time thereabouts, so long as we can possibly lengthen out our victuals, so that we may be able to get home, in case the victualling ships do not come in time; which we shall then be forced to do, or must perish in the sea. I have no more at present to trouble your Highness with (this already being I fear too much), but shall ever remain,

Your Highness's most humble

And faithful servant,

ROBERT BLAKE.

Aboard the (St.) George, in Cascaes Road,
August 30, 1655.[1]

The allusion to his own indisposition of body and trouble of mind, contained in this letter, though brief and by the way, is extremely touching. He had left a sick room to go on board. For nearly a year he had never quitted the " very foul and defective" flag-ship. Want of exercise and sweet food, beer, wine, water, bread and vegetables, had helped to develop scurvy and dropsy; and his sufferings from these diseases were now acute and continuous. In fact, his constitution was completely undermined. For three weeks after the date of the letter just quoted, he kept his station in the Spanish waters, when, finding no relief come in, and supposing that the Silver Fleet would now remain in America until spring, he reluctantly turned his bows towards the north, and brought his squadron home to repair and replenish.[2]

But there was no rest for him at home. Arrived in

---

[1] Thurloe, iii. 718, 719.

[2] Blake to Capt. Duncombe, Sept. 18, 1655, Dept. Mss.

England, he found that in the present posture of affairs his retirement from the service, even for a time, would be extremely detrimental to the country. The Council had no one to take his place. Deane, Penn, Ascue, Lawson, all the men who had served with him in the Dutch war with eminent ability and success, were now either dead or out of employment :—Ascue had been pensioned and dismissed on the alleged ground of his want of success against De Ruiter, but in reality because suspected of a leaning towards the exiles ; Penn had been ostensibly broken for the failure on Hispaniola, more likely because Cromwell had heard of his treacherous offers ; Lawson lay under a cloud, and was soon afterwards arrested as a Fifth-monarchy conspirator ; Deane was dead ; and Monk had neither the genius nor the desire for naval commands. But while the more experienced commanders were thus falling away, the duties and demands of the service were daily increasing. The nation was committed to a war with Spain. The Pope, ill at ease since the fright of the previous spring, was warmly engaged in a project for uniting all the Catholic maritime powers in a league against the formidable heretics ; and agents from Venice, Florence, Madrid and some other cities, had already met in Rome. Genoa also threatened : many merchants of that Republic being interested in the safe arrival of the Silver Fleet, they strongly urged that the Genoese armada should join with that of Spain for their protection. Holland was again wavering in her friendship, report affirming that the King of Spain had tempted them to declare war against England by the offer of Dunkirk and two other ports in the narrow seas. Nor was peace yet firmly established with the Barbary powers; at the very first reverse of fortune these corsairs would have gladly seized the moment of retaliation and revenge. What perhaps most of all annoyed Cromwell was that John King of Portugal, who had thus far found means to delay the final execution of the treaties entered into twenty months previous—especially the clause which secured to English subjects in his dominions immunity from the Holy Office—now manifested a disposition to withdraw from the compact altogether.[1]

In face of so many perils and uncertainties, Blake's services were indispensable. At such a time, his very name was worth a squadron of ordinary ships. Not to speak of the moral strength which his presence would give to any fleet going southward, the occasional sight of his flag would be pretty certain to keep the Barbary corsairs quiet; a sudden visit, paid by him to the Tagus, might bring John of Braganza to reason; and the dread of another call at Leghorn would probably be sufficient to frighten the Pope and the Grand Duke out of the proposed league of Catholic princes. However anxious for repose of mind and body, Blake could not decline the responsibilities of command without a breach of duty to his country; and ill as he then was, he lent his days and nights to the duties of his station, visiting the dockyards and arsenals, and urging the work of repair and replenishment by his presence and his counsels. But though he would not refuse the last pulse of his brain to his

---

[1] Heath, 323; Granville Penn, ii. 141; Thurloe, vi. 185, v. 93, 304, 338.

beloved country, his age and bodily sufferings warned
him of the fatal consequences which might result to the
service should he fall a victim to any sudden sickness
while in those distant seas, with no colleague on board
to whom in case of need he could devolve the supreme
command; he therefore begged the Council of State to
nominate another Sea-General to share his responsibilities and assist him with his knowledge. Whether he
actually named Montagu for the office is uncertain;
but true to the plan of their parliamentary predecessors,
the Council fixed on this soldier, a young man of good
family, and a confidential friend of Cromwell, as the
new general. The preparations of the fleet went on
rapidly. Towards the end of February, 1656, the Generals went on board the *Naseby*, then in the Downs
with part of the fleet, and they continued in the Channel, cruising between the river mouth and St. Helen's
road, for the better expedition of affairs. The trouble
of getting in the necessary provisions was almost incredible; every naval station on the coast was short of
stores; nor could they be procured in sufficient haste
at any price or favour. Blake's patience was at length
tired out, and he resolved to sail without them : —
" the expectation of the provisions and fire-ships," he
writes to Cromwell on the 8th of March, " shall be no
cause of stay; but as soon as ever we can get a supply
from the shore of the things that are essentially requisite, which we are labouring at, we shall with the
help of God be gone." At St. Helen's in the Isle of
Wight, he received his final instructions, and while his
fleet was getting under weigh for the south, he wrote

his last letter in England—a very simple and a very touching farewell:

General Blake to Secretary Thurloe.

SIR,—I have received yours of the 13th instant, together with the enclosed note of the galleons; as also your intelligence touching the end of the war between the Protestant and Popish cantons, and the peace settled there, and likewise the probabilities of a truce for six years betwixt France and Spain; and the being of Charles Stuart with his company in Flanders. These sudden transactions seem to have some great matters in the womb of them; but we know that God is the supreme disposer of all the counsels, designs, and confederations in the world; and we know He is able to order them all for the greater good of His people. And our trust is, that He will do so even for our good also, if we can believe in Him. The Lord help our unbelief, and subdue our hearts to the obedience of His holy will in all things. We are now getting an anchor aboard, making ready to sail, although there be little wind, or none at all. But we shall use our utmost endeavours to get to sea, not losing any opportunity that God shall afford us; as we have hitherto been careful, and hope that his Highness is confident we are and shall continue so, as far as God shall enable us; which is all at present from

Your very affectionate friend and servant,

ROBERT BLAKE.

Aboard the *Naseby* in St. Helen's Road,
    March 15, 1656 (new style).[1]

---

[1] Clarendon, vi. 19; Thurloe, iv. 545, 592, 620.

Two days before the date of this letter he had made his will, writing the whole of it out with his own hand. The document ran:

The last Will and Testament of me, Robert Blake, written with my own hand as followeth.

First, I bequeath my soul into the hands of my most merciful Redeemer, the Lord Jesus Christ, by Him to be presented to His heavenly Father, pure and spotless, through the washing of His blood which He shed for the remission of my sins, and, after a short separation from the body, to be again united with the same by the power of His eternal Spirit, and so to be ever with the Lord: Item, unto the town of Bridgwater.I give one hundred pounds to be distributed among the poor thereof, at the discretion of Humphrey Blake my brother, and of the Mayor for the time being:[1] Item, unto the town of Taunton I

---

[1] On a panel in the parish church appears the following inscription:—

" The Hon. Robert Blake, Esq., of this town, Captain-General of the fleet of England, did by his last will and testament bequeath unto the poor of this borough the sum of one hundred pounds; fourscore pounds and upwards whereof was disposed of in purchasing certain land within this parish, then known by the name of Jacob's Land, but now, in honour of the worthy donor, called Blake's Land, consisting of a piece of land without the East Gate, and two small tenements in Eastover, the yearly rents whereof for ever to remain to the use of the said poor, to be distributed in food or apparel at the discretion of the trustees of the said land. He died anno Dom. 1657.

" Unto the above is added another tenement in Eastover adjoining to the above mentioned, purchased by the present trustees of Mr. Richard for forty pounds, part of the money by them saved from the sale of lives in the two tenements aforesaid. Anno Dom. 1729."

The property purchased with the Admiral's bequest has, by a strange

give one hundred pounds to be distributed among the poor of both parishes at the discretion of Samuel Perry, once my lieutenant-colonel, and Mr. George Newton, minister of the gospel there, and of the Mayor for the time being: Item, I give unto Humphrey Blake my brother, the manor of Crandon-cum-Puriton, with all the rights thereto appertaining, to him and to his heirs for ever: Item, I give unto my brother Doctor William Blake three hundred pounds: Item, unto my brother George Blake I give three hundred pounds: Also, unto my brother Nicholas Blake I give three hundred pounds: Item, unto my brother Benjamin Blake I give my dwelling-house, situate in St. Mary's Street in Bridgwater, with the garden and appurtenances, as also my other house thereto adjoining, purchased of the Widow Coxe: likewise I give unto him all the claim I have in eleven acres of meadow and pasture (more or less) lying in the village of Ham, in the parish of Bridgwater, lately in the possession of the Widow Vincombe deceased: Item, unto my sister Bridget Bowdich, the wife of Henry Bowdich of Chard Stock, I give one hundred pounds; and to her children, of the body of Henry Bowdich aforesaid, I give the sum of nine hundred pounds, to be disposed among them according to the discretion of Humphrey, William, George, Nicholas, and Benjamin Blake aforesaid, my brothers, or any three of them: Item, unto my Brother Smythes, goldsmith in Cheapside, I give the sum of one hundred pounds:

---

perversity, been hitherto known in the town as Jacob's Land. Such is local fame! The property has passed into private hands; a church stands on part of the ground, a school and a number of elegant villas occupy the remainder. During a recent visit to Bridgwater, I had an opportunity of suggesting to the owner of the villas that the site should bear the illustrious name with which it is historically connected; he made me its sponsor, and I at once christened it *Blake Place.*

Item, unto my nephew, Robert Blake, son to Samuel Blake, my brother deceased, I give the gold chain bestowed on me by the late Parliament of England: also, all the claim I have in an annuity of twenty pounds, payable out of the farm of Pawlett: Item, unto my nephew Samuel Blake, younger son to Samuel, my brother deceased, I give two hundred pounds: Item, unto Sarah Quarrel, daughter of my late niece, Sarah Quarrell, by her husband Peter Quarrell, now dwelling in Taunton, I give the sum of two hundred pounds, to be disposed of for the benefit of the said Sarah Quarrell, according to the discretion of Humphrey, Nicholas, and Benjamin Blake, my brothers aforesaid: Item, unto my cousin John Blake, son unto my brother Nicholas Blake, I give one hundred pounds: Item, unto my cousin John Avery of Pawlett, once a soldier with me in Taunton Castle, I give fifty pounds: Item, unto Thomas Blake, son of my cousin William Blake, once commander of the *Tresto* frigate deceased, now aboard of the *Centurion* frigate in the service, I give fifty pounds: Item, all my plate, linen, bedding, with all my provisions aboard the ship *Naseby*, I give unto my nephews Robert and Samuel Blake aforesaid, and to my nephew John Blake aforesaid, to be divided between them by even and equal portions: Item, unto the negro called Domingo, my servant, I give the sum of fifty pounds, to be disposed of by my aforesaid nephew, Captain Robert Blake, and Captain Thomas Adams, for his better education in the knowledge and fear of God: Item, unto my servants, James Knowles and Nicholas Bartlett, I give to each of them ten pounds: Item, unto the Widow Owen of Bridgwater, the relict of Mr. Owen, minister, I give ten pounds: Item, unto Eleanor Potter, widow, I give ten pounds: All the rest of my goods and chattels I do give and bequeath unto George, Nicholas, and Benjamin Blake, my brothers aforesaid, and also to Alexander Blake my brother, to be equally divided among them, whom I do appoint and ordain to be the executors of this my last will and testament.   ROB. BLAKE.

> Signed and sealed aboard the *Naseby*, March the thirteenth, one thousand six hundred and fifty-five, in St. Helen's Road, in presence of Roger Cuttons, J. Hynde, John Bourne, Antho. Earming.

Oliver, Lord Protector of the Commonwealth of England, Scotland, Ireland, and the dominions, territories thereunto belonging, to all to whom these presents shall come, greeting : Know ye, that upon the twentieth day of August, in the year of our Lord one thousand six hundred fifty and seven, before the Judges for probate of wills and granting administrations lawfully authorised, the last will and testament of the Honourable Robert Blake, late General of the Fleet for the Commonwealth of England at sea, deceased, was at London in common form proved, which will is to these presents annexed : And administration of all and singular the goods, chattels, and debts of the said deceased which may any manner or way concern him or his said will, was granted and committed to George Blake, Benjamin Blake, and Alexander Blake, three of the executors named in the said will, they first having taken their oaths well and truly to administer the same goods, chattels, and debts according to the tenour and effect of the same will; and to make or cause to be made a true and perfect inventory of all and singular the goods, chattels, and debts of the said deceased, which have, shall, or may come to their hands, possession, or knowledge ; and also a true and just account in and concerning their said administration when they shall be assigned or lawfully called so to do ; which touching an inventory they were presently assigned to perform at or before the last day of December now next ensuing the date hereof. Power being nevertheless reserved to make like probate and grant like administration to Nicholas Blake, the other executor named in the will aforesaid, whenever he shall legally desire the same.

Given at London, under the seal of the Court for Probate of Wills and granting Administrations, the day and year above said.   R. HANKEY.

MARK COTTLE, *Register.*[1]

This solemn act accomplished, and the final instructions received from the Council of State, orders were given to get the ships under weigh. The squadron coasted as far west as Torbay, and as the white cliffs and verdant slopes of Devonshire faded from his sight, the departing hero saw his last of England. As the Sea-Generals passed down the Portuguese coast, they sent their letters to King John and assurances of support to Mr. Meadows, English envoy at the court of Lisbon, in his demand for a complete recognition of all the clauses of the late treaty; but they never once slackened sail until they were again in the Bay of Cadiz, where their dispositions soon made the inhabitants aware that their daring intention was to remain the entire summer, and to hold the royal harbour in a state of perpetual blockade. By these means the Silver Fleets would be kept at sea in imminent danger, and the usual trade of the Seville and Cadiz merchants would be destroyed. The Spaniards did not, however, dream of fighting with the renovated fleet. Now and then a slight skirmish took place between a couple of stray ketches, shallops or long-boats; and one morning in the

---

[1] Office copy, in Blake Mss.

Y

midst of a dead calm, when even the English frigates could not move a point of the compass, the royal galleon and two others rowed out and fought at a great advantage with some of Blake's outsiders. But the principal damage done on either side in this encounter was effected by a chance shot from one of the frigates lying close in shore, for this cannon-ball knocked down part of a church and killed two men.[1]

While these affairs were going on, serious news came in hot haste from Lisbon. King John, suffering from stone, and in the hands of his priests, absolutely refused to accept the treaty; and the majesty of England had been insulted in the person of its envoy. Don Pantaleone and his brother, the Conde de Torre, as was generally given out at the time, waylaid and pistolled Mr. Meadows in the streets of the capital,—probably out of revenge for the death of their brother, who had been executed in London for murder. No attempt was made to discover the assassins. The wound did not prove mortal; but Blake remembered the unatoned murders of Ascham and Dorislaus; and this time he was resolved to shew the world that England would cause the law of nations to be respected towards her servants. Leaving a few frigates to keep watch over Cadiz, the whole fleet weighed for Lisbon, and in the first week of June anchored in Cascaes road at the Tagus mouth. But fear and dismay travelled faster than the *Naseby*, and as soon as it was known in Lisbon that Blake's instructions were clear and ample, the people rose against the priest party and compelled the invalid King to make peace

---

[1] Thurloe, iv. 679, 762; Heath, 381.

with England. John sent for Mr. Meadows; and on receiving a promise that in case of compliance the Sea-Generals would not molest his ships or damage his ports, he consented to accept the treaty substantially as it then stood : — that is, with one or two verbal alterations, which, in the opinion of the resident English, would not unfavourably affect their just claims, while, on the other hand, they would have the effect of soothing the King's pride. The right of our nation to have Bibles and other pious books in their houses, without being considered as thereby breaking the laws of the country, was conceded. The proposal of an appeal to the Pope in all disputes about religion, previously insisted on by the Portuguese, was abandoned. The lives and proper-ties of English settlers were placed beyond the reach of the Holy Office. The customs were reduced to twenty-three per cent. And, finally, the King consented to pay down in silver 50,000*l.* sterling, besides 20,000*l.* and some other monies due to the English for demurrage and freight of ships. A careful perusal of all the cor-respondence of John and his agents with the English, would probably incline the reader to believe that the hasty admission of these various claims, after two years of intrigue and subterfuge, was intended only as a feint to gain time and induce the Generals not to enter the Tagus. But Blake knew the King of old, and he de-clared his fixed resolution to remain at Cascaes — or in case of need to sail up the river to Lisbon, and there wait the fulfilment of the treaty. Flurried by a mes-sage so energetic, the court sent to Mr. Meadows to beg that he would obtain for them some sort of assurance from the Generals that they would not molest their trade, if they, on their part, held fast to the terms of the treaty. Whereupon Blake and Montagu wrote:—" If his majesty of Portugal do perform on his part, and cause the money, which is by the treaty to be forthwith paid to his Highness's use, to be put into our possession, that it may be conveyed to England,—he may confidently assure himself that we shall never so far dishonour his Highness nor prostitute our own reputation, and bring a scandal on the faith and holiness of the religion we profess, as to violate any of the articles of the treaty." John had no resource but to pay the money, which was accordingly put on board and sent to England.[1]

A rather ludicrous incident served to shew the effect of Blake's southern campaigns in the capital of the Catholic world. Pope Alexander VII. had been active in his hostility to England. He had invited Spain, Genoa, Florence and other maritime states, to make common cause against Puritan intruders into the Mediterranean. He had been the chief abettor of the dying King of Portugal in his faithless attempt to evade treaties. He had interposed the strongest obstacles to a just settlement of the Protestant question of the Vaudois. His Holiness, therefore, listened with fear and trembling for the renewed echoes of that Puritan cannon which had already left so many records of its presence on the shores of Spain, Italy and Barbary. One morning in the middle of June, while the red cross of the Commonwealth was still floating in the Tagus and Blake occupied in

---

[1] Thurloe, iv. 758, v. 44, 98, 116, 123, 125.

taking on board the Portuguese dollars, it was suddenly announced in the streets of Rome that the English fleet was cannonading Civita Vecchia! The poor Pope, supposing in his terror that the formidable heretics would in a few hours be thundering at the gates of the Eternal City, caused earthworks to be thrown up, and the cannon of St. Angelo to be dismounted, carried into the streets, and placed in the most commanding positions for defence. But as no enemy appeared in sight, scouts were sent down to Civita Vecchia, when it turned out that no damage had been done—that no English vessel had been in that harbour—and that the firing which had given rise to the little comedy in Rome proceeded from a couple of Dutchmen, the crews of which were wasting their powder in a fit of drink![1]

The state of affairs remained unchanged before Cadiz. Cromwell, harassed for funds, was anxious to strike some sudden and tremendous blow against the great enemy of his country; and therefore sent out one Captain Loyd, "known to us to be a person of integrity," with a set of propositions as to how and where such a blow could be best dealt; "desiring to give no rule to you,"—Blake and Montagu,—but "rather as queries than as resolutions:"—a very remarkable instance of submission in a man of Cromwell's imperious character. The queries were:—Would it not be possible to burn the galleons at their moorings in the harbour? Could Cadiz itself be attacked with success? Or, failing both these, might not an attempt be made to carry the town

---

[1] Thurloe, v. 137.

and Castle of Gibraltar? All these were points to be maturely considered. Drake had once burnt a fleet in the Bay of Cadiz. Essex and Raleigh had once carried the city by assault. On their way from Cascaes road the Sea-Generals held many consultations, examined charts and compared opinions; intending, if the project of burning the Spanish fleet as it lay in the Carracas appeared feasible, to fall suddenly and fiercely to the work of destruction the moment of their arrival. But not a single pilot could be found willing to undertake the responsibility of carrying an English war-ship into that narrow and dangerous harbour. Times had changed since Drake surprised the Spaniards. The expedition under Essex had taught them their weakness and their strength. When he arrived in the Bay, Blake obtained exact information from spies, secret agents and others, as to the means of defence possessed by the city, from which it appeared,—that the navigation of the channel was extremely difficult at all times,—that the Spaniards had thrown a number of heavy chains across it,— that large vessels had been placed in convenient positions ready to be sunk at the first signal of an attempt to enter it by force,—that guns had been planted on both shores of the passage,—and that the preparations for defence were altogether of the most complete and formidable character. It was therefore obvious to the council of war, that in order to destroy the fleet in Carracas it would be necessary first to subdue Cadiz. And this point was considered; but only for a moment. That the city was strong by nature, and still stronger by art, was well known to military men; but Cromwell's spies had led him to believe that it was ill-supplied with troops, and it was on this circumstance that he had indulged in his dream of an attack. On the spot the council of war obtained more exact accounts, when it appeared that in Cadiz, town and island, Porto Santa Maria and Rotto, where the Duke of Medina commanded in person, there were about forty thousand regular troops, some regiments of which vast force enjoyed the well-won reputation of being the finest infantry in the world. Under these circumstances they voted it irrational to think of making any attempt on the mainland, unless a large body of troops could be sent from England to co-operate with the fleet, as had been the case when Essex and Raleigh forced their way into the town. An attack on Gibraltar was declared impracticable for similar reasons; the Spaniards having recently strengthened the works and thrown a powerful garrison into that important stronghold.[1]

On receipt of the letters in which these decisions of the war-council were reported, the Protector and his Council wrote to Blake and Montagu as follows:

GENTLEMEN,—We have seen a letter written by you to the Commissioners of the Admiralty, dated 9th May, from Tangier, which arrived here yesterday morning, whereby we understand the posture of the enemy, and that for the several reasons expressed by you in that said letter, it seems to you not rational to attempt the burning of the Spanish fleet in Cadiz; and thereupon apprehending that some of your ships may be spared into the Chan-

---

[1] Carlyle's Cromwell, iv. 64-67; Thurloe, v. 134.

nel for the better securing of trade, and the blocking up
of Dunkirk and Ostend, where the pirates and ships-of-
war grow so numerous, that lately eighteen or nineteen
of them in a body took twenty of our merchant-ships
in two fleets, being under a convoy of a Dutch ship of
thirty-six guns; therefore we have resolved to call into
these seas part of the fleet now with you; and to that
end we desire you, upon the receipt hereof, to give orders to ten ships, under a good officer, to sail with the
first opportunity of wind and weather into the Downs,
requiring them to give immediate notice unto us of their
arrival. We leave it wholly unto you which of the ships
you will send, conceiving you to be best able to judge
which of them will be fittest for this service and may be
best spared by you. Some thoughts we have had that
the lesser sort of ships, and especially frigates, will best
answer the aforesaid ends here. This we have resolved,
not knowing any thing of your posture or counsels more
than your aforesaid letter represents. But in case you
are upon any design, or if aught else hath emerged,
either upon our letter and instruction sent by Captain
Loyd, or from your own thoughts, with which these
orders will not well consist, we leave it to you, notwithstanding what we have herein written, whether you will
send these ships or not; our intentions not being to dis-
appoint any thing which may be in your eye or design
to be done there by the fleet.[1]

The fleet had barely taken up its former position
in the Bay before it began to experience some of that

---

[1] Thurloe, v. 101, 102.

extreme weather to which the hopes of the Spaniards seemed now chiefly turned as a means of compelling their enemy to go home. Several captains of ships were on board the *Naseby* receiving their instructions to sail for England in compliance with the request of the Council, when a gust of wind suddenly rose in the east and south-east, increased into a tremendous gale, snapt the anchor-chains, tore the cordage into shreds, and scattered the fleet — seven or eight ships, of which the *Naseby* was one, excepted — far and wide from Sagres to Tangier, doing serious damage to the entire squadron. The night which followed this terrible day was dark as well as tempestuous. Here and there the lights were hung out all night long as signals of distress, and in every pause of the storm the commanders heard signal-guns booming over the sea from great distances. About one o'clock, the *Naseby* had a narrow escape of wreck. The *Taunton*, her sails torn and rudder unmanageable, came drifting before the gale right on them. Lights were hoisted and orders given for Captain Vallis, her commander, to open a new sail; but the poor fellow seemed to have lost all power over her movements. On she came, stern foremost, against the *Naseby*, which vessel had hitherto kept her anchor. A few moments and a collision appeared inevitable. Blake ordered his cables to be cut as a last chance, when suddenly, as he says in his letter to Cromwell — "it pleased God in very much mercy that she" — the *Taunton* — "let slip, and getting a sail open with much ado steered clear off us, else one or both of us, in all likelihood, had immediately gone to the bottom." Nearly all the vessels of his fleet lost their long-boats, and many of them their cables and anchors:—the *Resolution* had one of her anchors snapt into two pieces, and the other bent almost double. But none were absolutely lost. The *Kent* and the *Taunton* were the longest absent from the general gathering; but after a few days of painful suspense, to the infinite joy of their comrades they also returned. In one of his letters Montagu says " the sea ran mountains high;" and he added suggestively—" Judge you what this sea is to ride in winter time!" Great damage was also done to the Spanish ships lying in harbour; many of the merchant-men being torn from their moorings and driven out to sea.[1]

Six of the English ships, including the *Kent*, *Bristol* and *Mermaid*, were judged to be no longer fit for so rude a service, and were sent home to England. Meantime the Generals did their utmost to exasperate the enemy to come out and fight. But neither insult nor spoliation could sufficiently stir their blood: as the Lisbon agent expressed it in his correspondence, " the Spaniard used his buckler rather than his sword." Hearing that a Sicilian and a Genoese galley had taken part with the Spaniards of Malaga against the English, Blake despatched the *Ruby*, *Nantwich*, and *Lyon*, with the *Fox* fire-ship, to that port, in search of the offenders, and with orders to infest and alarm the coast on that side from Gibraltar to Valentia. Still the Cadiz galleons would not venture out. Blake then drew off a number of frigates and good sailers for a temporary

---

[1] Thurloe, v. 178, 179, 195.

guard, and with the body of his fleet sailed for the African coast in search of water and provisions; intending also to pay a brief visit to Salee, on the west coast of Africa, and teach the lawless rovers of that city some respect for European commerce and civilisation. Success attended him and his chosen officers. The expedition against Malaga was brilliantly executed. The English ships rode into the harbour at mid-day, with colours and pennons flying, and anchored between the bulwark and the pier-head in three fathoms of water. The people on shore were taken quite aback, fancying they were some ships come in to give themselves up to the King of Spain. But they were awoke from this dream by a sudden declaration that, if the Genoa galley was not given up to them at once, they would proceed to fire every ship that was within the pier. After exchanging signals, the two galleys made an attempt to quit the port, the Genoese covering the Sicilian like a shield, when the frigates poured a broadside into the insolent Genoese, which broke her rudder, killed forty of her crew, and carried off her oars in splinters. The Sicilian slipt away in the confusion, but the Genoese was obliged to put back into the port, where she was grappled by the fire-ship and instantly wrapt in flames. The cannon of the land-works now opened on the English, and in return the ships began to bombard the town. A dozen resolute fellows leapt on shore from a long-boat, and in a few minutes they had spiked eight pieces of heavy ordnance under the very walls of the town. The people were in great confusion; many of the gentry fled away; the citizens hid themselves in their wine-casks; and it was thought that a force of 4000 men would have been able to capture and plunder the place, so great was the terror of the moment.[1]

Blake and Montagu returned to their old station, but the Spaniards still remained in port. No Silver Fleets appeared. July and August passed away in glorious but not very profitable cruises, skirmishes and blockades. Winter was drawing near, and every ship in the service required to be careened and refitted. Victuals of every kind ran short. To obtain supplies even of bread and water, it was necessary to seek the ports of a friendly power. Blake, therefore, appointed Captain Richard Stayner, of the *Speaker*, to watch the bay with a squadron of seven ships, the *Speaker*, *Bridgwater*, *Providence*, *Plymouth*, and three others; and with the remainder of his power he sailed early in September for the northern part of Portugal. The Generals, however, had not come to an anchor in Aviero Bay before a fortunate accident brought a division of the long-expected Silver Fleet in sight of Stayner's squadron. Four magnificent Spanish royal galleons and two great merchantmen of Indian build, all of them laden with precious cargoes of gold, silver, pearls and precious stones, hides, indigo, sugar, cochineal, varinas and tobacco, and having the Viceroy of Lima and his family, a general, an admiral, and vice-admiral, together with about two thousand inferior persons on board, had left the Havanna early in June bound for Cadiz, under the impression that their European fleets would be able to protect them against

---

[1] Thurloe, v. 195, 233, 234, 285, 337.

every enemy, and without touching land at any point, they had made the whole voyage in the short space of fifty-seven days. On their way they picked up a little French barque, laden with hides, and afterwards, among the Western Islands, a Portuguese corn-factor, both of which vessels they made prizes. Either from mistake or from malice, the Portuguese sailors, when their captors inquired from them where the English fleet lay, replied that the Spaniards had beaten Blake a month ago, and driven him away from their coast; they consequently continued their voyage towards Europe in the utmost confidence, instead of running to the Azores for a convoy. In passing San Lucar they noticed a long-boat in the act of crossing the bar ; but by some strange fatality they proceeded towards Cadiz without staying to inquire how an English long-boat could be entering the Gaudalquiver if Blake's squadron had been discomfited and driven home. Even when they observed Stayner's frigates, just at dusk on the 8th of September, some five or six leagues eastward towards Cadiz, they concluded that they must be Spanish guard-ships lying about the harbour, and therefore did their best to keep close to them all night, putting their own lights on for company, and occasionally firing guns to announce their fortunate arrival. At day-dawn, they discovered their serious mistake ; and, though they had a vast preponderance of force, they separated, and some of them ran ashore as the only means of saving the vast treasures with which they were freighted. A fresh gale, blowing hard from the north-east, had scattered the English squadron, and only the *Speaker*, the *Plymouth* and the *Bridgwater* were at first sufficiently near the galleons to engage with them. Stayner naturally made for the flag-ship of the Spaniard; but finding that it was one of the weakest in the fleet, and suspecting that the flag was raised on that vessel merely to deceive and draw off an enemy from the gold and silver galleons, he let her go, and she succeeded in making her escape with the Lisbon prize into Cadiz. The battle raged between the others for six hours. From the walls and towers of the city the Spaniards could see every turn of the engagement; two of their galleons were on fire at the same moment; two others of their ships went down to rise no more. After defending his charge with heroic valour, their Vice-admiral was overpowered, his vessel, on fire in several places, was hastily rifled by the conquerors of its gold and silver; the prisoners were removed to the *Speaker*, and it was then left to fill and sink. In this galleon went down the unfortunate Viceroy of Lima, with his wife and daughter. The *Plymouth* chased one of the traders to the shore, where she ran aground near Cape Degar; but it appeared by the statement of prisoners taken that she had no silver on board. The galleon of the Rear-admiral was taken, a prize of very great value. " The ship we took," says Stayner in his letter to Blake, " is worth all the rest of the fleet." It was a royal galleon of about 500 tons burden with 350 men on board when she struck her colours, and contained two million pieces of eight. Two other prizes were afterwards picked up; and of the whole eight vessels only two escaped capture or destruction. The money lost amounted to nine million pieces of eight. The loss in men on the English side was very slight; but

ROBERT BLAKE. 335

several of the frigates were much damaged, especially the *Speaker*, which had borne the chief brunt of the battle.[1]

Among the prisoners taken was the young Marquis de Badajoz, son of the Viceroy of Lima, whose melancholy and romantic story at once became a theme for poets and tale-tellers. His father was born a few leagues from Madrid, of a noble but reduced family of the pure Hidalgo blood. In early life his royal master made him Governor of Chili, in South America; afterwards he was translated to the Vice-royalty of Lima, which country he governed fourteen years; but his period of office being completed, his family grown up to youth, his own labours rewarded with wealth and honours, he embarked in the vice-admiral with his lady, his four sons, and his three daughters—two of them affianced brides, one to a son of the great Duke of Medina Cœli, the other to Don Juan de Joyas, Rear-admiral of the fleet, and now Stayner's prisoner. When the flames began to spread in the galleon, the marchioness and one of her daughters swooning with heat and fear fell on their faces and were soon scorched to death. One of the boys also fell a victim to the fire. The marquis might have escaped unhurt, but seeing the blackened bodies of his companions where they lay, he rushed towards them, threw his arms about his wife, and died in the embrace. The young marquis, his brothers and sisters, were saved by the English boarders and carried to the *Speaker*, where they were treated with great civility even by the rude sailors.

---

[1] Montagu to Thurloe, in a Select Collection of Original Letters (1755, 12mo), i. 202; Clarendon, vi. 19-20; Thurloe, v. 399, 400.

The eldest boy afterwards became quite a favourite with the two commanders: " He is a most pregnant, ingenious, and learned youth as I ever met with," said Montagu, " and his story is the saddest that ever I heard of or read of to my remembrance." The whole fortune of the family, consisting of 800,000 pieces of eight, was on board the vice-admiral; much of it was plundered by the boarders, and the rest went down with the wreck.[1]

Cromwell had already desired one of the Generals to return home for a short time, to consult with the Board of Admiralty on the state of the fleet and on the general conduct of the war; and he had named Montagu for this purpose, as his absence would be least severely felt. Blake was desired, if the plan met with his approval, to make a selection from the squadron under his command of such good sailors as would be best likely to stand the wear of a winter campaign, and with these vessels keep guard before the harbour of Cadiz, and utterly destroy its commerce. He thereupon removed the red cross of the Commonwealth to the mast of the *Swiftsure;* and collecting all Stayner's prizes with the other ships intended for home, he took farewell of his colleague, committing him to the mercies of God and the good-will of his countrymen. England soon rang with the new glories of its great seamen. Poems, plaudits and rewards without end met the victorious Montagu. A knighthood was reserved for Stayner. The bullion which he had captured was landed at Portsmouth, and some eight-

---

[1] Elegiac Enumeration, 22, 23; Waller's poem, " On our late War in Spain ;" Select Coll. of Orig. Letters, i. 202.

and-thirty wagons, attended by chosen picquets of soldiers, carried it triumphantly through the western towns
to London, where it was paraded through the City, and
then immediately carried to the Tower and coined into
money.[1]

---

[1] Whitelocke, 643; Clarendon, vi. 20; History and Life, 92-94.

CHAPTER X.

Santa Cruz.

STAYNER's brilliant success against the first division of
the Silver Fleets which had fallen in the way of an English squadron, encouraged Blake in the idea that by remaining out at sea all winter, he might perhaps be able
to strike such a blow at the naval power of Spain, as
would shake that overgrown and haughty empire to its
foundations. The Mexican galleons had been disposed
of by his lieutenant; those of Peru, known to be still
more richly laden with gold, silver, pearls and precious
stones, were on their way to Spain. Could he only keep
the mouth of the Carracas closed, so as to prevent any
caraval going out to warn them of their danger, it was
not unlikely that they would follow in the track of the
former fleet, and fall into his hands unprepared. But
this advantage was only to be gained by a winter at sea;
and in such a sea, with a fleet in the worst condition,
and in his state of increasing bodily infirmity! The best
of the great ships had gone home with the *Naseby*,
Cromwell believing from all past naval experience that
it would be impossible for them to ride through the
storms of December and January on that dangerous
coast: what remained as the Cadiz blockading squadron
were about twenty frigates, with the *Swiftsure*, a vessel

of 898 tons burden, carrying 380 men and 64 guns, as admiral. Yet the duties were numerous and of different kinds which this fleet of frigates was expected to perform. Simply to keep the seas would have been no easy task; but Blake was expected to hold the whole southern coast of Spain in a state of siege,—to close the Straits of Gibraltar against the enemy,—to intercept the Silver Fleets should they arrive,—to prevent the coming in of oak, hemp, tar, and other materials for shipbuilding from the north of Europe,—to entice out and then fight with the war-galleons known to be fitting up in Cadiz by the merchants of Seville for the defence of their property,—to cut off all communication over sea between Spain and Flanders,—to harass and destroy the enemy's trade, particularly that of their colonies and settlements in America,—to watch and check the movements of the Barbary corsairs,—and, finally, to protect the interests of English commerce with Portugal and the Straits of Gibraltar, then fiercely menaced by Biscayan and other Spanish privateers.[1]

The Commonwealth expected full and daring service from its officers. But however much was hoped in England from the great Admiral's genius and good-fortune, the wonders of this winter cruise and the brilliant action with which it closed in the early spring at Santa Cruz surpassed every expectation. For the first few weeks, the Spaniards affected to laugh at a madman who could dream of riding out in that tempestuous ocean for a whole winter. Nevertheless, October and November passed away; and though daily storms scattered the

---

[1] Clarendon, vi. 20, 38, 39; Carlyle's Cromwell, iv. 85, 86.

devoted squadron, carrying some of the frigates to the
African ports, others into the Straits, and now and then
an unfortunate vessel as far as Cape St. Vincent, the bay
was never free from the enemy; and after a day or two
of decent weather, the fleet was found riding in all its
strength across the entrance to Cadiz. Opinion then
worked gradually round. The citizens began to fear
that nature would probably not fight their battle as effectually as they had hoped. If the Mexican fleet was
to come in, other means of defence must be considered.
Some rich merchants at last offered to fit out a powerful
squadron. At their expense eight royal galleons were
prepared forthwith; guns were also put on board twelve
traders of heavy burden; and a solemn appeal was
made to the chivalry of Spain to go on board the relief
squadron as volunteers, and in that capacity make one
grand effort to dislodge the enemy from his insulting
position. Much was expected from this appeal; several
spirited gentlemen offered their services, and the agents
talked in heroic measures of their intended feats:—but
for some reason not known to the English, the squadron
did not venture outside the passage, and Blake continued undisputed master at sea. About mid-winter, De
Ruiter anchored off the bar of San Lucar with nine or
ten Dutch men-of-war; and the opinion current in di-
plomatic circles in the south of Europe was, that he
intended openly to join the Spaniards against England.
European diplomacy was probably well acquainted with
the secret leanings of the States-General; but it erred
in assuming that they would have the courage to declare
their preference, and take upon themselves the conse-

quences of their friendship for Spain. They rather chose to work for her in secret. Under false flags and with forged papers they from time to time carried succours to Cadiz and San Lucar; in the name of the Genoese they built and equipped in their dockyards as many frigates and men-of-war as would have formed a powerful fleet; and indeed at that very moment they had six magnificent ships, of from sixty to seventy guns each, on the stocks nearly finished. But De Ruiter carefully abstained from any offence against the red cross. He made a shew of the profoundest respect for Blake personally, and sailed away into the Mediterranean, as he pretended on a voyage against the pirates of Algiers and Tripoli.[1]

The English were compelled to rule the Barbary powers with a rod of iron. A few months ago the Admiral had paid his promised visit to Salee, when he summoned the formidable rovers of that port to a consultation; but as the barbarians did not for the space of two days comply with his request, he drove two of their fleetest vessels on the rocks and broke them into fragments, threatening to deal in like manner with their entire fleet if they persisted in their refusal to treat with him according to the usages of nations. The Prince of Salee had already learned by the example of Tunis that Blake never threatened in vain, and on receiving this peremptory intimation he sent an agent to the *Naseby*. The sudden recal of the fleet towards the Bay of Cadiz, in expectation of the Silver Fleet, had prevented the formal conclusion of a treaty; but the

---

[1] Thurloe, vi. 3, 4, 48, 49, 56.

rovers became more guarded from that time in their interference with English merchants. Early in February a violent storm in the Bay of Cadiz drove the blockading fleet towards the Straits, and the heavy gales increasing, Blake ran into Tetuan, a Morocco port just within the Straits, for shelter; and as some questions had arisen between him and the Dey of Algiers, ere he returned to Cadiz, he ran along the coast to that city, paid the Dey a flying visit, and arranged all his difficulties without having to fire a single shot. The affair of Porto Ferino had relieved him from the necessity of any more fighting with the pirates. In passing Tangier, then a settlement of the Portuguese, he found it closely invested by the Moors, and so severely distressed as to be not unlikely to fall into their hands. In the high spirit of Christian chivalry he detached a part of his fleet to relieve the garrison, break the besiegers' lines and support the interests of the new King of Portugal, Alphonso VI., on those shores: — a service which had the happy effect of saving the town and drawing still closer the bonds of friendship already established by his means between London and Lisbon.[1]

Discontents arose and multiplied in Spain. The loss of one and the long delay of the other Silver Fleet rendered money scarce, crippling both public and private means. New taxes had to be imposed. Voluntary gifts and loans were tried,—and many Hidalgo families stript themselves of part of their ancient wealth to uphold the glory of their King. The Church also contributed its

---

[1] Thurloe, v. 285, 6; vi. 48.

blessing and its money towards the support of a war against heretics. But these donations went but a short way towards meeting the enormous expenditure; and in its hour of need government was compelled to exact a fifth part of the estates, stock and property of every merchant in the empire. Thousands were ruined by this sweeping measure. Trade almost ceased. The Spanish dollar rose in value; debts were left unpaid; and many of the most princely residents of Cadiz and Seville were completely broken in their fortunes. In England the splendour of victory, the humiliation of a haughty foe, and now and then the sight of wagons filled with captured gold and silver, helped to sustain the popularity of the war; but the trading interests suffered severely from the corsairs of Brest and the Bay of Biscay. The amount of money taken from the enemy was slight when compared with the losses of private persons. Few indeed gained by the war except the privateers of the two nations, and that band of lawless adventurers who plundered peaceful traders under cover of any flag which it suited them for the moment to unfurl.[1]

Nothing excites more wonder and admiration than the poverty of means with which this bold watch and guard was maintained. Hardly a single ship was seaworthy. The *Fairfax*, the *Worcester*, the *Plymouth*, the *Newcastle*, the *Foresight*, were all seriously damaged. Some were short of a mast, others had no powder; all were in want of spars, canvass, hemp and stores.[2] Worst of all, sickness had carried off the ablest seamen of the

---

[1] Thurloe, v. 89, 153.

[2] Blake Despatch, Add. Mss. 9304-122.

fleet; and more than one of the frigates had not sufficient hands for the ordinary working service, much less for war. On the 11th of March, 1657, Blake writes from before Cadiz to the Admiralty:

" Our fleet at present, by reason of a long continuance abroad, are grown so foul, that if a fleet outward bound should design to avoid us, few of our ships would be able to follow them up. I have acquainted you often with my thoughts of keeping out those ships so long, whereby they are not only rendered in a great measure unserviceable, but withal exposed to desperate hazards: wherein, though the Lord hath most wonderfully and mercifully preserved us hitherto, I know no rule to tempt Him, and therefore again mind you of it, that if any such accident should for the future happen to the damage of his Highness and the nation—which God forbid—the blame may not be at our doors, for we account it a great mercy that the Lord hath not given them [the Spaniards] the opportunity to take advantage of these our damages. Truly our fleet is generally in that condition, that it troubles me to think what the consequence may prove if such another storm, as we have had three or four lately, should overtake us before we have time and opportunity a little to repair. Our number of men is lessened through death and sickness, occasioned partly through the badness of victuals and the long continuance of poor men at sea. The captain of the *Fairfax* tells me, in particular, that they are forced to call all their company on deck whenever they go to tack. Therefore (I) desire that, if you intend us to stay out this summer, or any considerable part thereof, that you will forthwith send us a sufficient supply of able seamen."[1]

But Cromwell was too busy with his own schemes of personal aggrandisement to think of the brave men who were fighting the battles of their country on a distant station. No succours were sent out; nothing but apologies and excuses. The Lords of Admiralty said they were sorry to hear of his illness; sorry also to hear of the wretched state of his ships; but they could not promise him any immediate aid, because the Lord Protector's time was completely taken up with Parliamentary intrigues, the great question of Kingship being then under consideration.[2] The events of the next few days, however, put an end to the tasks which held the sick Admiral a sort of prisoner in those waters. Letters of intelligence came to hand announcing that the second Silver Fleet, consisting of six royal galleons and sixteen other great ships, was on its way towards Europe; but that having heard of the former disaster, and learning that the enemy was still in some force before the Bay of Cadiz, it had run for safety into harbour in one of the Canary Islands. At first this news was of a doubtful nature, perhaps an invention of the Spaniards to draw him off from his post; certainly it was too vague a report to justify a run with his whole squadron into a latitude so remote; but several hands, unknown to each other, furnished him with the same intelligence, and his habitual caution at last admitted that there were grounds for trusting to the general accuracy of his information.

[1] Blake Despatch, Add. Mss. 9304.

[2] Ms. Orders and Instructions, May 2, 1657, Admiralty Office.

Finding that the fleet already prepared for sea did not
venture forth, he arranged his plans, called in his cruisers,
and on the 13th of April set sail with his whole force,
now recruited to twenty-five ships and frigates, for those
islands. Don Diego Diagues, the Spanish Admiral at
Santa Cruz, had news of Blake's intended movement, and
he made instant preparations to give the assailants a
warm reception should they venture to attack his fleet.
The port of Santa Cruz was then one of the strongest
naval positions in the world. The harbour, shaped like
a horse-shoe, was defended at the north side of the
entrance by a regular castle, mounted with the heaviest
ordnance and well garrisoned; along the inner line
of the Bay seven powerful forts were disposed; and
connecting these forts with each other and with the
castle was a line of earthworks, which served to cover
the gunners and musketeers from the fire of an enemy.
Sufficiently formidable of themselves to appal the stout-
est heart, these works were now strengthened by the
whole force of the Silver Fleet. The precious metals,
pearls and other jewels, were carried on shore into the
town ; but the usual freightage, hides, sugar, spices, cochineal and other valuable commodities, remained on
board, Don Diego having no fears for their safety. The
royal galleons were then stationed on each side the narrow entrance of the Bay; their anchors dropped out,
and their broadsides turned towards the sea. The other
armed vessels were moored in a semicircle round the inner line, with openings between them so as to allow full
play to the batteries on shore in case of necessity. Large
bodies of musketeers were placed on the earthworks

uniting the more solid fortifications; and in this admirable arrangement of his means of resistance Diagues waited with confidence the appearance of his enemy.

On the evening of Saturday, April 18th, the foremost of the English frigates sighted what they believed to be the nearest point of land in the Canary Islands; but the weather was so extremely thick and hazy that doubts were entertained, and it was noon on Sunday before they were certain of their exact bearings. This circumstance afforded Diego timely warning of their approach. Next morning, Monday, the red cross of the Commonwealth was descried at daybreak from the royal galleons; the fleet appearing about three leagues distant, under crowded sail and bearing in before a stiff breeze.[1] A Dutch captain, who had seen something of the late war, happened to be lying at that moment in the Santa Cruz roadstead with his vessel; when he saw the Sea-General's pennon floating on the wind, and the frigates in advance making direct for the harbour, he felt they were bent on mischief, and anxious to avoid any portion of the hard knocks likely to be given in the coming fray, went straight to the Spanish Admiral to ask his permission to retire. Diagues affected to smile at his fears. Why, his naval force alone was almost equal to the enemy. The royal galleons were mounted with the finest brass ordnance in the world. Their broadsides would oppose a living wall of fire against assault. With his castles, batteries and earthworks, his powerful and spirited garrison, his double line of war-ships, he considered, and not unreasonably considered, that his posi-

---

[1] Narrative of the Passages of these Times of the Commonwealth, 25.

tion was impregnable. The Dutchman shook his head: "For all this," he said, "I am very sure that Blake will soon be in among you."—"Well," replied the haughty Spaniard, "go, if you will; and let Blake come if he dare."—The applicant returned to his vessel, hoisted sail and escaped the destruction which awaited every spar and canvass afloat within the Bay of Santa Cruz that fatal morning.

As soon as day dawned on the English fleet, a frigate, which had been sent forward in the night for that purpose, signalled to the *Swiftsure* the welcome intelligence that the whole body of the Silver Fleet lay at anchor within the harbour. Thereupon Blake, roused from his sick-bed by the prospect of immediate action, called a council of war, stated the case in a few brief and pregnant words, and ended with a proposal to ride into the port and attack the enemy in his formidable position.[1] The shape of the harbour, the situation of the great castle, and the direction of the wind—then blowing steadily landwards—made it useless to think of bringing off the royal galleons. It only remained therefore to destroy them where they stood, with their threatening broadsides pointing towards the English ships. Many thought this scheme would be equally impossible to carry out; but the captains who had served in the attack on Porto Ferino had no doubt but that the bold conception of their general might be as brilliantly executed. At least it was resolved to make the attempt. Between six and seven o'clock, a solemn prayer was offered to the Disposer of events: no oath, no irreverent

---

[1] Ms. Orders and Instructions, May 2, 1657, Admiralty Office.

ribaldry, was ever heard on board that fleet; no rum or brandy was given out on the eve of battle; but every man on those gallant ships knelt down humbly, and in that fervent spirit which was in all trials and temptations the Roundheads' sustaining fire, asked the God of battles to bless His people, and put forth His right arm in support of the good cause.[1] At seven all was ready —the sailors had breakfasted and prayed. A division of the best-equipped and most powerful ships was then drawn off and sent forward under the gallant Captain Stayner to attack the royal galleons and force an entrance into the harbour; Blake reserving to himself the task of silencing the castles and batteries on land. Stayner's old frigate, the *Speaker*, now bearing his pennon as Vice-admiral, rode in the van of this attacking squadron right at the entrance, unchecked by the tremendous broadsides of the galleons and regardless of the terrific flanking fire from the castle and batteries. In a space of time almost incredibly short he had passed the outer defences and established himself near the royal galleons, in the centre of a huge semicircle of shot. Blake instantly followed with the remainder of his fleet, and covering Stayner's flank with his frigates, so as to leave him free to fight the great ships without interruption from the batteries on shore, he commenced a furious cannonade on the whole line of defences, and especially against the castle. The Spaniards fought throughout with desperate valour, and for some hours the old peak of Teneriffe witnessed a scene which might almost be compared with one of its own stupendous outbursts.

---

[1] Narrative of the Passages of these Times of the Commonwealth, 26.

The Spanish musketeers kept up a most destructive fire from behind the covered way. Yet in spite of the highest courage, unanimity and conduct on the side of the defence, the cannonade along the earthworks gradually slackened. One by one the batteries ceased to answer. Before twelve o'clock Blake was able to leave the completion of this part of his task to a few well-stationed frigates, while he turned with the main body to the assistance of Stayner, engaged for four hours in an unequal contest with galleons of greatly superior force in men and guns. Diagues made heroic efforts to recover his failing ground; but it was now too late to turn the tide of victory. By two o'clock the battle was clearly won. Two of the Spanish ships had gone down, and every other vessel in the harbour, whether royal galleon, ship-of-war, or trader, was in flames. Miles and miles round the scene of action, the lurid and fatal lights could be seen, throbbing and burning against the dull sky. The fire had done its work swiftly and awfully. Not a sail, not a single spar was left above water. The charred keels floated hither and thither. Some of them filled and sank. Others were thrown upon the strand. Here and there the stump of a burnt mast projected from the surface; but not a single ship — not a single cargo — escaped destruction. All went down together in this tremendous calamity.[1]

Their victory complete, the next care of the English was to get away safely from the Bay, as the great guns of the castle at its entrance, supplied with fresh gunners,

---

[1] Bates, Elenchus Motuum nuperorum in Anglia, part ii. 227; Heath, 391; Clarendon, vi. 39, 40.

kept up a deadly fire from all its embrasures. Blake's
plan, when he rode with a strong breeze into Santa Cruz,
seems to have been to fight and destroy the Spanish
galleons, first silencing as many of the land-batteries as
might be necessary to that end, and then to retire with
his fleet from the harbour at the ebb-tide; but just as
the devouring flames had got safe hold of the Spaniards'
hulls, ensuring the complete destruction of their ships,
the wind began to veer a little towards the south-west—
a change, as the pious sailors remarked, which had not
been known to occur on that coast for many years—and
by skilful management the whole squadron came out of
the Bay with one slight accident, the striking of a frigate
on an unknown rock. But she was got off without serious damage; and by seven o'clock in the evening all the
ships were out in the Bay beyond gun-range.[1] The loss
of the Spaniards was immense. The finest part of their
Silver Fleets was utterly annihilated: ships, guns, equip-
ments, cargoes, all were gone. Considering the many
disadvantages under which they had fought, the losses
of the English were comparatively unimportant. Not
a single ship was missing at the muster; but several
frigates, particularly the *Speaker*, were rendered unfit
for further service. The slain amounted to no more
than 50; the wounded were about 150 in number.[2]

Perhaps no naval action has ever been more warmly
admired and more curiously criticised than this attack
on Santa Cruz. "Of all the desperate attempts," says
royalist Heath, "that were ever made in the world

---

[1] Narrative of Passages, 27.

[2] Parl. Hist. xxi. 144; Burton's Diary, ii. 142.

against an enemy by sea, this of the noble Blake's is not inferior to any."—" The whole action," writes Clarendon, " was so miraculous, that all men who knew the place concluded that no sober man, with what courage soever endued, would ever undertake it; whilst the Spaniards comforted themselves with the belief that they were devils and not men who had destroyed them in such a manner. And it can hardly be imagined how small loss the English sustained in this unparalleled action; no one ship being left behind, and the killed and wounded not exceeding two hundred men, when the slaughter on board the Spanish ships and on the shore was incredible." On the other side, it has been alleged by Sir Philip Warwick and later writers, that when Blake rode into the bay of Santa Cruz there was no reasonable probability that the wind would change when the work of destruction was effected; that had it not changed, the squadron would have been wind-bound within reach of the great artillery of the castle for an indefinite period; that, in short, nothing less than the unexpected turn of wind could have saved the fleet which his rashness had placed in such imminent peril.[1]

To these criticisms it would probably be a sufficient answer to say, that during his whole naval career the great Admiral never made a serious mistake: even his unequal and disastrous encounter with Tromp in the Downs was defensible on political grounds. The best proof, however, that he could bring his fleet out of the harbour when its work was done, is the fact that he did bring it out; had it appeared to him desirable

---

[1] Warwick's Memoirs, 421-2, edition of 1702.

for the ships to remain at anchor under the castle-guns, there is no reason to believe that they would have been unable to hold their position. Masters of the harbour for twelve hours, it would have been easy to remain masters for twelve days. Nor is it clear that the change of wind took place before the fleet quitted the bay—as accounts written on the spot represent that change as occurring after the muster in the offing—when a speedy return to Spain, not an escape from Santa Cruz, figures as the great object of providential interposition.[1]

Intelligence of this great naval exploit reached London as Cromwell's second Parliament was drawing its first session to a close. The excitement was extreme.[2] Popular ballads, in which Antichrist and the Inquisition were treated with disdainful waggery, were sung at every street-corner under the fantastic and picturesque gables of old London. The Lord Protector sent his secretary down to the House with the letter of details; and when honourable members had heard the whole story from Blake's own hand, they tendered him the thanks of the country for his eminent services, and voted five hundred pounds for the purchase of a jewel to be given him as a mark of honour and respect. The House partook of the liberal enthusiasm which filled the cities of London and Westminster. The representatives gave one hundred pounds to Captain Story, the messenger of such glorious news. They ordered a letter of thanks to be written to the officers of the fleet. Finally, they set apart an early day for a solemn national thanksgiving.[3]

---

[1] Narrative of Passages, 27.   [3] Parl. Hist. xxi. 145.
[2] Ms. Orders and Instructions, June 11, Admiralty Office.

Cromwell himself wrote to the dying General a letter of thanks and congratulation :

SIR,—I have received yours of the [20th April], and thereby the account of the good success it hath pleased God to give you at the Canaries, in your attempt upon the King of Spain's ships in the Bay of Santa Cruz. The mercy therein to us and this Commonwealth is very signal, both in the loss the enemy hath received, as also in the preservation of our ships and men, which indeed was very wonderful, and according to the wonted goodness and loving-kindness of the Lord, wherewith His people hath been followed in all these late revolutions ; and call for on our part, that we should fear before Him, and still hope in His mercy. We cannot but take notice also, how eminently it hath pleased God to make use of you in this service, assisting you with wisdom in the conduct, and courage in the execution ; and have sent you a small jewel, as a testimony of our own and the Parliament's good acceptance of your carriage in this action. We are also informed that the officers of the fleet and the seamen carried themselves with much honesty and courage, and we are considering of a way to shew our acceptance thereof. In the meantime we desire you to return our hearty thanks and acknowledgments to them. Thus beseeching the Lord to continue His presence with you, I remain your very affectionate friend.[1]

One unhappy incident had occurred to dash this great public triumph with a private grief. His brother Humphrey, removed from the Board of Prizes to the

---

[1] Thurloe, vi. 342.

command of a frigate, saw his first real service in this most trying engagement, and in a moment of extreme agitation failed in his duty. After the muster-call in the offing, whispers began to circulate through the fleet that the General's brother had not done his part like an English captain, and certain voices accused him openly of cowardice. Humphrey seems to have been one of those jovial, plastic and good-natured men whom every one likes, and no one respects. Only a few months in the fleet, he was already a favourite with his brother officers; and when the accusation first arose against him, they tried to stifle it, and by every means in their power sought to prevent the affair from coming under the notice of a court-martial. But the great Admiral was inexorable. Humphrey was his favourite brother; he was the next to him in age, and he had been his chief playfellow in boyhood; when on shore he always shared with him his house, his table and his leisure: but above and before all private affection for this favourite brother rose up in his mind the stern sense of public duty. For years it had been his office to purge that navy of all ungodly, unfaithful and inefficient officers with a rigorous hand; and how could he spare his own flesh and blood? The captains went to him in a body, and endeavoured to shew him that Humphrey's fault was a neglect rather than a breach of duty; and that the ends of justice would be met without the disgrace of a public sentence. They ventured to suggest that without taking formal notice of the scandal which was abroad in the fleet, he might be sent away to England until his fault was forgotten. Blake looked grave and angry. They nevertheless pressed their suit, believing that nature itself would prevent a failure of their application. They appealed to his private affection—they glanced at the offender's want of experience at sea. But it was all to no purpose. Blake answered that his first duty was to the service. Their very reasoning proved more clearly that this was not a case which could be allowed to pass into a precedent; and, at the conclusion of the interview, he ordered a court-martial to be summoned. "If none of you," said he, "will accuse him, I must myself be his accuser." The officers forming the court could only give one sentence on the evidence laid before them; but they sent with it a petition, signed by the entire court, to their Admiral, praying him to remit the sentence, and allow the culprit to return to England in his own ship. This prayer was granted, as it would have been in any ordinary case ; but the Commander added to the painful document the stern words—" He shall never be employed more." Yet to the brother thus sternly rebuked he left the greater part of his property.[1]

The favourable wind which brought the squadron out of Santa Cruz carried it once more at a steady and rapid pace to the shores of Andalusia; but intelligence of the terrible disaster at the Canaries had already reached the merchants of Cadiz, and new endeavours were made to induce the States-General of Holland to unite with Spain in a league against the proud and victorious islanders. Dutch statesmen, alarmed at the extraordinary growth of English influence at sea, were

---

[1] History and Life, 104, 5; Copy of Will in Blake Mss.

disposed to entertain the advances made to them by their ancient and mortal enemies; they expedited the preparations of their fleet, and raised it to a force of seventy sail. Cromwell's ministers could obtain no satisfactory explanation of the reasons for this armament or of the service on which it was to be employed; and as soon as the battle of Santa Cruz had disabled Spain for some time, they wrote to inform Blake of their fears and uncertainties, and to beg that he would return with convenient haste to England.[1] Warned of these intrigues with the States-General, the English frigates kept strict watch over the motions of the Dutch squadron in those seas, and soon found that, while declining to commit themselves to the hazards and expenses of another naval war, the officers readily engaged themselves to bring into Cadiz and other ports the gold and silver landed at Santa Cruz, by order of Don Diego Diagues, before the late attack. Aware of the contract, Blake declared these Dutchmen lawful prizes; and instructed the captains of his cruisers to chase, capture or destroy them whenever found with Spanish cargoes on board. By these prompt measures several of their ships and frigates were taken, laden in great part with gold and silver from that island. One of these Dutch vessels was reported to have a million pieces of eight on board. Another of his captures, the *Flying Fame* of Amsterdam, ran on shore near Suebra, in order to save the cargo; but it was got off again at full tide by the English frigates: it had 448 Spaniards, passengers from the Canaries, on board, besides a very valuable freight. Re-

---

[1] Ms. Orders and Instructions, June 11, Admiralty Office.

monstrances were of course made by the Ambassadors of Holland against this rigorous policy. But Blake had little patience with the wiles and subterfuges of diplomacy. His object in those seas was to destroy the trade, the resources, the fleets of Spain; he considered its gold and silver, its pearls and precious stones, its spices, sugar, hides and cochineal lawful prey; and in whatever bottoms or under whatever flag he found these articles, he believed his right to seize them indisputable. The Dutchmen railed and spouted — but they kept the peace. From Norway to Barbary the echoes of Blake's thunder had been heard. The wavering were confirmed in their friendship for the Commonwealth; States which had so far proudly held aloof evinced the desire to cultivate a closer alliance; false friends suddenly grew eager and demonstrative in their civilities. To use the emphatic words of our agent at Lisbon, the English were " every where held in terror and honour."[1]

But the hero's health was now failing fast. The excitement of Santa Cruz had fearfully augmented his disorders; his attached friends could see that he was nigh to death; and the dismissal of his brother had therefore been a most severe addition of sacrifice to his stern sense of duty. Confined to his cabin by sickness, he began to feel the whole loneliness of his position. Humphrey had been his companion from a child. No one clung to him like his brother Humphrey; no one knew so much of his inward life; no one was possessed so thoroughly of his thoughts and opinions on all subjects; no one had learned to conform to his habits so

---

[1] Thurloe, vi. 364, 388, 399, 401, 485.

completely as this favourite. Few commanders have
ever won so entirely the love, devotion, adoration of
their officers and men. It was an article of faith for
the captains to believe in his genius and fortune. The
common sailors would have leapt into the sea, or rushed
into the cannon's mouth, to gain a word of approbation
from his lips. But the brother's place by the sick bed
could not be supplied by any stranger to his blood. For
himself, his work was nearly done. And he was most
anxious, if God were willing, to go home, and die in
his native town. He had his country's express permission to return should he think it useful to the service;[1]
but it lay on his conscience to perform one other task
before he quitted for ever the seas in which he had kept
this glorious watch; and that was to pay a second visit
to Salee, and compel the Moorish corsairs to restore the
Christian captives to their freedom, and enter into a
treaty of peace with England. This was his last, and,
in the opinion of his biographer, his most illustrious
action. An accident had formerly defeated his attempt
to exact reparation from these formidable pirates for the
injuries inflicted by them on English commerce; before
he finally quitted the southern waters, he considered it
a sacred duty to return to Salee and complete the negociations then suddenly interrupted.

Unlike the pirates of Tunis, Tripoli, and Algiers, who
went out to sea in the largest class of war-ships, the Moors
of Salee, a town forming part of the dominions of the
Emperor of Fez and Morocco, made their excursions in
small but well-built and extremely fast-sailing vessels;

[1] Ms. Orders and Instructions, June 11, Admiralty Office.

the bar of the river on which their town was built not
affording, even in good weather, more than a depth of
ten or twelve feet of water. After a short prevalence of
south-west winds, a strong swell of sea always broke on
the bar, rendering it impassable for craft of any but the
smallest size; so that in winter the pirates were usually
compelled to lie still. But with the approach of spring,
they would set out in their powerful little frigates, scour
the European waters as far as the Bay of Biscay and the
Sardinian sea, rifling unarmed traders, and even making
occasional descents on the coasts of Spain and Italy in
search of spoil and prisoners. On his second visit to
this nest of corsairs, Blake succeeded, without firing a
gun, or shedding a drop of blood, in bringing the Moorish Prince to reason:—he had conquered the rovers of
Salee at Santa Cruz! The very day on which his frigates
appeared off the bar, they accepted his proposed terms;
and in less than a week he departed for the north, having
taken on board supplies of fresh water, cleared the whole
body of Christian captives, and made peace with them
for the future.[1]

This crowning act of a virtuous and honourable life
accomplished, the dying Admiral turned his thoughts
anxiously towards the green hills of his native land.
The letter of Cromwell, the thanks of Parliament, the
jewelled ring sent to him by an admiring country,—
all reached him together out at sea. These tokens of
grateful remembrance caused him a profound emotion.
Without after-thought, without selfish impulse, he had
served the Commonwealth, day and night, earnestly,

---

[1] Harl. Misc. viii. 399, 403; Thurloe, vi. 492.

anxiously and with rare devotion. England was grateful
to her hero. With the letter of thanks from Cromwell,
a new set of instructions arrived, which allowed him to
return with part of his fleet, leaving a squadron of some
fifteen or twenty frigates to ride before the Bay of Cadiz
and intercept its traders; with their usual deference to
his judgment and experience, the Protector and Board
of Admiralty left the appointment to the command entirely with him; and as his gallant friend Stayner was
gone to England, where he received a knighthood and
other well-won honours from the Government, he raised
Captain Stoaks, the hero of Porto Ferino and a commander of rare promise, to the responsible position of
his Vice-admiral in the Spanish seas.[1]

Hoisting his pennon on his old flag-ship the *St.
George*, Blake saw for the last time the spires and cu-
polas, the masts and towers, before which he had kept
his long and victorious vigils. When he put in for fresh
water at Cascaes road he was very weak. " I beseech
God to strengthen him," was the fervent prayer of the
English Resident at Lisbon, as he departed on the homeward voyage. While the ships rolled through the tempestuous waters of the Bay of Biscay, he grew every day
worse and worse. Some gleams of the old spirit broke
forth as they approached the latitude of England. He
inquired often and anxiously if the white cliffs were yet
in sight. He longed to behold once more the swelling
downs, the free cities, the goodly churches of his native
land. But he was now dying beyond all doubt. Many

---

[1] Ms. Orders and Instructions, May 2, Admiralty Office; Thurloe,
vi. 401.

of his favourite officers silently and mournfully crowded round his bed, anxious to catch the last tones of a voice which had so often called them to glory and victory. Others stood at the poop and forecastle, eagerly examining every speck and line on the horizon, in hope of being first to catch the welcome glimpse of land. Though they were coming home crowned with laurels, gloom and pain were in every face. At last the Lizard was announced. Shortly afterwards the bold cliffs and bare hills of Cornwall loomed out grandly in the distance. But it was now too late for the dying hero. He had sent for the captains and other great officers of his fleet to bid them farewell; and while they were yet in his cabin, the undulating hills of Devonshire, glowing with the tints of early autumn, came full in view. As the ships rounded Rame Head, the spires and masts of Plymouth, the wooded heights of Mount Edgecombe, the low Island of St. Nicholas, the rocky steeps at the Hoe, Mount Batten, the citadel, the many picturesque and familiar features of that magnificent harbour rose one by one to sight. But the eyes which had so yearned to behold this scene once more were at that very instant closing in death. Foremost of the victorious squadron, the *St. George* rode with its precious burden into the Sound; and just as it came into full view of the eager thousands crowding the beach, the pier-heads, the walls of the citadel, or darting in countless boats over the smooth waters between St. Nicholas and the docks, ready to catch the first glimpse of the hero of Santa Cruz, and salute him with a true English welcome,—he, in his silent cabin, in the midst of his lion-hearted comrades, now sobbing like little children, yielded up his soul to God.[1]

The mournful news soon spread through the fleet and in the town. The melancholy enthusiasm of the people knew no bounds, and the national love and admiration expressed itself in the solemn splendour of his funeral rites. The day of his death the corpse was left untouched in its cabin, as something sacred; but next morning skilful embalmers were employed to open it; and, in presence of all the great officers of the fleet and port, the bowels were taken out and placed in an urn, to be buried in the great church in Plymouth. The body, embalmed and wrapt in lead, was then put on board again and carried round by sea to Greenwich, where it lay in state several days, on the spot since consecrated to the noblest hospital for seamen in the world. On the 4th of September a solemn procession was formed on the river. The corpse was placed on a state barge, covered with a velvet pall, adorned with pencils and escutcheons. Trumpeters in state barges, bearing his pennons as General-at-Sea, surmounted by the great banner of the Commonwealth, preceded the body. Humphrey and all his other brothers, all the nephews and other members of his family, together with the secretaries and servants attached to his immediate household, dressed in the deepest mourning, followed. After them came the Protector's Privy Council in their state barge, the Lords of the Admiralty and Navy, the Lord Mayor

---

[1] Wood's Mss. E. 4, no. 8560, art. iv. 3, in Ashmol. Museum; Hist. Parl. xxi. 145; Thurloe, vi. 401; Heath, 402; Mercurius Politicus, 375; Clarendon, vi. 41.

and Aldermen of the City of London, the Admirals, Vice-admirals and Captains of his fleet, the Field Officers of the army, and a vast procession of civil notables.[1]

In this order they moved slowly up the river from Greenwich to Westminster, where they were received by a military guard and greeted with salvoes of artillery. At the stairs, the heralds re-formed the procession, which then marched slowly through Palace-yard to the venerable Abbey. A new vault had been made for his remains in Henry the Seventh's chapel, and close to that of the great Tudor monarch,[2] and they were lowered into it amidst the tears and prayers of a grateful and admiring nation. Other heroes of the Commonwealth had been already buried within those regal precincts; and on every such occasion loyal tongues had not feared to accuse the new rulers with upstart and indecent pride. But no voice was raised against the interment there of the conqueror of Tromp, the hero of Tunis and Santa Cruz, the liberator of Christian slaves. In some unaccountable manner, this illustrious man escaped the common lot of greatness; perhaps no one ever played so conspicuous a part in the drama of history who was followed by less envy, hatred and other uncharitableness. Personal foes he seems not to have known; and even the bitter enemies of his political creed spoke of what they deemed his errors more in sorrow than in anger. All parties owned, as they stood by that silent grave, that its occupant was

---

[1] Add. Mss. 12, 514-234.

[2] Elegiac Enumeration, 27 :

    " Amongst the kings interred, and neer to one,
    That Prince of peace, which joyned in Hymen's band
    The two divided houses of our land."

one who had merited, by brilliant public services and the rarest disinterestedness, the highest rewards a grateful country could bestow. When the imposing ceremonial was closed, a stone slab was laid on the vault,—and they left him there in the old Abbey, with no other monument than that of his imperishable renown.[1]

To their eternal infamy, the Stuarts afterwards disturbed the hero's grave. It was a mean revenge in them to touch the bones of Cromwell; but in his case they could urge the plea of moral and political retribution. The great usurper had been the chief cause of their father's tragic death; he had hunted them for years from land to land; he had shot their most faithful followers and confiscated their richest estates. But Blake had ever been for mild and moderate councils. He had opposed the late King's trial. He had disapproved the usurpation. When he found the sword prevail against law and right, he abandoned politics, like Sidney, Vane, and other of his illustrious compeers, giving up his genius to the service of his country against its foreign enemies. Surely after a life of the most eminent services, the ashes of such a man might have been allowed to rest in peace! The House of Lords, in their ardent zeal for the restored family, gave orders that the bodies of Cromwell, Ireton and Bradshawe should be dug out of their graves and treated with gross indignity; but even these zealots did not deem it decent to include the remains of Blake in their order. That infamy was reserved for Charles himself. In cold blood, nearly seven-

---

[1] Wood's Mss. iv. 3; Heath, 402.

teen months after his landing at Dover from the deck of
the *Naseby*, a royal command was issued by this prince
to tear open the unobtrusive vault, drag out the embalmed body, and cast it into a pit in the Abbey yard.
Good men looked aghast at such an atrocity. But what
could the paramour of Lucy Walters, Barbara Palmer,
Kate Peg, and Moll Davies, know of the stern virtues
of the illustrious sailor! What sympathy could a royal
spendthrift have with the man who, after a life of great
employments and the capture of uncounted millions,
died no richer than he was born! How could the prince
who sold Dunkirk and begged a pension from Versailles
feel any regard for a man who had humbled the pride of
Holland, Portugal and Spain, who had laid the foundations of our lasting influence in the Mediterranean, and
in eight years of success had made England the first
maritime power in Europe!

A hole was dug for the reception of these hallowed
bones near the back door of one of the prebendaries of
Westminster:—and the remains of Cromwell's mother,
of the gentle Lady Claypole, and of sturdy John Pym,
were all cast into the same pit. How lightly Englishmen
should tread that ground![1]

---

[1] Lords Journals, xi. 205; Bliss's Wood's Fasti, ii. 371; Oldmixon,
i. 421; Kennett's Register, 536.

THE END.

Index

Vandruske, 84, 87
Vendome, duke of, 208, 209, 210, 215, 271
Venice, 278, 289–90

Welden, 96, 98, 100, 101
Wyndham, 32, 50, 78, 79, 82, 90